"Set me as the seal on your heart,
The seal on your arm."
–Song of Songs 8:6

THE SONG OF SONGS

The Song of Songs

A WOMAN IN LOVE

TRANSLATION & COMMENTARY BY

BENJAMIN J. SEGAL

gefen
publishing house
JERUSALEM • NEW YORK

Copyright © Benjamin J. Segal
Jerusalem 2009 / 5769

Typesetting: KPS, Jerusalem
Cover Design: S. Kim Glassman

ISBN 978-965-229-445-6

Edition 1   3   5   7   9   8   6   4   2

Gefen Publishing House Ltd.   Gefen Books
6 Hatzvi Street, Jerusalem 94386, Israel   600 Broadway, Lynbrook, NY 11563, USA
972-2-538-0247 • orders@gefenpublishing.com   1-800-477-5257 • orders@gefenpublishing.com

www.israelbooks.com

Printed in Israel   *Send for our free catalogue*

To Judy

"אַחַת הִיא יוֹנָתִי תַמָּתִי"

(שיר השירים ו:ט)

"One is she, my dove, my perfect one"

(Song of Songs 6:9)

Benjamin J. Segal

To Sheri with Love

"רַבּוֹת בָּנוֹת עָשׂוּ חָיִל
וְאַתְּ עָלִית עַל־כֻּלָּנָה"
(משלי לא:כט)

*"Many daughters have done worthily,
but you excel them all"*

(Proverbs 31:29)

Paul

In loving memory of Blanche Dimston

"תְּנוּ־לָהּ מִפְּרִי יָדֶיהָ
וִיהַלְלוּהָ בַשְּׁעָרִים מַעֲשֶׂיהָ"
(משלי לא:לא)

*"Extol her for the fruit of her hands,
and let her works praise her in the gates"*

(Proverbs 31:31)

Contents

Introduction: The Song of Songs

In this section, we briefly introduce the Song of Songs and the principles which have guided this translation and commentary. A full exposition and explanation of matters touched upon here will be found in the "Overview" which follows the text and commentary. Readers who have previously studied the Song in depth might prefer to read that Overview prior to the commentary, in lieu of this introduction.

A UNIQUE POEM

"*T*he Supreme Poem" – this is the primary implication of "Song of Songs." So attested by many generations, this is no idle boast. A relatively short work, the Song is the only biblical book devoted to human love, and it has attracted and fascinated readers for century upon century.

Across the millennia, there have been various base perceptions of the Song. For two thousand years, the dominant approach saw the Song as an allegory. (Most often, the human lovers are seen only as symbols for God and humanity.) This understanding possibly accounts for the inclusion of this poem, which is otherwise devoid of divine reflections, in the Bible.

Much later views saw the Song as a drama or as reworked pagan literature. In more modern times, the poem was understood to be simply love literature – though often understood to be an anthology of short poems and fragments. Over the last fifty years, an increasing number of researchers have come to appreciate the Song's unity, implying that even if older sources are included, the final work is that of a single poet who rewrote all into a unified work. Such is the starting point of this commentary, which seeks to identify the poem's tone, contentions and basic story line, as well as the poet's techniques.

The Song was set down in its current form in the fourth or third century BCE, by a now unidentified author. There is reason to believe that the author was either a woman or a male seeking to capture the female voice. Support for that contention is found in the dominant voice being female (most verses are spoken by the woman), the heroine's relative assertiveness, the prominence accorded a female chorus (the "Girls of Jerusalem"), the frequent references to the mother, the emphasis on equality between the sexes and the metaphors of strength describing the woman.

As opposed to some other ancient love poetry, dialogue is the chosen format of the Song. It may be that the poet sought simply to reflect on the two lovers who are the principle speakers. However, the most repeated words in the poem are "love," "loving" and "darling." (As we shall point out, word repetition in the Song indicates centrality.) Further, the concluding chapter includes a rapturous encomium of love. The poem has an encompassing tenor, and an overview of love emerges. Here we find, then, an ideal of love.

In painting its picture, the poem often employs comparison, the colors of this love set against a different background. Consistent with its dependency on meaning through repetition, the Song reveals its primary contrast through repeated use of a single Hebrew letter pattern, *sh-l-m*, as found in Solomon, Jerusalem, Shulammite (see 7:1) and shalom (peace). While the implication of this pattern will be revealed gradually by the text (and detailed in the Overview there-following), we note that its use indicates a world of man-woman relationship very different than that of the couple — it is a city ethos (they are from the countryside), one of harems and of multiple partners, one often lacking emotional love,

devotion and/or commitment. This world of *sh-l-m* is rejected.

This is not to say that physical love is denigrated by the Song, which is clearly neither puritanical nor prudish. In fact, few works of literature have so successfully celebrated the rapture of physical love. Rejected are *incomplete* relationships — those lacking devotion, mutuality, exclusivity and commitment.

At the same time, the Song does paint a picture of the relationship that the couple shares, as follows. The young woman is single, as is, presumably, her lover. There is much physical contact, alongside beautiful metaphoric descriptions of the body. The lovers long to lie with each other, and kisses dominate their dreams. The Song celebrates physical love, and between the lines, coition does occur. The language is not pornographic, but ever the more erotic for its resort to gentle symbols and metaphors. Throughout, the context of all that happens sexually is love, an exclusive relationship of loyalty one to the other, a mutual admiration marked by equality.

Though the lovers are single, marriage and even childbearing appear on the (hoped for) horizon, usually indicated by references to the mother as model.

While the love is strong and unwavering,

the Song sharply emphasizes movement and change. Physically, the lovers constantly move across the landscape and call on each other to be in motion. A rhythm of togetherness and separation pulsates throughout. Furthermore, the poem is marked with a grand movement of change, as former situations, previously used words and prior accounts continuously reveal themselves anew, with different implications. Some of these are in flux between dream and reality. As the Song progresses, one also senses a general movement toward the future. The concentration is on hope.

The poet implies that nothing approaches the scope or power of love, which therefore requires varied and multitudinous images. Reborn nature (the spring) – more specifically, its fragrance – signals the time of love, with plants cited from around the world. Many pleasing odors, animals, plants and spices are noted throughout. There is also a plethora of other similes and metaphors, including precious metals, rare materials, expensive woods, jewels, locations and celestial bodies. Locales span Israel at its greatest moment of historical expansion.

The scope, in short, is simply enormous. Love, says the poet, "is as mighty as death, jealousy as relentless as the grave (8:6)."

THIS TRANSLATION AND INTERPRETATION

The discovery of meaning through repetition is one of the oldest techniques of biblical interpretation. The Song of Songs adopts the reuse of words, roots, phrases, sections, metaphors, etc., as its basic literary technique. Many have seen the large number of recurrences as a prime indication of the poem's unity. In fact, *every* repetition in the Song can be seen as meaningful and we shall, in this commentary, explore possible connections in each instance.

Given the import of word and root repetition, we translate accordingly (literally), seeking (to a maximal extent) to use the same term in English for parallel root uses in Hebrew, and different English terms for each Hebrew root. The cost is clear: we are unable to seek modern metaphors for biblical ones, paraphrase is eschewed and the text reflects a biblical esthetic, not a modern one. On the other hand, the reader, with effort, is able to hear the echoes that dominate the Song, and to constantly reread early verses in light of later ones.

Double entendres are also among the poet's favorite techniques. Where possible, we include both levels of meaning in the translation itself. More often, the alternate

or complementary reading is indicated in the commentary.

In the translation, the reader should recall that "love" and "loving" represent two different Hebrew roots in the Song. We use "love" for *'-h-v*, a general term, one less often associated in Hebrew with physical lovemaking and/or coition (though it can be). We use "loving" for *dodim*, a term which always has physical overtones in the Hebrew. The word "lover," *dod*, is connected by root to "loving," not "love."

We feel compelled to adopt the usual usage: "lover" for male, "beloved" for female, despite the woman being the more active and assertive member of the couple. Draft versions to the opposite effect merely confused readers. We do so with regret, hopeful that linguistic patterns may some day evolve toward greater flexibility.

All great literature bears rereading. In the case of the Song, the consistent use of guide words and repetition is sufficient reason to argue that the Song can *only* be understood on rereading, and that several times over. Only then will the reader begin to appreciate the interaction of terms, phrases, situations, etc.

The poet evidently wished to reveal these layers of meanings gradually. In translating and commenting, we try to walk the thin line between revealing too little and too much.

We refer to future developments only where we feel it necessary, but more often comment assuming no knowledge of what follows. In order to appreciate future readings, however, we add an extensive chapter at the end, "On Rereading the Song of Songs." There we review many verses that change significantly on a second reading. (To allow for a smooth and unified rereading of the commentary at a later date, each verse in the first commentary that is reinterpreted in the "Rereading" chapter is marked after the comments by a double asterisk in parentheses.)

In the instances wherein we encounter two or more possible meanings of a word, phrase, metaphor, etc., we assume that the poet was sensitive to the range of meanings. Hence we include, at times, alternative or complementary understandings. In addition, on those occasions where implications are not clear, we opt for translations that are more flexible, and the reader will find occasional unanswered questions in the commentary. These are not rhetorical, but unresolved considerations.

Our purpose is to provide new insight, not to survey all prior works. We feel free to refer readers to earlier commentaries for details that might not be of immediate interest to all. Where a significant degree of controversy exists, we cite either the reasons for our

interpretation or scholars who have detailed the same.

We shall here divide the Song into smaller units, but these should not be seen as separate poems. In no case do we intend so to imply, given our conviction that the poem is one. Rather, we seek to accommodate the need to read longer works in smaller sections. In order to emphasize that these are not self-contained poems, we have labeled each only with a short quote from the text itself, numbering each as a consecutive chapter, as of one book.

Prologues

Love is longing. Love is dreaming. Love is memory reexplored and a future envisioned. Love is determination and anticipation. It is the struggle against all those forces that keep lovers apart. Love is spiritual and physical at one and the same time. Love is a struggle against a society dehumanizing sexual relationships and challenging loyalty. Love is mutuality. Love is an echo of spring. Love demands daring, and love must suffer separation. Love is as mighty as death. So speaks the Song of Songs, the love poem of the Bible.

Rashi (eleventh century), from his prologue: *"'God spoke once, and I heard twice' (Ps. 62:12). Any verse has many interpretations, but in the final analysis, every verse remains with its simple, direct meaning. And even though the prophets spoke allegorically, one must understand the allegory by the specifics and their order..."*

Ibn Ezra (twelfth century), from his prologue: *"This is a noble book, entirely a delight, and none of Solomon's one thousand and five songs can match it, for which reason it begins, 'The song of songs of Solomon...'"*

The Song of Songs

שיר השירים

Chapter 1   **פרק א**

1:1   *The Song of Songs – of Solomon.*   א   שִׁיר הַשִּׁירִים אֲשֶׁר לִשְׁלֹמֹה:

1:1 The title: **The Song of Songs** – the greatest, or most sublime of poems (which were often sung in antiquity). Secondarily, "the greatest among Solomon's songs." As a pun, it is also "a song made up of (smaller) songs," as reflected in the poem, which skips from one scene to another.

The Hebrew "**of**" (*asher*) appears everywhere else in Song in an abbreviated form (*she*), one reason that some see the title as a later addition. However, the use of the full term creates a beautiful alliteration ("*shir hashirim asher lishlomo*"), a technique dear to the author. This would argue that the title was original. Later considerations will confirm that.

This is a poem of King **Solomon**, implying "by" him, one known for his extensive writing (1 Kings 5:12 – 1,005 poems!). It could alternatively mean "concerning Solomon." He indeed will become a subject of concern, but not in a way one could guess here.

I. Let him kiss me

1:2   *Let him kiss me with the kisses of his mouth,*   ב   יִשָּׁקֵנִי מִנְּשִׁיקוֹת פִּיהוּ
For your loving is better than wine.   כִּי־טוֹבִים דֹּדֶיךָ מִיָּיִן:

1:2. Let him kiss me – the Song opens with desire and longing – **with the kisses of his mouth**. Some take the strange emphasis on the mouth (what other kisses are there?) as implying that both partners mouths' meet (Rashi, Ibn Ezra). The full implication unfolds gently through the Song, as the many references to the mouth (last, 7:10) are framed by the only two mentions of the kiss (here; 8:1 – where she kisses him, creating mutuality and balance). The intimate kiss encompasses all elements of the mouth.

For your loving is better – she says to him, establishing a tension between coexistent presence and absence. It is better **than wine** ("which cheers the hearts of men" – Psalm 104:15), perhaps giving more permanent joy. He will later offer her (4:10) similar praise, one of many expressions of mutuality. Wine will evolve into an important symbol of their love (e.g., 7:10, 8:2), allowing for a metaphorical complementary translation: "for your loving, (consisting of) wine, is good."

1:3   *For fragrance, your oils — so good!*
      Excellent oil — thus are you known,
      Therefore do the damsels love you.

לְרֵיחַ שְׁמָנֶיךָ טוֹבִים   ג
שֶׁמֶן תּוּרַק שְׁמֶךָ
עַל־כֵּן עֲלָמוֹת אֲהֵבוּךָ:

1:3 **For** their **fragrance, your oils** are **so good!** she calls out, reflecting their proximity, and echoing herself ("so good" is identical to the Hebrew of "better," in verse 2). Fragrance will become a major motif (1:12; 2:13; 4:10, 11; 7:9, 14).

Excellent oil — thus are you known, literally, "this is your name," implying reputation. "Name" (*shem*), echoes "oil "(*shemen*), a treasured commodity. (In II Kings 20:13 Hezekiah displays his treasure: silver, gold, spices, armor and precious oil!) He later praises her good oils (4:10). **Therefore do the damsels love you** — introducing a third party, who, while verifying the woman's high estimation of her lover, present a possible challenge. Others love him! (Elsewhere – 6:8 – they are said to be numerous, "without number.")

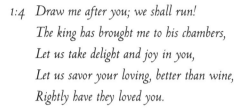

1:4 *Draw me after you; we shall run!*
The king has brought me to his chambers,
Let us take delight and joy in you,
Let us savor your loving, better than wine,
Rightly have they loved you.

ד מָשְׁכֵנִי אַחֲרֶיךָ נָּרוּצָה
הֱבִיאַנִי הַמֶּלֶךְ חֲדָרָיו
נָגִילָה וְנִשְׂמְחָה בָּךְ
נַזְכִּירָה דֹדֶיךָ מִיַּיִן
מֵישָׁרִים אֲהֵבוּךָ:

1:4 At this early point the poet hints at complexity, in creating with great virtuosity a verse that can be understood in multiple ways. Two readings are:

Draw me after you she cries out, competing with the damsels, who respond in kind: **After you** (the lover) **we shall run!** (See notes on reading "after you" twice.) She need not fear, for already **the king** – her lover in all his glory – **has brought me**, perhaps in response to her "draw me after you," **to his chambers**, a locus of privacy and intimacy. The damsels continue: **Let us take delight and joy in you, let us savor your loving, better than wine**, as 1:2, above, confirming her evaluation by further testimony. Indeed she understands them: **Rightly have they loved you.**

Alternatively, and more intimately (since this reading omits other speakers), she may not quote other damsels, but her lover, as follows. She begins: **Draw me after you, we** – she and he – **shall run** through an envisioned romantic setting. (Alternatively, she says, "Draw me after you" and then he, or they, call out, "Let us run.") **The king has** once **brought me to his chambers!** she exults in recollection, quoting his words then: **Let us**, he replies in royal plural, **take delight and joy in you** (the Hebrew "you" can be feminine). To this she responds: **Let** both of **us savor your loving**, which is in fact **better than wine**. She confirms, **Rightly have they** – the damsels – **loved you.**

We assume the poet created both readings, making them complementary. In both, the sense of movement, to be echoed throughout the Song, takes center stage.

Using a literary device (see notes) the poet here concludes the opening section. The stage is set with all its principle props: love, intimacy and longing. The motif has also been established – a dialogue of love, recited within a tension of absence and presence, and contrasted to a potential threat of competition from others. The phrases of this opening will be used near the end of the Song when the lover awakes from a fantasy to realize that his sexual desire is really for his beloved (7:10). (✱✱)[1]

II. Black, but comely

1:5 *I am black, but also comely,*	ה שְׁחוֹרָה אֲנִי וְנָאוָה
O Girls of Jerusalem,	בְּנוֹת יְרוּשָׁלָיִם
Like the tents of Kedar,	כְּאָהֳלֵי קֵדָר
Like the pavilions of Solomon.	כִּירִיעוֹת שְׁלֹמֹה:

1:5 **I am black**, unlike pale, indoor-oriented city girls, **but** – either "nevertheless" or "in addition" – **also comely**, beautiful, **O Girls of Jerusalem**, the city women, experts in beauty and love. Her beauty is different than theirs, and the Girls need an explanation. Implied is a certain expertise of the Girls, which will become basic to further encounters. He will often (1:10, 2:14, 4:3, 6:4) describe her as comely, once as "comely as Jerusalem" (6:4). Surely the Girls from Jerusalem should have seen this!

She is dark but comely, **like** other beautiful items: **the tents of** the tribe **Kedar** (the Hebrew name implies darkness), the dark tents of desert nomadic tribes, and **like the** woven dark beautiful **pavilions of Solomon**. "Solomon" seems cited only incidentally, identifying a type of tent. Later the Song will make this connection between the Girls of Jerusalem and Solomon more meaningful.

---

1.   This symbol (✱✱) indicates that the verse just discussed is interpreted in the chapter "Rereading the Song of Songs" (p. 108 ff)

1:6   *Do not set your sight on me*

     Because I am blackish,

     Because the sun has glared at me.

     My mother's sons waxed hot in anger at me.

     They set me as guard to the vineyards.

     My very own vineyard I did not guard.

ו   אַל־תִּרְאַנִי
שֶׁאֲנִי שְׁחַרְחֹרֶת
שֶׁשֱׁזָפַתְנִי הַשָּׁמֶשׁ
בְּנֵי אִמִּי נִחֲרוּ־בִי
שָׂמֻנִי נֹטֵרָה אֶת־הַכְּרָמִים
כַּרְמִי שֶׁלִּי לֹא נָטָרְתִּי:

1:6 Do not set your sight on – look at – **me because I am blackish.** This is not the way she usually is! She is so now only **because** of unusual circumstances: **the sun has glared at me.** They should understand that **my mother's sons,** her brothers (who had a leading familial role in pastoral society, specifically charged with overseeing their sister), **waxed hot** (a pun, given the effect of the sun) **in anger at me.** In consequence, **they set me as guard to the vineyards.** That is why she is presently sunburned. **My very own vineyard I did not guard** – explaining either that usually she is not so dark, or possibly why her brothers were angry in the first place. (**)

III. Where do you pasture

1:7   *Tell me, you whom my soul loves:*

     Where do you pasture,

     Where do you lie down at noon?

     Lest I be as one who wanders

     Beside the flocks of your fellows.

ז   הַגִּידָה לִּי שֶׁאָהֲבָה נַפְשִׁי
אֵיכָה תִרְעֶה
אֵיכָה תַּרְבִּיץ בַּצָּהֳרָיִם
שַׁלָּמָה אֶהְיֶה כְּעֹטְיָה
עַל עֶדְרֵי חֲבֵרֶיךָ:

1:7 Tell me, you whom my soul loves: so she differentiates herself from the damsels whose love is not associated with the soul, the depth of being, an image to which the poet will return. The longing tone perhaps reflects the lover's absence, to which she immediately refers: **Where do you pasture** your sheep, **where do you lie** them **down at noon,** when

the heat forces shepherds and flocks to rest. She does not know where he, a shepherd who must seek available pasture, has gone. She is determined to find him, **lest I be as one who wanders** – the last thing a lover would want for his beloved – **beside the flocks of your fellows**, again, ominous others. (******)

1:8 *If you do not know,*
   O most beautiful of women,
   Then follow the tracks of the sheep
   And pasture your kids
   Next to the shepherds' huts.

ח אִם־לֹא תֵדְעִי לָךְ
הַיָּפָה בַּנָּשִׁים
צְאִי־לָךְ בְּעִקְבֵי הַצֹּאן
וּרְעִי אֶת־גְּדִיֹּתַיִךְ
עַל מִשְׁכְּנוֹת הָרֹעִים:

1:8 If you do not know, O most beautiful of women, the lover begins his response, encouraging her by recalling the physical beauty of which they alone are aware. To the damsels, she is "only" a swarthy country maid (verses 5, 6). If you do not know, **then follow the paths of the tracks of the sheep and pasture your kids next to the shepherds' huts.** Before he had responded to her call by inviting her to his chambers (1:4); he now tells her that she must take initiative and seek him out. (******)

IV. How comely

1:9　*To a mare in Pharaoh's chariotry*
　　Have I likened you, O my darling.

ט　לְסֻסָתִי בְּרִכְבֵי פַרְעֹה
　דִּמִּיתִיךְ רַעְיָתִי:

1:9 To a mare in Pharaoh's chariotry, have I likened – or imagined – **you.** Perhaps the thought of his beloved among the shepherds sparks the image of a mare among Egyptian warhorses, which were all stallions. This worrisome picture quickly moves beyond the immediate association, for the horses evoke images of strength, speed, pride and possibly well-groomed beauty. (Ancient drawings testify to the beautiful accouterments placed on horses.) **O my darling.** "Darling" (*ra'ayah*) echoes "pasture" and "shepherd," 1:7, 8 (*ro'eh*). These are similar words, using the same letters, with different meanings. "My darling" is subsequently used most often in conjunction with "my beautiful one" (1:15; 2:10, 13; 4:1, 7; 6:4), leading one to guess that beauty is emphasized here, reflecting the attention she draws from those other shepherds.

1:10　*How comely your cheeks with circlets,*
　　Your neck in beads.

י　נָאווּ לְחָיַיִךְ בַּתֹּרִים
　צַוָּארֵךְ בַּחֲרוּזִים:

1:10 How comely – the same term as her self-description to the Girls of Jerusalem (1:5) – **your cheeks with circlets,** either of plaited hair, a style known in the ancient world, or of circular jewelry (cf. Rashi – "earrings"), **your neck in beads,** a style also well known in the ancient world. He seems less assertive than she. Whereas he circles around the intimacy of the mouth, citing her cheek and neck, she had immediately cited the intimacy of the mouth and kiss (1:2). He describes only her cheeks as comely, whereas she had applied that term to her entire self (1:5).

1:11 *Circlets of gold we shall make for you*
With spangles of silver.

יא תּוֹרֵי זָהָב נַעֲשֶׂה־לָּךְ
עִם נְקֻדּוֹת הַכָּסֶף:

1:11 Circlets of gold we shall make for you as befits her beauty **with spangles of silver.** (******)

v. On his couch

1:12 *While the king was on his couch*
My spikenard gave forth its fragrance.

יב עַד־שֶׁהַמֶּלֶךְ בִּמְסִבּוֹ
נִרְדִּי נָתַן רֵיחוֹ:

1:12 While the king — again, her lover in all his glory (1:4), the fine jewelry (verse 10f.) returning attention to royal imagery — **was on his couch** — she is again in his house, in the privacy of his chambers — **my spikenard**, an expensive, refreshing, Indian spice, **gave forth its fragrance**, complementing the smells of his oils, which are so good (1:3).

1:13 *A bag of myrrh is my lover to me,*
Lying between my breasts.

יג צְרוֹר הַמֹּר
דּוֹדִי לִי בֵּין שָׁדַי יָלִין:

1:13 A bag of myrrh, another strong, pleasant and long lasting spice, originally from southern Arabia but grown also in Israel, **is my lover to me.** Subsequently the poet will use the image to bond the lovers: first, as myrrh falls from his lips, and later, as a description of her, and it thus becomes a shared attribute. It, or he, is **lying** — by way of double entendre, either the myrrh, in a fragrant bag between her breasts, or the lover himself, setting his head there, or both. The core meaning of the term "lying" is "to spend the night." Is that also implied? He – and/or it – lies **between my breasts**, close to the heart, intimately near. Cloth bags were used as amulets hung round the neck in ancient Egypt. (**)

1:14 A cluster of henna is my lover to me
  In the vineyards of Ein Gedi.

יד   אֶשְׁכֹּל הַכֹּפֶר

דּוֹדִי לִי בְּכַרְמֵי עֵין גֶּדִי:

1:14 A cluster of henna, yet another pleasant spice, **is my lover to me**, just as he is a bag of myrrh. Alternatively, once placed between her breasts, as is the bag of myrrh, he seems to her as a cluster of henna blossoms, which she would naturally clutch close to her, holding them there for enjoyment. This henna is **in the vineyards of Ein Gedi**, the oasis in the Judean desert that is Israel's only suitable environment for growing the tropical henna, which itself does not grow on vines (so "in" must imply "among"). The symbolic valences of "spices" and "vineyard" will be clarified later. Complementarily, the lovers themselves could be placed in Ein Gedi. The lover will later apply "cluster" and "vineyard" to her (7:9, 13), an added reflection of the mutuality of their love.

VI. You are beautiful

1:15 Indeed you are beautiful, my darling,
  Indeed you are beautiful; your eyes – doves.

טו   הִנָּךְ יָפָה רַעְיָתִי

הִנָּךְ יָפָה עֵינַיִךְ יוֹנִים:

1:15 Indeed you are beautiful, my darling, whom he has called the "most beautiful of women" (1:8). **Indeed you are beautiful**, he repeats, overwhelmed; **your eyes** are like **doves**. Many implications have been attributed to this image:

the shape of the eyes (in some ancient drawings a woman's eyes appear as doves), beauty, gentleness, softness (as feathers), innocence, sparkle and even monogamy. (The dove has only one mate, with an implied parallelism – "you are beautiful/ you are my darling/ you are beautiful/ you are mine alone.") The poet might have had several or all of these in mind. Subsequently both she and her eyes will be compared to doves, possibly implying a more central role to the eyes in representing her person. Is the image shared because doves transcend distance, the separation they wish to overcome?

1:16 Indeed you are beautiful, my lover,
   Truly lovely;
   Truly our pallet is verdant.

טז   הִנְּךָ יָפֶה דוֹדִי
אַף נָעִים
אַף־עַרְשֵׂנוּ רַעֲנָנָה:

1:16 Indeed you are beautiful, my lover, she replies in symmetry and in mutuality, **truly lovely** – she emphasizes; **truly our pallet is verdant**, as she will detail immediately. Through "truly" his beauty and that of the environment meld. (**)

1:17 The beams of our houses — cedars;
   The rafters — junipers.

יז   קֹרוֹת בָּתֵּינוּ אֲרָזִים
רַחִיטֵנוּ בְּרוֹתִים:

1:17 The beams of our houses – the plural, "houses," may be either a veiled reference to the many places of their meetings, or a late form of writing, indicating the singular, "house." These beams are **cedars; the rafters – junipers.** Both are luxurious trees, evergreens indigenous to north Israel and Lebanon. Cedars are often considered the finest of building materials in the Bible. The poet seems determined to "sweep" the countryside, taking the reader from southern Ein Gedi to the north.

Chapter 2

פרק ב

א אֲנִי֙ חֲבַצֶּ֣לֶת הַשָּׁר֔וֹן
שֽׁוֹשַׁנַּ֖ת הָעֲמָקִֽים:

2:1 I am a Sharon-rose
A valley-lily.

2:1 I am a Sharon-rose, a valley-lily. Having cited the trees supporting their "house of love," the woman recalls herself in much smaller terms – slight flowers that bloom in Israel. Scholars differ on the identity of the plants. The biblical references (which include their use as symbols of the promised restoration of Zion) indicate that both bloom regularly and across a wide area. The metaphor would seem to rest on the plants being commonplace ("I am just one of the girls") with an undertone of strength and determination (they appear annually, and are sure to blossom). The poet will develop the image, and later usages indicate that the lily is a pink plant. "Sharon," applied to several areas in Israel, most often to the coastal plain, refers either to the woman's (or the plant's) location or to a type of rose. (On "lily" – see note.)

ב כְּשֽׁוֹשַׁנָּה֙ בֵּ֣ין הַחוֹחִ֔ים
כֵּ֥ן רַעְיָתִ֖י בֵּ֥ין הַבָּנֽוֹת:

2:2 As a lily among the brambles,
Such is my darling among the girls.

2:2 If she claims to be only a lily, he replies that for him she is much more. She is **as a lily among the brambles**, exceptional. Her beauty is not lost within the context of a love forest (1:17), but is a burst of color among dry and useless thorns. **Such is my darling** – whose beauty he has previously affirmed – **among the girls**, either all women, or particularly among the Girls of Jerusalem to whom she has proclaimed her beauty (1:5). (**)

2:3 *As an apricot among the trees of the forest,*
Such is my lover among the boys.
I delight to linger in that shadow,
And that fruit is sweet to my palate.

כְּתַפּוּחַ בַּעֲצֵי הַיַּעַר ג
כֵּן דּוֹדִי בֵּין הַבָּנִים
בְּצִלּוֹ חִמַּדְתִּי וְיָשַׁבְתִּי
וּפִרְיוֹ מָתוֹק לְחִכִּי:

2:3 As an apricot, she replies, citing a fruit-bearing tree, **among the trees of the forest**, which do not bear fruit, a parallel appreciation to his citing her as a lily among brambles, **so is my lover** who is thus differentiated sharply from his environment both by beauty and usefulness. The imagery is natural given their forest location of love (1:17). Indeed, the end of chapter 1, referring to both spices and forest, has laid the groundwork for the strong nature similes here. She places him **among the boys**, a parallel to his "among the girls" in verse 2. Both stand out. His preeminence may indicate superiority to the shepherds, above (1:8). "Boys" were also mentioned (1:8, there translated "sons"), referring to her brothers. Is she also declaring his superiority to them?

She continues, **I delight to linger in that** – "that" could imply "its" or "his," referring to the tree or the lover – **shadow**, protecting her from the hot mid-Eastern sun that has already burnt her (1:5, 6). She prefers him despite the fact that fruit trees cast less shade than forest trees, as a rule. **And that fruit** – again, the Hebrew can be "its" or "his" fruit – **is sweet to my palate.** The verse thus flows from tree imagery to a kiss, one already longed for and declared part of their love, better than wine (1:2). Now the kiss is celebrated for its sweetness, artfully integrating the images of fruit and wine. (**)

VIII. To the wine house

2:4 *He brought me to the wine house,*
And he viewed me with love.

הֱבִיאַנִי֙ אֶל־בֵּ֣ית הַיַּ֔יִן ד
וְדִגְל֥וֹ עָלַ֖י אַהֲבָֽה׃

2:4 Having recalled his kiss, she is transported from the metaphors of nature back to another moment of intimacy.

He brought me, she recalls. Before she had recalled his "bringing her" to the chambers, but here he brings her **to the wine house**, a markedly different locale, a public place and therefore a public declaration of his love. (The poet has already prepared the reader for a connection of wine to love – 1:2). **And he viewed me with love.** Literally, his view upon me was love, the term "view" to be subsequently developed in several ways. Here, the connection of the eyes isolates the lovers, dimming the import of their surroundings. (**)

2:5 *Sustain me with cakes,*
Cushion me with apricots,
Because I am lovesick.

סַמְּכ֙וּנִי֙ בָּאֲשִׁישׁ֔וֹת ה
רַפְּד֖וּנִי בַּתַּפּוּחִ֑ים
כִּי־חוֹלַ֥ת אַהֲבָ֖ה אָֽנִי׃

2:5 Sustain me with raisin **cakes**, she calls out, an apparent need in the heady atmosphere of the wine house to mollify the effect of the wine, allowing her to sit or stand straight. The true need, however, is other, as she goes on to articulate. She is lovesick. Furthermore, similar raisin cakes are mentioned elsewhere in the Bible (see notes) in connection with fertility cults, and therefore one senses that she here anticipates moments beyond the shared look of love – moments of lovemaking, even fertility. **Cushion me** – a term used metaphorically, since the request to do so is **with apricots**, recalling her description of him as an apricot tree (2:3).

Those around her may hear a call for food. She utters a desire for a romantic kiss. Further, one wonders if the fruit-bearing nature of the tree is related to the fertility emphasis of the cakes. Sustain me and cushion me, she requests, **because I am lovesick**, weak from his stare of love, or from her love of him. (**)

2:6 *His left hand under my head,*
And his right hand embracing me.

שְׂמֹאלוֹ תַּחַת לְרֹאשִׁי
וִימִינוֹ תְּחַבְּקֵנִי:

ו

2:6 His left hand underneath my head, and his right hand embracing me, she describes. In approaching the crescendo of her description of their intimacy, the picture focuses more sharply on the couple alone. As was accomplished by the stare, the concentration on the physical contact has the effect of obscuring the background and the presence of others.

2:7 *I adjure you, O Girls of Jerusalem,*
By the gazelles and by the hinds of the field,
That you neither rouse nor disturb love,
Until it so desires.

הִשְׁבַּעְתִּי אֶתְכֶם בְּנוֹת יְרוּשָׁלַם
בִּצְבָאוֹת אוֹ בְּאַיְלוֹת הַשָּׂדֶה
אִם־תָּעִירוּ וְאִם־תְּעוֹרְרוּ אֶת־הָאַהֲבָה
עַד שֶׁתֶּחְפָּץ:

ז

2:7 The moment is intimate – too intimate. She breaks off, turning to address that ever-present audience and threat:

I adjure you, O Girls of Jerusalem, the city girls to whom she has already defended her beauty, **by the gazelles and by the hinds of the field** – i.e., by all that is holy. The free running, graceful gazelles and hinds represent her ideal, as opposed to the affected beauty of the city. In addition, their loyalty may appeal as referent: after choosing a mate from the herd, the hind is loyal to that single mate. In another vein, the animals' names are also appropriate, for their pronunciations resemble terms used for the deity, and can therefore serve as a replacement, as is common in many cultures. (See notes.) I adjure you **that you neither rouse nor disturb love**, that they not intrude upon this love idyll, **until it** – love itself – **so desires.**

The words are ambiguous. With equal degrees of validity, they may be understood differently. On one hand, the girls could be "called off," asked not to interrupt with extraneous matters until this matter works itself out. On the other hand, the call might be that love not be roused too soon, i.e., that it be allowed to blossom slowly, lest haste destroy its chances. In the first case, she pleads with the girls not to interrupt. In the second case, she uses them and the attraction of the life they lead as a sounding board, while essentially addressing herself: allow love its own steady progress and do not rush the process. Both meanings may have been intended.

Later, the Girls also will be seen as competitors for his love. With that, this verse will take on a third level of meaning – they are not to compete. She was there first.

This adjured noninterference also will become a repeated refrain. It is not this one incident alone, then, that demands noninterference, but the love relationship itself.

IX. Come away

2:8   *Hark, the voice of my lover!*

      Behold, it comes;

      Leaping across the mountains,

      Skipping across the hills.

ח קוֹל דּוֹדִי

הִנֵּה־זֶה בָּא

מְדַלֵּג עַל־הֶהָרִים

מְקַפֵּץ עַל־הַגְּבָעוֹת:

2:8 Hark, the voice of my lover! Having "escaped" from the intimacy of the description in verses 2:1–6 by turning to an outside party, she now sharply changes the subject. "Hark!" the Hebrew *kol* can be understood as either "hark" or "the voice of." Both are included in the translation. **Behold,** – now – **it** – or he – **comes**. While she hears her lover's voice coming to her, the verse also reflects her seeing him coming to her, **leaping across the mountains, skipping across the hills.** He moves swiftly across the countryside, and the scene is again far from the city.

    "Voices" will echo through the Song – hers and nature's. Similarly, the broad sense of movement first cited here will be developed throughout.

2:9   *My lover is like a gazelle*

      Or the young hart.

      Behold!

      He stands behind our wall,

      Gazing through the windows,

      Peering through the lattices.

ט דּוֹמֶה דוֹדִי לִצְבִי

אוֹ לְעֹפֶר הָאַיָּלִים

הִנֵּה

זֶה עוֹמֵד אַחַר כָּתְלֵנוּ

מַשְׁגִּיחַ מִן־הַחַלֹּנוֹת

מֵצִיץ מִן־הַחֲרַכִּים:

2:9 My lover is like a gazelle or the young hart, she concludes, having heard him bounding so swiftly across the hills. These graceful, wild animals are precisely those by which she adjured the Girls of Jerusalem. (The hart is the male, the hind the female. She here uses masculine nouns for the animals, including the gazelle, while in her oath, 2:7, she referred to the feminine of the species.) Now her lover appears as these animals, which represent "all that is holy." As physical attributes, they foretell his ability to reach her.

Behold! She superimposes on her previous call to "behold" (verse 8) a new, subsequent scene: Now **he stands**, in marked contrast to his flight across the hills, the text leaving the referent (the lover or the animal) vague, implying both, **behind our wall**, present, but still cut off. The wall being "ours" (not "mine") she hints that she is not alone, probably among family. Subsequently, she will seek to bring him in (8:2) and her brothers will seek to keep the lovers apart (8:8), strengthening the pain of the separation here. He is **gazing through the windows, peering through the lattices.** If this is the animal, the reticence to come closer is natural. If this is the lover, this is a poignant scene, the lover cut off from the beloved he had come to see, a reflection not only of the moment, but also of the situation of the poem. He has come as close as he might. Now the woman, observer of the previous verse, becomes the observed.

2:10 *My lover responded,*

    Saying to me:

    Rise up, my darling,

    My beauty, come away.

י   עָנָה דוֹדִי

וְאָמַר לִי קוּמִי

לָךְ רַעְיָתִי יָפָתִי

וּלְכִי־לָךְ:

2:10 My lover responded from behind the wall, to a gesture, to his beloved's attention or the like, **saying to me** – as she recalls not only his arrival, but also that of his voice. (The Hebrew "responded…saying" implies "began to speak." We translate literally in light of later use of the verb "respond.") **Rise up, my darling, my beauty** – the two terms seem connected. He can hardly use the term "my darling" without referring to her beauty (cf. 1:9, 15; 2:2). **Come away.** The terms "rise up" and "come away" are in the ethical dative, an intensive form translated in earlier style,

"rise ye" and "come ye." This form had been used before, in his message to her to follow the tracks of the sheep to seek him out, with the verbs "know" and "follow" (1:8 – not reflected in the translation there). He seems to regret his previous instructions, given from afar, and now replaces them. No longer is the instruction to conduct a vague search, but to come with him. His statement is chiastic (a-b-b-a, rise-darling-beauty-come), isolating this opening call and heightening its effect. (**)

2:11 *For behold,*
  The winter is past,
  The rains are over, gone away.

יא כִּי־הִנֵּ֥ה
הַסְּתָ֖ו עָבָ֑ר
הַגֶּ֕שֶׁם חָלַ֖ף הָלַ֥ךְ לֽוֹ׃

2:11 For behold, the poet repeats a third time (2:8, 9) maintaining the sense of immediacy, **the winter is past,** and there is now free access to the fields and hills, for **the rains,** the winter rains of Israel, which has two seasons, rainy and dry, **are over, gone away** – using both the same Hebrew verb and the same ethical dative form as "come away" in the previous verse. The sense is "long gone." She is asked, as it were, to join both him and nature.

2:12 *The buds are seen in the land,*
The time of singing has arrived,
And the voice of the turtledove
is heard in our land.

יב   הַנִּצָּנִים֙ נִרְא֣וּ בָאָ֔רֶץ
עֵ֥ת הַזָּמִ֖יר הִגִּ֑יעַ
וְק֥וֹל הַתּ֖וֹר
נִשְׁמַ֥ע בְּאַרְצֵֽנוּ׃

2:12 The buds are seen in the land, promising the blossoming and green-ery with which the two have described their love (cf. 1:14, 16, and 17). This is a renewal of the environment. Here the poet moves smoothly from spring as a time of easy movement to spring as a symbol of love. **The time of singing** – the Hebrew can also be translated "pruning," and some have suggested that both are intended. In any case, this new spring is an appropriate occasion for song. The time **has arrived, and the voice of the turtledove**, perhaps echoing his voice (2:8) **is heard in our land**. (**)

2:13 *The fig tree puts forth its young fruit*
And the vines, in blossom,
give forth fragrance.
Rise up, my darling,
My beauty, come away.

יג   הַתְּאֵנָה֙ חָֽנְטָ֣ה פַגֶּ֔יהָ
וְהַגְּפָנִ֥ים ׀ סְמָדַ֖ר
נָ֣תְנוּ רֵ֑יחַ
ק֥וּמִי לָ֛ךְ רַעְיָתִ֥י
יָפָתִ֖י וּלְכִי־לָֽךְ׃

2:13 The fig tree puts forth its young fruit, he continues the picture of early spring, **and the vines, in blossom, give forth fragrance**, certainly an indication of nature's readiness for love, just as her spikenard "gave forth its fragrance" as the lover was on his couch (1:12). **Rise up, my dar-ling, my beauty, come away**, he repeats, closing his appeal exactly as he began (2:10).

Spring reflects both the new and the renewed. The lovers seek to go off for the first time or to reunite. Both possibilities are inherent in the verse – perhaps even reflecting two different stages at one time. The reader awaits clarification.

x. Let me hear

2:14 *My dove,*

 In the crannies of the rock,

 in the covert of the terrace,

 Let me see the sight of you,

 let me hear your voice;

 For your voice is sweet,

 and the sight of you is comely.

יד   יוֹנָתִ֞י

בְּחַגְוֵ֣י הַסֶּ֗לַע

בְּסֵ֨תֶר֙ הַמַּדְרֵגָ֔ה

הַרְאִ֨ינִי֙ אֶת־מַרְאַ֔יִךְ

הַשְׁמִיעִ֖ינִי אֶת־קוֹלֵ֑ךְ

כִּי־קוֹלֵ֥ךְ עָרֵ֖ב

וּמַרְאֵ֥יךְ נָאוֶֽה׃

2:14 My dove, he addresses her in a term of endearment, and then continues with the simile, **in the crannies of the rock, in the covert of the terrace,** where doves customarily nest, far away and inaccessible in distant hills or in the mountains' agricultural terraces. This is in stark contrast to the previous imagery, though the appeal for her to appear approximates his prior appeal to her to "come away." The poet effectively extends the dove imagery, with a call that applies equally well to the dove and to the woman: **Let me see the sight of you, let me hear your voice;** he longs for her presence. Nature in its readiness is both "seen" and "heard" (2:12 – same roots). How much more so should you be seen and heard, **for your voice is sweet, and the sight of you is comely,** "comely" being the term she has used for her own beauty (1:5) and which he has confirmed (1:10). His appeal to her is another chiastic structure (a-b-b-a, appearance-voice-voice-appearance), echoing his call to her to come out (2:10, 13). Thus the use of both terms ("see," "hear") and the chiastic structure connect this section to the preceding verses. In 1:6 the Girls saw (looked at) her, seeing only external blackness. He here sees her true comeliness immediately.

 The dove image takes on complexity. Previously compared to her eyes (1:15), it is now a term for her. The poet will continue to develop the image. (**)

2:15 *Hold off foxes for us!*
    Little foxes that ruin vineyards,
    And our vineyard is in blossom.

טו אֶחֱזוּ־לָנוּ שֻׁעָלִים
שֻׁעָלִים קְטַנִּים מְחַבְּלִים כְּרָמִים
וּכְרָמֵינוּ סְמָדַר:

2:15 Hold off — an admonition to an anonymous audience — **foxes for us** two lovers. (He spoke the previous verse, she speaks the next, so this verse blends both speakers, or can be either, the poet leaving the identification blurred.) For **little foxes** are creatures **that ruin** — evidently an immediate and serious threat — **vineyards**, the place of his abode (1:14) and that which she had to guard, though she had not guarded her own (1:5f.). Foxes in antiquity were commonly conceived to be destroyers of vineyards. (See notes.) (The Song does not repeat mention of foxes, as it does with all vital terms, so we need seek no further implication of the foxes than their endangering vineyards.) **And our vineyard** — the speaker(s) transfers the threat to a personal, immediate plain — **is in blossom**, like the rest of nature (2:13), "ready." However, the possessive, "our" vineyard, hints that the reference is deeper than yet another citation of nature. One senses that the vineyard, in its present and previous uses (1:5f.) is a value-laden symbol, but it remains, at this juncture, still vague. (**)

2:16 *My lover is mine, and I am his;*
    He who pastures among the lilies.

טז דּוֹדִי לִי וַאֲנִי לוֹ
הָרֹעֶה בַּשּׁוֹשַׁנִּים:

2:16 My lover is mine, she declares, taking a phrase from previous sentences (1:13f., there translated "is my lover to me"), now used as a declaration. Despite the danger (foxes), the relationship remains present and strong, **and I am his**, the equality and balance of the relationship serving as the best possible defense against any threats. She is his, **he who pastures** — like the English "feed," the Hebrew (used also in 1:7, 8) can be causative (pasture the sheep) or active (eat). Despite being near other shepherds (1:8) she seeks only him, he who feeds **among the lilies**. Since she is a lily (2:1), if "feed" is taken as "eat," the imagery is erotic and intimate. The plural, however, also recalls the existence of other women who love him (1:3). The previous verse is thus starker – their commitment is undertaken in the presence of others. It recalls 2:2, his declaring that she is a lily among brambles, the best of women.

The echo noted above (1:9) is repeated: he is now called one who pastures (*ro'eh*), recalling her as "darling" (*ra'ayah*) – 1:9, 15; 2:2, 10, and 13. There is an implied mutuality.

2:17 *Until the day breathes,*
    And the shadows flee,
    Circle about, my lover,
    Make yourself like a gazelle,
    Or a young hart,
    On the cleft mountains.

יז עַד שֶׁיָּפוּחַ הַיּוֹם
וְנָסוּ הַצְּלָלֵים
סֹב דְּמֵה־לְךָ
דוֹדִי לִצְבִי
אוֹ לְעֹפֶר הָאַיָּלֵים
עַל־הָרֵי בָתֶר:

2:17 Until the day breathes, when the winds blow, morning or evening, **and the shadows flee**, the sun being near the horizon, the edges of the shadows move quickly; until then, **circle about** – i.e., "turn," but related to later uses of same root with an implication of circling. Turn, **my lover** – away from this intimacy, or from those other lilies? **Make yourself like a gazelle, or a young hart**, as she has just heard him, skipping over the mountains (2:8f.). She hopes he will return to that grand movement, again approaching her. His similarity to these animals (2:9) augurs well for his ability to meet her requests. She hopes to see him skipping **on the cleft mountains**, the terrain now accentuated. The mountains are split, sharply cragged, lending an ominous tone to the surroundings, making access to one another difficult.

His circling about, while waiting, is soon to be balanced (3:2) by her circling about while looking for him. (✽✽)

XI. On my bed at night

Chapter 3

פרק ג

3:1   *On my bed at night*

     I sought him whom my soul loves.

     I sought him, but found him not.

א   עַל־מִשְׁכָּבִי בַּלֵּילֹות

בִּקַּשְׁתִּי אֵת שֶׁאָהֲבָה נַפְשִׁי

בִּקַּשְׁתִּיו וְלֹא מְצָאתִיו:

3:1 On my bed at night – the preceding reference to the change of light to dark recalls to her a nighttime scene, which would seem to straddle dream and reality. Literally, "at nights" (plural) is used, a poetic form, indicative of a general description, best translated "at night." However, there may be a secondary implication of consecutive nights, as in a recurring dream. **I sought him whom my soul loves** – so she has addressed her lover before (1:7), also emphasizing his absence. **I sought him**, still either in fact or in fantasy, **but found him not**, scarcely a surprise if he took to the hills at her request (2:17). (**)

3:2   *I will rise and I shall circle through the city,*

     Through the streets and the squares.

     I shall seek him whom my soul loves.

     I sought him, but found him not.

ב   אָקוּמָה נָּא וַאֲסֹובְבָה בָעִיר

בַּשְּׁוָקִים וּבָרְחֹבֹות

אֲבַקְשָׁה אֵת שֶׁאָהֲבָה נַפְשִׁי

בִּקַּשְׁתִּיו וְלֹא מְצָאתִיו:

3:2 I will – as opposed to "shall," the Hebrew reflecting determination – **rise**, she says to herself, possibly responding to his appeal that she "rise up" (2:10, 13), but too late. He had called in her presence, but now she seeks him in his absence. Was her delay responsible for that? She will rise **and I shall circle through the city**, "circling" as she asked her lover to circle back to be like a gazelle (2:17 – the roots are related, not identical). There is a tone of rapid circular movement to the poem, as she moves **through the streets and the squares**, an audacious and perhaps

dangerous act for the young woman at night. **I shall seek him whom my soul loves. I sought him**, now perhaps in actuality, in response to her musings of the previous verse, **but found him not**, just as she was unable to do in her musings. (✲✲)

3:3 *The watchmen, circling within the city, found me.* מְצָאֻנִי֙ הַשֹּׁמְרִ֔ים הַסֹּבְבִ֖ים בָּעִ֑יר ג
"He whom my soul loves – have you seen him?" אֵ֛ת שֶׁאָהֲבָ֥ה נַפְשִׁ֖י רְאִיתֶֽם:

3:3 The watchmen, who are charged with protecting the city, **circling** as she was doing, **within the city** – all the parties seem to be in rapid movement, as the scene itself seems to swirl – **found me**. This she notes ironically. She hoped to find her lover; instead, the watchmen found her. "**He whom my soul loves** – the object is emphasized by appearing first – **have you seen him?**" The watchmen do not respond, a silent stark contrast to the desperation of her search. (✲✲)

3:4 *Scarcely had I passed them by,* כִּמְעַט֙ שֶׁעָבַ֣רְתִּי מֵהֶ֔ם ד
When I found him whom my soul loves. עַ֣ד שֶֽׁמָּצָ֔אתִי אֵ֥ת שֶׁאָהֲבָ֖ה נַפְשִׁ֑י
I held him and shall not let him go אֲחַזְתִּיו֙ וְלֹ֣א אַרְפֶּ֔נּוּ
Until I have brought him עַד־שֶׁהֲבֵיאתִיו֙
To the house of my mother, אֶל־בֵּ֣ית אִמִּ֔י
To the chamber of her who conceived me. וְאֶל־חֶ֖דֶר הוֹרָתִֽי:

3:4 Scarcely had I passed them by – she passes them, not they her, for hers is the principle movement – **when I found**, finally, **him whom my soul loves. I held him** (the dangers having been "held" off for the meantime – 2:15) **and shall not let him go.** The movement of the search comes to a sudden halt in an embrace, but still with anticipation. She will not let go **until I have brought him**, renewed movement, as he has "brought" her twice, for intimate moments, to his chambers (1:4) and to the wine house (2:4), **to the house of my mother, to the chamber** – the same term used before for a room of intimacy (1:4) – **of her who conceived me.** She here moves her hopes up a degree. Her mother is a model – implying not only love, but also marriage and childbearing! She sees beyond intimacy to family. (✱✱)

3:5　*I adjure you, O Girls of Jerusalem,*
　　By the gazelles and by the hinds of the field,
　　That you neither rouse nor disturb love,
　　Until it so desires.

ה　הִשְׁבַּ֨עְתִּי אֶתְכֶ֜ם בְּנ֤וֹת יְרוּשָׁלִַ֙ם֙
בִּצְבָא֔וֹת א֖וֹ בְּאַיְל֣וֹת הַשָּׂדֶ֑ה
אִם־תָּעִ֧ירוּ | וְֽאִם־תְּע֥וֹרְר֛וּ אֶת־הָאַהֲבָ֖ה
עַ֥ד שֶׁתֶּחְפָּֽץ׃

3:5 I adjure you, O Girls of Jerusalem – exactly as she did before (2:7). This third mention of the Girls would indicate that they must be central to the poem, even if it is not yet clear how or why. She adjures **by the gazelles and by the hinds of the field, that you neither rouse nor disturb love, until it so desires.** As before, she has reached a peak of intimacy in her description, and discretely cuts that off with a dual plea neither to interrupt nor to rush love. Both meanings are appropriate.

XII. Solomon's own

3:6 *Who is this, ascending from the desert,*
Like shafts of smoke,
Perfumed by myrrh and frankincense,
With all the peddler's powder?

ו   מֵי זֹאת עֹלָה מִן־הַמִּדְבָּר
כְּתִימְרוֹת עָשָׁן
מְקֻטֶּרֶת מֹר וּלְבוֹנָה
מִכֹּל אַבְקַת רוֹכֵל:

3:6 Who is this woman? The question appears to be a response by the Girls of Jerusalem to the woman's speaking. The continuation, however, clarifies that the poet has, like before (2:8), changed scenes entirely after addressing the Girls. Who is this **ascending from the desert**? In the previous sharp change of scene (2:8), a literal translation would have read, "Hark! My lover — behold *this* (masculine) is coming…" Here the poet asks, "Who is *this* (feminine) ascending…," a balance to that previous verse.

The desert supplements previous scenes (Jerusalem, pastures, mountains, valleys, oasis, cliffs, forests, vineyards, etc.), possibly an attempt to be all-embracing. In addition, ascent from the desert may suggest renewed life, a return to the vegetation and nature in blossom mentioned previously. The ascent also recalls Jerusalem, which is in the mountains above the Judean desert. She is **like shafts of smoke**, a jarring image — perhaps dust clouds rising from a caravan. She is **perfumed** (translation fits the terms following, though the Hebrew could also be construed "clouded," describing the smoke pillars. Perhaps both were intended, a double entendre) **by myrrh**, a sign of mutuality — her lover was a bag of myrrh between her breasts (1:13) **and frankincense, with all the peddler's powder?** Spices were a major export of South Arabia, across the desert. (**)

3:7 *Behold — the bed, Solomon's own.*
Encircling it are sixty warriors
Of Israel's warriors.

ז   הִנֵּה מִטָּתוֹ שֶׁלִּשְׁלֹמֹה
שִׁשִּׁים גִּבֹּרִים סָבִיב לָהּ
מִגִּבֹּרֵי יִשְׂרָאֵל:

3:7 Behold — the same terms and sense of immediacy the poet used describing the lover, skipping over the hills (2:8, 9) — **the bed** (the term can indicate a portable couch), **Solomon's own.** Apparently, no answer is offered to the question of the previous verse. Was the question rhetorical? Is the woman presumed to be the one who ascended, and is she somehow now in Solomon's presence? Alternatively, is the picture of her ascending to be contrasted to this picture of Solomon?

Solomon's reappearance is itself a surprise. His appearance in the title all but forgotten, he now seems more important to the Song, though the import is not yet clear. It should be noted that Solomon, third king of Israel, inherited an extensive kingdom from his father David, and he was known for his great wealth.

Encircling it, his bed, **are sixty warriors** who stand statically around the bed, as opposed to her self-assured, rapid "circling" movement through the town (3:2), **of Israel's warriors,** the national, martial tone reinforcing the "authenticity" of the mention of Solomon. The number here cited is very impressive. David had thirty or thirty-seven warriors (II Sam. 23). (**)

3:8 *All of them held fast to their swords,*
Trained for war,
Each man with his sword on his thigh
Because of the terror at night.

כֻּלָּם אֲחֻזֵי חֶרֶב ח
מְלֻמְּדֵי מִלְחָמָה
אִישׁ חַרְבּוֹ עַל־יְרֵכוֹ
מִפַּחַד בַּלֵּילוֹת:

3:8 All of them held fast to their swords — meaning "skilled soldiers," here translated literally because of the striking contrast to the lovers. The warriors are "held" to their swords, involuntarily bound. They might resemble only the foxes that are "held" off (2:15). The lovers are active holders — "holding" each other in love after her intense search (3:4). These warriors are **trained** — literally, "taught" — **for war** — meaning "expert in battle." **Each man** stands in that circle, **with his sword on his thigh because of the terror at night.** These great heroes are afraid at night! The contrast is extreme. At night (same word — *ballelot* — 3:1f.) she goes out into the city to seek her lover, circling through it; the warriors form a protective circle of fear. (**)

3:9 *A litter he made for himself, the king, Solomon,*
Of wood from Lebanon.

אַפִּרְיוֹן עָשָׂה לוֹ הַמֶּלֶךְ שְׁלֹמֹה ט
מֵעֲצֵי הַלְּבָנוֹן:

3:9 A litter he made for himself, did **the king** — the reader wonders for a moment if this is the "king," i.e., the lover (1:4, 12), but is immediately informed that we continue to speak about **Solomon,** his name being held until this point in the verse somewhat unnaturally, emphasizing his presence. The connection of "king" with "Solomon" is also somewhat puzzling. While the title certainly fits Solomon, it has been used in the Song only for the lover, and unless the lover is totally a symbolic person, he and Solomon cannot be the same. The reader is left puzzled at this point.

The litter is made **of** precious and strong **wood from Lebanon.** (**)

3:10 *Its pillars he made of silver,*
Its cushioning of gold,
Its seat of purple yarn,
Its interior inlaid with love
By the Girls of Jerusalem.

עַמּוּדָיו עָשָׂה כֶסֶף

רְפִידָתוֹ זָהָב

מֶרְכָּבוֹ אַרְגָּמָן

תּוֹכוֹ רָצוּף אַהֲבָה

מִבְּנוֹת יְרוּשָׁלָם:

י

3:10 Its pillars he made of silver, its cushioning of gold, the comparison continues, for the lover preferred to use these two precious metals as jewels for his beloved (1:11). She preferred natural cushions – apricots (2:5). **Its seat** is **of purple yarn**, an expensive, honorific fabric; **its interior inlaid with love by the Girls of Jerusalem.** This last phrase has several possible implications. "Inlaid with love" might be adverbial ("lovingly wrought by"). It could indicate pictures and/or statements of love physically inlaid or it might refer to physical acts of love that there took place. All might be implied. "By the Girls" might also be translated "for the Girls." The litter may be inlaid with pictures of love for them, and possibly acts of love by them! The identity of the Girls of Jerusalem is here further clarified. They are experienced in the ways of love, at the "highest" level. It is they to whom she has made her claim of beauty (1:5), and whom she has sworn to noninterference (2:7; 3:5). They seem as much threat as audience. (✶✶)

3:11 *Go out and see, O Girls of Zion,*

The king, Solomon,

Wearing the crown his mother placed on him

On his wedding day,

On the day of his heart's delight.

יא צְאֶינָה ׀ וּרְאֶינָה בְּנוֹת צִיּוֹן
בַּמֶּלֶךְ שְׁלֹמֹה
בָּעֲטָרָה שֶׁעִטְּרָה־לּוֹ אִמּוֹ
בְּיוֹם חֲתֻנָּתוֹ
וּבְיוֹם שִׂמְחַת לִבּוֹ:

3:11 Go out and see, O Girls — formerly, she asked them not to set their sights (same root) upon her (1:6). She now suggests the proper object. She addresses the Girls **of Zion**, a synonym for "Girls of Jerusalem" (the term used elsewhere in Song). Look at **the king**, again clarified to be **Solomon**, whose couch and litter were just described. Surprisingly, however, the verse does not focus on him in the litter, but instead removes to another occasion — he is **wearing the crown placed on him by his mother** — a stark contrast to the preceding. Certainly we did not expect to encounter his mother while describing his love-inlaid litter! The scene obviously changes, but is confusing. What kind of crown is this, given by a mother? Clearly it is not the coronation crown. In fact it is the crown she placed on him **on his wedding day**. As per custom, all grooms wore crowns, and were dubbed "king." (See notes.) It is this Solomon, the "king" of the wedding, whom the Girls should note. By way of double entendre "King" Solomon has been relocated, away from his royal, indiscreet lifestyle, to the joy dominant **on the day of his heart's delight**. The wedding — not the royal bed and not the love-inlaid litter — represents the best of Solomon. The involvement of Solomon's mother in the wedding might also clarify her previous desire to bring the beloved's lover to her *mother's* chamber (3:4). Was she thinking marriage, not just intimacy?

In retrospect, then, the phrase "Girls of Zion" may well have been purposely substituted for "Girls of Jerusalem," a clue that this was a different scene, a different emphasis.

Chapter 4

פרק ד

4:1 *Indeed you are beautiful, my darling,*
Indeed you are beautiful,
Your eyes: doves, from behind your veil.
Your hair is like a flock of goats
Streaming down Mount Gilead.

א הִנָּךְ יָפָה רַעְיָתִי

הִנָּךְ יָפָה

עֵינַיִךְ יוֹנִים מִבַּעַד לְצַמָּתֵךְ

שַׂעְרֵךְ כְּעֵדֶר הָעִזִּים

שֶׁגָּלְשׁוּ מֵהַר גִּלְעָד:

4:1 His admiration of her "coming up from the desert" (3:6) was interrupted by the section on Solomon. Now he continues.

Indeed you are beautiful, my darling, indeed you are beautiful, your eyes: doves, repeating verbatim his previous statement (1:15), now further to expand. While descriptions of both lovers proceed from the top down (with one purposeful later exception), there may be special significance to his beginning with her eyes, which will enthrall him (4:9; 6:5). Your eyes appear **from behind your veil,** lending a sense of motion to his observation, as befits the tone of this verse and the next. The veil and the term "from behind" (used of a wall, 2:9) emphasize their separation. The biblical range of uses of the veil is so broad (from modesty to a symbol of prostitution — see notes) that further specific implications cannot be drawn. **Your hair is like a flock of goats,** which are mostly black in Israel, **streaming down Mount Gilead.** A flock of goats will descend along twisting, varied paths, thus resembling braids of hair. Once again, the list of locales mentioned is expanded (see 3:6, commentary).

4:2 *Your teeth are like a flock of woolly ewes,*
Ascending from the washing,
All of them properly twinned,
None of them barren.

ב שִׁנַּ֙יִךְ֙ כְּעֵ֣דֶר הַקְּצוּבֹ֔ות
שֶׁעָל֖וּ מִן־הָרַחְצָ֑ה
שֶׁכֻּלָּם֙ מַתְאִימֹ֔ות
וְשַׁכֻּלָ֖ה אֵ֥ין בָּהֶֽם׃

4:2 Your teeth are like a flock of woolly ewes, ascending from the washing. An opposite movement is created, ascent to balance the descent, "completing" the picture. These are shining, wet teeth, **all of them properly twinned.** Sheep move orderly, by twos, guided after washing, providing a second counterweight to the goats, whose descent is a random twisting down the hills. The Hebrew is delightfully ambiguous, meaning both "bearing twins" (i.e., the sheep, an unusual achievement) and "matched" (i.e., the teeth). (The translation approximates the double entendre.) **None of them** — evidently, the sheep — are **barren.** By way of application of the simile, we conclude also that no teeth are missing. The Hebrew of these lines includes a particularly clear echo ("all of them," *shekulam*, and "barren," *shakulah*, which the translation approximates with other terms: "all of them," "none of them"). The mention that they are not barren may be a subconscious reflection of the man looking forward to the woman's ability to bear children.

4:3 *Like a scarlet thread are your lips,*
And your mouth is comely.
Like a pomegranate slice is your smile
From behind your veil.

ג כְּח֤וּט הַשָּׁנִי֙ שִׂפְתֹתַ֔יִךְ
וּמִדְבָּרֵ֖ךְ נָאוֶ֑ה
כְּפֶ֤לַח הָֽרִמֹּון֙ רַקָּתֵ֔ךְ
מִבַּ֖עַד לְצַמָּתֵֽךְ׃

4:3 Like a scarlet thread so red and delicate, the color sharply contrasting with the black (goats) and white (sheep) above, **are your lips, and your mouth** — here, literally, "organ of speech," a unique usage, incorporating appreciation of her appearance and her words, **is comely**, as she and her appearance have been termed (1:5, 10; 2:14) – in the last instance, associated with her sweet voice. The mouth stands out as an exception in this section, described directly, without simile or metaphor, recalling the mouth's centrality at the beginning (1:2). **Like a pomegranate slice is your smile** – since the pomegranate approximates the composite picture of white teeth surrounded by gums, lips or the curve of the smile (or all of these) **from behind your veil**, a position shared with the eyes (4:1). The re-mention of the veil seems to mock the item, for it does not prevent the lover from seeing what is to be praised, seeing the unseen, so to speak, or implying knowledge from other, private moments.

4:4 *Like the Tower of David is your neck,*	ד כְּמִגְדַּל דָּוִיד צַוָּארֵךְ
Built row on row,	בָּנוּי לְתַלְפִּיּוֹת
A thousand are the shields hung thereon,	אֶלֶף הַמָּגֵן תָּלוּי עָלָיו
All the bucklers of the warriors.	כֹּל שִׁלְטֵי הַגִּבֹּרִים:

4:4 Like the Tower of David is your neck, he continues, moving down the body, now using an image of strength and beauty. Either hyperbole or different standards of beauty explain the appeal of the long neck. It is **built row on row**, presumably indicating jewelry. **A thousand are the shields hung thereon** – so he describes the component parts of the necklace (in the Hebrew, there is an echo from "row on row," *talpiot*, to the combination of "hung," root, *t-l-h* with "thousand," root, *'-l-f*) – **all the bucklers of the warriors**. Thus the poet uses the description of the necklace to expropriate the very armor of Solomon's "warriors" (3:7). The use of shields as symbolizing the necklace is appropriate, for in antiquity shields could be hung on city walls and towers. The "warriors" are thus here assigned their more significant role – adorning the woman!

4:5 *Your breasts are like two young harts,*
   Twins of a gazelle,
   Who pasture among the lilies.

שְׁנֵי שָׁדַיִךְ כִּשְׁנֵי עֲפָרִים ה
תְּאוֹמֵי צְבִיָּה
הָרֹעִים בַּשּׁוֹשַׁנִּים:

4:5 Your breasts are like two young harts, the very animals with which she had described him (2:9) and urged him (2:17). She implied agility and speed, and he reapplies the images as shape and proportion. The breasts are, naturally, **twins** – implying both balance and perfection, as "twinning" did above (4:2) – **of a gazelle**, the oft repeated image (2:7, 9, 17; 3:5). More specifically, these are gazelles **who pasture among the lilies**. Physically, the breasts are compared to the heads of two fawns bent over to eat, with possible reference to the nipples (the lilies). With this metaphor, the lover is using the same description for her breasts as she used for his person (2:16 – he who pastures among the lilies). The poet thus accomplishes through parallel images the same intimate connection implied by a previous metaphor (1:13 – a bag of myrrh is my lover to me, lying between my breasts), bringing his head to her breasts.

The "lily" image thus draws them ever closer (cf. commentary, 2:16). In addition, the previous awkwardness of the phrase "among the lilies" is somewhat ameliorated. It may not refer to other women, but rather to her breasts. Alternatively, both could be implied as distinct levels of meaning. (✱✱)

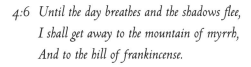

4:6   *Until the day breathes and the shadows flee,*
       I shall get away to the mountain of myrrh,
       And to the hill of frankincense.

ו   עַד שֶׁיָּפוּחַ הַיּוֹם וְנָסוּ הַצְּלָלִים
אֵלֶךְ לִי אֶל־הַר הַמּוֹר
וְאֶל־גִּבְעַת הַלְּבוֹנָה:

4:6 Mention of the gazelle and hart recall her request that he imitate those animals to flee *from* her on the mountains (2:17), precisely **until the day breathes and the shadows flee.** He now responds, **I shall get away** — but now he uses her terminology to come *with* her, "get away" being the same Hebrew term as "come away" and "gone away" in 2:10f. Indeed he intends to go not to the *cleft* mountains (2:17), but **to the mountain of myrrh, and to the hill of frankincense.** He evidently refers to her breasts, given the context of the preceding verse, the use of the two references (mountain, hill) and the recollection of myrrh (1:13 – "a bag of myrrh is my lover to me, lying between my breasts"). Frankincense has also perfumed her whole person (along with myrrh – 3:6).

He has already crossed "mountains" and "hills" (2:8). Now he moves on to a higher level of determination, to be with his beloved. She had previously asked him to bide his time, but now he responds, in a much more determined manner, that he will act. He is inspired in part, no doubt, by his description of her in the previous verses.

The ascent from the desert (3:6) also now appears ever the more important, for she was then perfumed with myrrh and frankincense. Does he here express his desire to join her in ascent? This could well explain his use soon (4:8 and beyond) of "bride."

4:7 *You are totally beautiful, my darling,*
There is no blemish in you.

כֻּלָּ֤ךְ יָפָה֙ רַעְיָתִ֔י
וּמ֖וּם אֵ֥ין בָּֽךְ׃

ז

4:7 His loving description of her body having led him to an exclamation of desires, he has only to return to complete the description, which he does in all-embracing terms. **You are totally beautiful, my darling,** he ends, using words similar to the opening description (4:1), again joining "darling" and "beautiful" (as 1:15; 2:10, 13; 4:1). Her beauty is overwhelming and encompassing. **There is no blemish in you** – implying total praise and total familiarity. She will later confirm the mutuality of their love – he terms her "totally" beautiful; she will term him "totally" a delight (5:16).

XIV. Come with me

4:8 *With me from Lebanon – O bride,*
Come with me from Lebanon.
Trip down from atop Amana,
From atop Senir and Hermon,
From the lions' dens,
From the leopards' mountains.

אִתִּ֤י מִלְּבָנוֹן֙ כַּלָּ֔ה
אִתִּ֖י מִלְּבָנ֣וֹן תָּב֑וֹאִי
תָּשׁ֣וּרִי ׀ מֵרֹ֣אשׁ אֲמָנָ֗ה
מֵרֹ֤אשׁ שְׂנִיר֙ וְחֶרְמ֔וֹן
מִמְּעֹנ֣וֹת אֲרָי֔וֹת
מֵהַרְרֵ֖י נְמֵרִֽים׃

ח

4:8 With me, he continues, beginning the sentence with a preposition, emphasizing his desire to be together with this perfect woman, **from Lebanon – O bride,** a striking new term. While it is usually taken as a general romantic term, it is hard to escape the inference of thoughts of marriage.

Come with me from Lebanon. As he departs for the mountains of spice, he calls her to join him. The Song again enhances movement by geographical expansion (see 4:1). "Lebanon" may also hint that he calls her away from the values represented by Solomon's litter, made of trees from Lebanon (3:9). **Trip down from atop Amana, from atop Senir and Hermon**, names associated with mountain ranges in the north and northeast of Israel. She is far, but she is to descend, which makes the way easier. The descent also balances her ascent from the desert (3:6), as the descending goats and the ascending ewes balanced each other (4:1, 2). Get away **from the lions' dens, from the leopards' mountains.** He is either seeking to protect her from danger, embodied in natural mountain enemies (similar to the use of foxes, 2:15), or he emphasizes that her habitat is a wilderness, the opposite of the city girls. Like the foxes (2:15), the lions and leopards do not reappear, and we therefore need seek no further implication than danger. (***)

4:9 *You have stolen my heart, my sister-bride,*	ט לִבַּבְתִּנִי אֲחֹתִי כַלָּה
You have stolen my heart	לִבַּבְתִּנִי
With one of your eyes,	בְּאַחַד מֵעֵינַיִךְ
With one jewel of your necklace.	בְּאַחַד עֲנָק מִצַּוְּרֹנָיִךְ:

4:9 Come because **you have stolen my heart** – or "given me heart" (similar implication) – **my sister-bride**, "sister" being an ancient term of affection whose range included sibling status, friendship, love and marriage. (See note.) The pairing with "bride" clarifies that romance is implied. **You have stolen my heart**, he repeats, this term (*libavtini*) recalling the repeated "Lebanon" (*Levanon*) of verse 8. This she did **with one of your eyes**, her eyes that first drew his attention (4:1). The reference to "one eye" is striking. Eyes form a unit not normally divided. She stole his heart even **with** but **one jewel of your necklace**, evidently the necklace described above (4:4) as having a thousand parts – but one is enough to capture him. (***)

4:10 How beautiful is your loving, my sister-bride,
   How much better is your loving than wine,
   The fragrance of your oils than all spices.

י   מַה־יָּפוּ דֹדַיִךְ אֲחֹתִי כַלָּה
מַה־טֹּבוּ דֹדַיִךְ מִיַּיִן
וְרֵיחַ שְׁמָנַיִךְ מִכָּל־בְּשָׂמִים:

4:10 How beautiful (as she herself is – 4:7) **is your loving**, he gushes, enthralled, **my sister-bride** – he continues with this motif. **How much better is your loving** (there is also an echo effect in this section) **than wine**. Thus he praises her exactly as she praised him (1:2), reflecting mutuality. The recollection of the opening of the Song alerts the reader to the centrality of this section. So, too, **the fragrance of your oils** is better, another note of mutuality, recalling the opening of the Song (1:3), **than all spices**, going beyond the single spices appreciated before (1:13, 14; 4:6). (✳✳)

4:11 Your lips drip nectar, O bride,
   Honey and milk are beneath your tongue,
   And the fragrance of your robes
   Is like the fragrance of Lebanon.

יא   נֹפֶת תִּטֹּפְנָה שִׂפְתוֹתַיִךְ כַּלָּה
דְּבַשׁ וְחָלָב תַּחַת לְשׁוֹנֵךְ
וְרֵיחַ שַׂלְמֹתַיִךְ
כְּרֵיחַ לְבָנוֹן:

4:11 Your lips drip nectar, a liquid honey, known for its sweetness. The tastes and odors lead the lover back (as 4:3) to her lips and to the sweetness of the kiss. **O bride**, he continues the motif, **honey and milk**, sweet and sustaining (and a biblical metaphor for abundance), are stored **beneath your tongue**, again reflecting the centrality of the mouth. "Beneath the tongue" can be used as the place of origin of speech (Ps. 10:7; Job 20:12) and honey is compared elsewhere to God's words (Ps. 119:103). Thus there may be two levels of description: the kiss, and pleasant words.

  And the fragrance, he continues as per the previous verse, reflecting the Song's acute awareness of pleasing odors (1:3, 12; 2:13), **of your**

robes, whose presence imposes a certain halt to the growing intimacy of the section, **is like the fragrance of** the trees or the wine (see note) of **Lebanon**, from which he asked her to come to him (4:8).

4:12 *A locked garden, my sister-bride,*
A locked cistern, a sealed spring.

יב גַּן | נָעוּל אֲחֹתִי כַלָּה
גַּל נָעוּל מַעְיָן חָתוּם:

4:12 A locked garden, my sister-bride — while continuing the bride motif, the lover dramatically shifts to an image of enclosure, emphasizing the gap that separates. (Here construed as a continuing address to the woman, the statement can also be a declarative sentence to an anonymous audience — "A locked garden is my sister-bride," further emphasizing the distance.) The growing closeness achieved through a progression of sight, smell and taste, already somewhat jarred by the robes, is put aside. A frustration of inaccessibility now dominates.

She is **a locked cistern, a sealed spring**. Most commentators properly understand this as a reference to sexual chastity. Water is the life-blood of societies in rain-dependent Israel, where springs or cisterns were covered to keep them from unwanted intruders. It is an ultimate image, in that water, the difference between life and death, is inaccessible to the lover. (**)

4:13 *Your limbs are an orchard:*
Pomegranates with delectable fruits,
Hennas with spikenards.

יג שְׁלָחַיִךְ פַּרְדֵּס
רִמּוֹנִים עִם פְּרִי מְגָדִים
כְּפָרִים עִם־נְרָדִים:

4:13 Your limbs — the Hebrew being ambiguous, either plant shoots in the garden or her body's limbs (or both, of course) — **are an orchard.** If he cannot see the garden, he can observe the overhanging branches. He sees **pomegranates**, a symbol of fertility (it is filled with seeds), along **with**

delectable fruits — as she delighted in the taste of his fruit (2:3). There are also **hennas with spikenards**, the plural emphasizing lushness. The garden is fictional — the plants grow in different climates. Spikenard has appeared before, as hers gave off fragrance while she was on her lover's couch (1:12).

4:14 *Spikenard and saffron, cane and cinnamon,*
 with all incensed woods,
 Myrrh and aloes, with all the top spices.

יד   נֵרְדְּ | וְכַרְכֹּם קָנֶה וְקִנָּמוֹן
עִם כָּל־עֲצֵי לְבוֹנָה
מֹר וַאֲהָלוֹת עִם כָּל־רָאשֵׁי בְשָׂמִים:

4:14 Spikenard and saffron, cane and cinnamon, he continues listing aromatic plants, **with** — he here picks up on the rhythm of the previous verse, a specific followed by "with," and then a more general term — **all incensed** ("incensed," *levona*, echoes "Lebanon" and "you have stolen my heart," *libavtini*, verses 8–9, and is related to "frankincense," used previously with myrrh to indicate her presence — 3:6, 4:6) **woods**, a nonspecific category. There are **myrrh and aloes, with all the top spices**, ending the list with a most general description. "Top" echoes "atop" the mountains from which she descended (4:8). Were they, too, aromatic?

This verse has echoed (in its use of structure: specific terms followed by the word "with," and then a more general term) the previous verse, expanding its scope. The lover has built to a crescendo, attributing almost every good odor to this orchard. (The fictional nature of the orchard remains. Like the spikenard and myrrh, cinnamon was an import to Israel from the Far East.)

There is a sexual overtone to the mention of spices as well. Note Prov. 7:17, the "smooth talking" stranger (woman) who tries to entice the young man: "I have sprinkled my bed with myrrh, aloes and cinnamon. Let us drink our fill of love…"

4:15 *A garden spring,*
A well of living water
Flowing from Lebanon.

טו   מַעְיַ֣ן גַּנִּ֔ים

בְּאֵ֖ר מַ֣יִם חַיִּ֑ים

וְנֹזְלִ֖ים מִן־לְבָנֽוֹן׃

4:15 A garden spring (literally, a spring of gardens) – having completed the description of the orchard, he returns to the images of 4:12, now setting the water in the garden. You are **a well of living**, indicating "fresh" or "running" **water**, which would seem to conflict with the "sealed" nature of the spring – but indeed, these waters are **flowing**, a direct contradiction to the previous description, **from Lebanon**, from which the lover called his darling to come (4:8).

The reversal is complete. The waters, previously locked and sealed, now flow. Did his will force the matter? The life-giving water he needs cascades down from Lebanon to him. The image bridges back across the change of metaphor (4:12) to his praise of her in terms of Lebanon. (One also hears now a third level of meaning for "limbs," 4:13. The Hebrew could also indicate "tributaries" of a river or stream. Might the poet have also been indicating that as she, the water, flows from the "sealed" environment, she indeed grants life to all these wonderful trees in the orchard?)

(The next verse opens the possibility that our verse is stated by the woman, the change of the waters being her response. To his claim that they are sealed, 4:12, she responds that it is not so. When the speaker changes is ambiguous. Perhaps the poet would have us wonder which of them spoke the words, or whether they spoke together.)

4:16 Rouse, O north wind,

    Come, O south wind,

    Breathe upon my garden,

    Let its spices flow.

    Let my lover come to his garden,

    Let him eat its delectable fruits.

טז   עוּרִי צָפוֹן

וּבוֹאִי תֵימָן

הָפִיחִי גַנִּי

יִזְּלוּ בְשָׂמָיו

יָבֹא דוֹדִי לְגַנּוֹ

וְיֹאכַל פְּרִי מְגָדָיו:

4:16 Rouse – she adjured the Girls of Jerusalem, that they not "rouse" love (2:7, 3:5) – **O north wind** – she is presumably north, in Lebanon. **Come**, as he called her to do, from Lebanon (4:8), **O south wind**, presumably his position in relation to her. The effect of the opposites is intense agitation. That the two winds cannot blow simultaneously befits the fictional and symbolic nature of the garden. It also echoes other balancing movements in the Song (see commentary, 4:8).

    Breathe, for she requested that he circle about the mountains until the day breathes, a request he rephrased as an intention to be with her (2:17, 4:6) – the "time" of love seems to have arrived! – **upon my garden** – she is both the garden (4:12) and the water thereof (4:15). Now he takes possession – she is "my garden." **Let its spices**, which he has detailed, **flow**, just as the waters flow from Lebanon.

    Let my lover – suddenly, she speaks – **come**, as he has asked of her (4:8) and of the wind (here) **to his garden**. She accedes to his taking possession. She – the garden – is his. **Let him eat**, for now it is fully accessible, **its** – the Hebrew can also be translated "his" – **delectable fruits**. His request has been answered with an invitation to love.

    With the change of speakers, the identity of the speaker(s) of the previous verse and a half blurs. Perhaps she called on the winds to blow, and perhaps she united the ownership of the garden, first calling it hers and then his. Perhaps she had declared that the waters were no longer to be locked up. The ambiguity leaves multiple levels of meaning, and a possible testimony to the couple's agreement.

Chapter 5

פרק ה

5:1   *I have come to my garden, my sister-bride,*
I have gathered my myrrh with my spice,
I have eaten my honeycomb with my honey,
I have drunk my wine with my milk.
Eat friends; drink, be drunk with loving.

א בָּאתִי לְגַנִּי אֲחֹתִי כַלָּה
אָרִיתִי מוֹרִי עִם־בְּשָׂמִי
אָכַלְתִּי יַעְרִי עִם־דִּבְשִׁי
שָׁתִיתִי יֵינִי עִם־חֲלָבִי
אִכְלוּ רֵעִים שְׁתוּ וְשִׁכְרוּ דּוֹדִים:

5:1 I have come to my garden, answering her call, **my sister-bride**. He returns to the appellation of 4:8–12, thus recalling those emphases: his call to her, his praise of her, etc., in this climactic verse celebrating sexual coition. **I have gathered my myrrh with my spice**, he declares, now continuing to emphasize "my." Myrrh, the most cited spice (1:13; 3:6; 4:6, 14) and "spice," the summary word of the fragrant inventory (4:14), transport all the odors of the orchard to this verse. **I have eaten my honeycomb with my honey**, the honey he found under her tongue (4:11). The possessive still dominates. **I have drunk my wine**, previously used as a comparison to loving (1:2, 4; 4:10), now as a metaphor for it, **with my milk**, which was also under her tongue (4:11).

Even the form of this beautiful description of coition declares closure. The echoes of previous terms are supplemented by an echo of a previous form (the use of "with," taken from 4:13f.), and the possessive "my" now is applied to all symbols. The verbs alone grant a clear, concise picture: I came, I gathered, I ate, I drank. Considering the single (indirect) object of the first verb and the double objects of the next three, one hears seven accomplished acts, emphasized by the use of "my" with each of them — seven being a biblical indication of completion. All reach a climax in this fictitious garden, reflected in fictitious pairings and actions. (One could scarcely gather spices not grown in Israel. Wine and milk are both refreshing, but not together.) The lovers have been united in the act

of love, and the poet chooses, as poets have for time immemorial, to use symbols to convey the overwhelming moment.

Eat friends, drink, be drunk, for mere drinking is not enough, **with loving**. "Eat" and "drink" – both literally, in celebration, and symbolically, enjoying love as he has done, as reflected in the metaphors of eating and drinking in this verse. He can wish them no greater joy. This address to the friends is a radical break. Who is the speaker, who the addressed? There were similar turns to others, the Girls of Jerusalem, at discrete moments (2:7, 3:5). There she spoke. Now he seems to turn to another group, male, under similar circumstances. Again a discrete closure is achieved.

Alternatively, the statement can be even more radical. The Hebrew *dodim*, "loving," can also mean "lovers," and *re'im*, "friends," is the plural of the word elsewhere used for "darling." Thus, the poet could step out of role and address the couple! "Eat, dear ones (darlings); drink, be drunk O lovers." (If the poet wishes us to read the Hebrew term *dodim* twice, we achieve, "Eat, dear ones; drink, be drunk, lovers, on love.")

Perhaps the poet intended us to hear both the address to outsiders and the address to the lovers. If so, the readers find themselves addressed and speaking at the same time – a remarkable poetic effect. (For double entendre, using one word with two meanings, see appendix.) (******)

XVI. My heart was aroused

5:2　*I was asleep, but my heart was aroused.*
　　Hark! The voice of my lover — he knocks:
　　Open for me,
　　My sister, my darling, my dove, my perfect one,
　　For my head is filled with dew,
　　My locks with the mist of night.

ב　אֲנִי יְשֵׁנָה וְלִבִּי עֵר
　　קוֹל | דּוֹדִי דוֹפֵק
　　פִּתְחִי־לִי
　　אֲחֹתִי רַעְיָתִי יוֹנָתִי תַמָּתִי
　　שֶׁרֹּאשִׁי נִמְלָא־טָל
　　קְוֻצּוֹתַי רְסִיסֵי לָיְלָה׃

5:2 Following previous "breaks" of turning to outside groups, the Song shifted to a different time and locale (2:8, 3:6). So it does again.

I was asleep, she declares, **but my heart was aroused**. The description borders consciousness and sleep, and the reader must keep both in mind. The "heart" is awake — the heart used previously in terms of Solomon's marriage (3:11) and in terms of her having stolen his heart (4:9). The context is emotional attachment. (However, outside of the Song, "heart" in the Bible is the locus of thought, and the verse also implies, therefore, "my mind was alert.") Her heart is "aroused" — recalling that she asked the Girls not to rouse love prematurely (2:7, 3:5). Perhaps the climax of 5:1 has made her ready — but the poet clarifies that not all is complete. She is still at least half asleep.

Hark! The voice of my lover — the precise words, with the precise double entendre, used after the first "break" (2:8), the translation again reflecting two translations of a single Hebrew term (*kol* – see 2:8). **He knocks:** and thus the poet again separates the couple. He is outside, she inside. The Hebrew for "my lover, he knocks" is onomatopoeic (*dodi dofek*).

Open for me — a phrase appropriate to the moment, after 5:1, and to their relationship as well — **my sister**, recalling their closeness (4:9–5:1), **my darling**, recalling her beauty and his call to go with him (1:15; 2:10, 13; 4:1, 7), **my dove**, recalling their distance and separation (2:14), **my perfect one**, a new epithet, perhaps another attempt (as 4:14) to end with an all-embracing

term. He remains committed to repeated use of the possessive "my" (see 5:1), the string of nouns emphasizing their closeness both through meaning and quantity. **For my head is filled with dew, my locks with the mist of night.** Did his use of adoration fail? He turns to practical reasons, perhaps coyly or humorously. His being out at night contrasts favorably with the night fears of Solomon's warriors (3:8) and recalls her night foray (3:1–4).

There is an erotic double entendre to these words as well. After 5:1, this pragmatic argument certainly recalls both his desires and his readiness for sexual encounter. (**)

5:3 *I took off my tunic,*	פָּשַׁטְתִּי אֶת־כֻּתָּנְתִּי ג
Should I now put it on?	אֵיכָכָה אֶלְבָּשֶׁנָּה
I washed my feet,	רָחַצְתִּי אֶת־רַגְלַי
Should I now dirty them?	אֵיכָכָה אֲטַנְּפֵם:

5:3 I already **took off my tunic, should I now put it on?** It is unclear whether she addresses herself or offers him a coy or delaying response. In either case, the result is the same. **I washed my feet, should I now dirty them?** Her response or reaction seems condemnable, more that of a spoiled princess than a lover. She, however, has done no more that adopt the somewhat frivolous tone of his request to come in because of the weather. The two play a game of sorts, not uncommon among lovers.

5:4 *My lover stretched forth his hand through the hole,*	דּוֹדִי שָׁלַח יָדוֹ מִן־הַחֹר ד
My innards were stirred for him.	וּמֵעַי הָמוּ עָלָיו:

5:4 My lover stretched forth his hand in longing, or as a doomed effort to reach a latch. The Hebrew for "stretched" the hand uses the root of the "limbs" of the orchard or of the woman (4:13). He stretched **through** –

the same preposition (*min*) used in his efforts to call "through," from beyond the wall (2:9), in a verse that also emphasizes their separation. He stretched through **the hole** in the door, the exact nature of this lock or door opening unknown. Seeing this, **my innards** – literally, intestines, the biblical seat of emotion – **were stirred for him.**

After 5:1, the actions of the lover, fully logical in context, cannot but bear a symbolic erotic tone for the woman, his hand stretching forth through the hole in the door.

5:5 *I did rise to open for my lover.*	ה קַמְתִּי אֲנִי לִפְתֹּחַ לְדוֹדִי
My hands dripped myrrh,	וְיָדַי נָטְפוּ־מוֹר
My fingers, passing myrrh	וְאֶצְבְּעֹתַי מוֹר
Upon the handles of the lock.	עֹבֵר עַל כַּפּוֹת הַמַּנְעוּל:

5:5 I did rise – the Hebrew is emphatic, and the verb indicates a response not only to his request that she open (5:2) but also to his former request that she "rise" and go with him (2:10, 13) **to open for my lover. My hands,** going to meet his hand, **dripped myrrh,** a recollection of their closeness, and particularly their greatest intimacy (4:14, 5:1). (The Hebrew includes a sound play, "dripped" – *natfu* – providing a reverse response to her not wanting to dirty her feet – *atanfem*. Now she is ready.) **My fingers, passing myrrh** – evidently, a superior, liquid form of the spice, perhaps based in the oils that had been mentioned. Her hands were **upon the handles of the lock,** the bolt holding the door closed. She, whom he had characterized as a "locked garden, a locked cistern" (4:12) takes lock in hand to open for him. She is scented and ready for love. (✲✲✲)

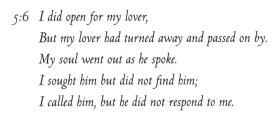

5:6 *I did open for my lover,*
But my lover had turned away and passed on by.
My soul went out as he spoke.
I sought him but did not find him;
I called him, but he did not respond to me.

ו פָּתַ֙חְתִּֽי אֲנִי֙ לְדוֹדִ֔י
וְדוֹדִ֖י חָמַ֣ק עָבָ֑ר
נַפְשִׁי֙ יָֽצְאָ֣ה בְדַבְּר֔וֹ
בִּקַּשְׁתִּ֙יהוּ֙ וְלֹ֣א מְצָאתִ֔יהוּ
קְרָאתִ֖יו וְלֹ֥א עָנָֽנִי:

5:6 I did open for my lover, she declares, again with emphasis, as in the previous verse, **but my lover had turned away and passed on by**. She was too late. Things "passed" are gone – the winter (2:11), the guards of the city (3:4). She was ready with liquid (literally "passing") myrrh, but ironically, he has "passed" on by. **My soul went out as he spoke**, she explains, expressing her devotion and explaining her delay. She had "lost her soul" (a phrase used elsewhere even for dying!), that soul which had previously been known only as the bearer of her love for him (he whom my soul loves – 1:7; 3:1–4). His voice simply overwhelmed her – hence her delay.

I sought him but did not find him. She undertakes a search, unsuccessfully, reported in almost identical words to her previous search (3:1f.). The reader is puzzled. In that search, eventually she found him. Is this, then, another search, or do we have a retelling of the former incident, in greater or different detail? The references to her soul and to seeking while not finding bind the two accounts together. **I called him, but he did not respond to me.** Once, he had "responded" even when not addressed (cf. 2:10). Now when she has "arisen" as he requested (2:10), unfortunately it is too late. He asked to hear her voice (2:14), and now it is sounded after he has passed on by, and he cannot hear. (✱✱)

5:7   *The watchmen, circling through the city, found me.*
They struck me, they bruised me,
They stripped off my mantle,
The watchmen of the ramparts.

ז   מְצָאֻנִי הַשֹּׁמְרִ֛ים הַסֹּבְבִ֥ים בָּעִ֖יר
הִכּ֥וּנִי פְצָע֑וּנִי
נָשְׂא֧וּ אֶת־רְדִידִ֛י מֵעָלַ֖י
שֹׁמְרֵ֥י הַחֹמֽוֹת׃

5:7 The watchmen, circling through the city, found me. With the identical words used in the previous search (3:3) she reports her encounter with the watchmen. Here the watchmen circle, and were it not for the previous account, the reader might even assume that she was motionless — seeking him only by calling.

They struck me, they bruised me, they stripped off my mantle. (How ironic, that they should remove part of the clothes she had previously refused to put on!) The strong sense of movement of the previous account is absent, and a darker, more violent element is added. The tone is less one of their search at this point than of confrontation. She is grossly physically abused by **the watchmen of the ramparts.** The reason for their violence is unclear (perhaps just the theft of the mantle), but of little import. She is vulnerable, and hurt by brute application of force.

The citation of the watchmen confirms that this is a retelling of 3:1–4. The tone here is calmer, lacking the staccato repetition of phrases and the emphasis on movement. She seems free to tell the tale with more detail and more accuracy, and even the violent moments seem reported more dispassionately. Possibly the placement of this section after the celebration of coition (5:1) accounts for the difference: though the poem reflects separation, it has also told of their moment of bliss. They look forward to renewed union, and their past struggles are now seen anew, in that light. (******)

XVII. **Totally a delight**

5:8 *I adjure you, O Girls of Jerusalem:*
    If you find my lover, what shall you tell him?
    That I am lovesick.

ח הִשְׁבַּ֧עְתִּי אֶתְכֶ֛ם בְּנ֥וֹת יְרוּשָׁלָ֖͏ִם
אִֽם־תִּמְצְאוּ֙ אֶת־דּוֹדִ֔י מַה־תַּגִּ֖ידוּ ל֑וֹ
שֶׁחוֹלַ֥ת אַהֲבָ֖ה אָֽנִי׃

5:8 I adjure you, O Girls of Jerusalem, just as she had after her last search for him (3:5). The circumstances, however, are different: this time she has not found her lover. Before (2:7, 3:5, 5:1), the turn to outsiders served to escape from a moment of intimacy. That this adjuration might be different is indicated by the absence of "gazelles" and "hinds." Indeed, it would seem momentarily that the Girls are being enlisted as allies, a clear contrast to the watchmen who beat her.

Proceeding word by word, one would probably translate the next phrase, *"that you not* find my lover," for the Hebrew term *im* was used for the negative in previous oaths (2:7, 3:5). Thus the woman seeks to keep him for herself, an appropriate sentiment. The verse continues otherwise — the translation here ("if you find") is the proper one — but the first impression lingers as an echo. The woman wants this man for herself.

She adjures them, then: **if you find my lover**, as she has been unable to do, **what shall you tell him?** she asks by way of announcing the message. Tell him **that I am lovesick**. She had so declared earlier (2:5), but not directly to him. Perhaps he did not know, and perhaps that is why he left before she opened the door. This word, "lovesick," used previously for being momentarily overwhelmed, now indicates a condition. Is this one of the changes that take place after the coition of 5:1? This is a steady, ongoing lovesickness, one reflecting his absence, not his presence.

Her message is all the more impressive in light of the preceding incident. She was physically abused, but her message to her lover is only of her lovesickness. (✱✱)

5:9 *How is your lover more than any lover,*
     O most beautiful of women?
     How is your lover more than any lover,
     That you thus adjure us?

ט מַה־דּוֹדֵךְ מִדּוֹד
   הַיָּפָה בַּנָּשִׁים
   מַה־דּוֹדֵךְ מִדּוֹד
   שֶׁכָּכָה הִשְׁבַּעְתָּנוּ:

5:9 How is your lover so special, ask the Girls, speaking for the first time. The question is revealing, as their question is one of comparison and of competition, a reflection of their position vis-à-vis the woman. How is he **more than any lover?** These experts in love, who "inlaid" Solomon's litter with love (3:9f.), are taken with this loyalty and devotion. After all, there must be many lovers for her, whom they address, **O most beautiful of women.** They here accept her declaration to them that she is comely (1:5f.). Alternatively, they here mock her by use of a wry superlative. If it is mockery, her forthcoming response will be not just a reply, but also a defense. Ironically, in mocking her, they resort to the same phrase with which he praised her beauty (1:8). She must hear the echo of his voice.

How is your lover more than any lover, they repeat in emphasis, explaining the reason for their question: **that you thus adjure us?** The message of lovesickness is a powerful one. He must be very special! In addition, the Girls may have heard the second, veiled request of the previous verse — i.e., that they not find him.

The confrontational tone of the previous verses continues and is enhanced, now incremented by the mocking and the direct challenge which the Girls present.

5:10 My lover is radiant and ruddy,
    Visible among ten thousand.

י   דּוֹדִי צַח וְאָדוֹם
דָּגוּל מֵרְבָבָה:

5:10 My lover is radiant and ruddy, she responds, as if beginning a physical description that might help them to identify him. He is both bright and reddish, strikingly **visible among ten thousand**, i.e., the masses. ("Ten thousand" is the largest numerical term in the Bible, and therefore might best be translated "millions.")

His being among masses does not separate the couple. Instead, sight overcomes distance. First, he stands out and is seen. Second, when in a group before, he "viewed" (same root as "visible" here – *d-g-l*) her with love (2:4). It was that viewing which made her lovesick (2:5)! The two uses of the root *d-g-l* draw them together.

5:11 His head is finest gold,
    His locks are curls, black as a raven.

יא   רֹאשׁוֹ כֶּתֶם פָּז
קְוֻצּוֹתָיו תַּלְתַּלִּים שְׁחֹרוֹת כָּעוֹרֵב:

5:11 His head – seeing him above the masses, she naturally begins at the top, which is where he began his description of her (4:1) – **is finest gold**. If the Girls thought for a moment that she was really about to describe her lover, they here learn otherwise. Evidently, they are to be treated to her romantic impressions – not who or where he is, but what he is to her. **His locks**, which had been paired with his head before, when he sought entrance because he was wet with dew (5:2), **are curls, black** – as she is black, evidently in contradistinction to the Girls (1:5f.) – **as a raven.**

5:12 His eyes are like doves by the water courses, עֵינָיו כְּיוֹנִים עַל־אֲפִיקֵי מָיִם **יב**
Bathed in milk, sitting by full ponds. רֹחֲצוֹת בֶּחָלָב יֹשְׁבוֹת עַל־מִלֵּאת:

5:12 His eyes, she continues, focusing on what had marked his appreciation of her (1:15; 4:1, 9), **are like doves** – as hers were equated to doves (1:15, 4:1). She draws him close to her eyes, but also to herself (she was termed a dove – 2:14, 5:2). These doves are **by the water courses**, the arroyos through which the rain descends from the mountains. The image seems to move in two separate, but complementary, directions. On one hand, the doves, moving by the water, resemble the irises set in the eyeballs. However, his eyes, like doves, are also "by" the water itself, for she is living water, flowing from Lebanon (4:15). In the latter case, she uses imagery that she – but not the Girls – will understand, declaring that his attention is given her. Further, his eyes, the doves, are **bathed in milk**, evidently, set in white. So the girls hear. For her, the recollection is also of their loving, of the "milk" he wanted to, and then did, taste (4:11, 5:1). The eyes are **sitting by the full ponds**, an enigmatic phrase (see notes), which, in any case, recalls his head "filled" with dew (5:2). The white doves are evidently intended to present a contrast in extreme to the black ravens of the previous verse. This balance echoes similar structures in the Song (cf. commentaries, 4:8, 10).

5:13 His cheeks are like the bed of spice, לְחָיָו כַּעֲרוּגַת הַבֹּשֶׂם **יג**
Towers of aromatics; מִגְדְּלוֹת מֶרְקָחִים
His lips are lilies, שִׂפְתוֹתָיו שׁוֹשַׁנִּים
They drip passing myrrh. נֹטְפוֹת מוֹר עֹבֵר:

5:13 His cheeks – he had praised her cheeks (1:10) – **are like the bed of spice**, aromatic oils, placed on the face or beard, possibly implying a sharply defined cheekbone, grooved in the face like a furrow in the earth. More likely, the similarity is only to the scent. She undoubtedly also

recalls his delight in partaking of her love, her "spices" (4:10, 14, 16) and of gathering those spices to himself (5:1). Now they are his. (Again, the Girls "hear" a physical description, while she recalls their relationship.) The cheeks are **towers of aromatics**, a parallel poetic expression for the bed of spice.

His lips – he had praised her lips (4:3, 11) – **are lilies.** The poet continues to bring the lovers closer through the image of the lilies. First these described her, then he was called the one who "pastures among the lilies," and then her breasts were described as fawns pasturing there. (See commentary, 4:5.) Now his lips are so described, the image, as it were, joining his lips to her breasts. **They drip** – as her lips dripped nectar (4:11) – **passing myrrh**, which dripped from her fingers as she rose to let him in, myrrh symbolizing their greatest intimacy (5:5). (**)

5:14 *His hands are rods of gold,*
    Filled with beryl;
    His belly, a plate of ivory,
    Overlaid with lapis lazuli.

יד יָדָיו גְּלִילֵי זָהָב
מְמֻלָּאִים בַּתַּרְשִׁישׁ
מֵעָיו עֶשֶׁת שֵׁן
מְעֻלֶּפֶת סַפִּירִים:

5:14 Having described his lips as flowing myrrh, as her hands had been described, her attention is drawn to **his hands** – the term also means arms – stating that they **are rods of gold.** She continues the dazzling description, now attributing to him the gold that decorates Solomon's litter (3:10). These are **filled** – a literal translation of a root now used three times in connection with him (also 5:2, 12), probably indicating "studded" here – **with beryl** (precise identity of stone unknown). **His belly** – the same term as her "innards," which were stirred at the sight of his hands (the belly and hand were again both mentioned in that verse, 5:4) – is **a plate of ivory, overlaid with lapis lazuli**, a precious jewel, the tone remaining one of strength and splendor.

5:15 His legs are marble pillars,
    Set upon sockets of fine gold.
    The sight of him is like Lebanon,
    A young man singular as the cedars.

טו   שׁוֹקָיו עַמּוּדֵי שֵׁשׁ
מְיֻסָּדִים עַל־אַדְנֵי־פָז
מַרְאֵהוּ כַּלְּבָנוֹן
בָּחוּר כָּאֲרָזִים:

5:15 His legs – literally, thighs – **are marble pillars**, recalling that Solomon's litter included a description of silver "pillars" (3:9), **set upon sockets of fine gold**, the latter term (*paz*) being part of "finest gold" used to describe his head (5:11). He is splendid from top to bottom, and as the metaphor at the beginning of the description was divorced from all reality, so are the metaphors at the end, at best bringing to mind imagined statuary. She manages to impress the Girls, without informing them.

    The sight of him – the whole now draws her attention, as an act of mutuality, for he had declared the sight of her to be comely (2:14). His appearance **is like Lebanon**, another comparison to Solomon's litter (3:9). Lebanon in the Song implies the finest wood (3:9), pleasing odor (of wood or wine – 4:11) and a majestic mountain to the North (4:8f.). All – majesty, delicacy and strength – are implied in a single phrase. This lover is in fact **a young man, singular** – the Hebrew (*bachur*) means either "choice" or "young man," and the translation reflects both, assuming the reader was meant to hear both (similar to double implication of "loving" and "lovers," 5:1) – **as the cedars**, also known for beauty, strength and majesty. (In retrospect, the transition of 1:16f. from his beauty to the description of their being among the cedars seems much more natural now, given the simile of this verse.)

5:16 *His palate is sweetness, and he is totally a delight.*
This is my lover, this is my darling,
O Girls of Jerusalem.

טז חִכּוֹ מַמְתַקִּים וְכֻלּוֹ מַחֲמַדִּים
זֶה דוֹדִי וְזֶה רֵעִי
בְּנוֹת יְרוּשָׁלָם:

5:16 His palate is sweetness, she declares, recalling that his apricots were "sweet" to *her* "palate" (2:3), thus bringing their mouths together in a deep, intimate kiss. The order of description, however, seems wrong, for it has heretofore proceeded from top down. **And he is totally a delight**, recalling her "delight" in sitting in the apricot tree's shade (2:3). (The connection is particularly appropriate, for in 2:3 she compared her lover favorably to all men, and indeed here the Girls have requested a comparison to all lovers.) As he concluded his earlier description of her with a "total" appreciation (4:7), so she replies in kind here. (That the poet tends to end lists with general descriptions was noted with "all the chief spices," 4:14.)

One now understands the inclusion of the palate at this point. "Palate" is used in parallelism with "totality" (a noun in the Hebrew). The apparent centrality of the mouth has been noted (cf. commentary 4:3). The Song began with the kisses of his mouth (1:2) and detailed the mouth in all its component parts — mouth, lips, teeth, organ of speech, palate, smile, tongue. The kiss, evidently, is the best articulation of their love. The "palate," therefore, appears here not as one body part, but as *pars pro toto*, that part which can best symbolize all of him.

This is my lover, this is my darling, she concludes, echoing his possession ("my") of her (5:2) and thereby reconfirming to these Girls that he is not for them. She here first uses "darling" for him, as he had for her (1:9, 15; 2:10, 13; etc.). Those contexts stressed her beauty (cf. commentary 4:7), making the term particularly apt here after her description of his beauty. "This" is the term (*zeh*) indicating immediate presence in 2:8, 9 (translated "he" — "*he* comes...*he* stands"), almost as if she is pointing. One wonders whether the woman does not "feel" his presence at this moment as well, after the description. Such is her lover, **O Girls of Jerusalem**, possibly another comparison to Solomon's litter (as above), which these Girls have inlaid with love (3:9f.). (**)

XVIII. **I am my lover's**

Chapter 6

פרק ו

6:1 *Where has your lover gone,*
    O most beautiful of women;
    Where has your lover turned,
    That we may seek him with you?

א אָנָה הָלַךְ דּוֹדֵךְ
הַיָּפָה בַּנָּשִׁים
אָנָה פָּנָה דוֹדֵךְ
וּנְבַקְשֶׁנּוּ עִמָּךְ:

6:1 Where has your lover gone? the Girls ask. Having failed to receive a very helpful description, the Girls seek directions. Again (as 5:9), they address the woman as **O most beautiful of women**, possibly still mocking her. **Where has your lover turned**, they repeat, using almost the same terms. This repetition echoes the literary form of their initial address to her (5:9). The repetition reflects their determined opposition to her evident desire to keep them away from her lover. Tell us, so **that we may seek him with you.** They are clearly moved to find him, with a variety of possible motives — admiration of her devotion, curiosity to see this wonderful creature and/or desire to have him for themselves.

6:2 *My lover has gone down to his garden,*
To the beds of spice,
To pasture in the gardens,
To pick lilies.

ב דּוֹדִי יָרַד לְגַנּוֹ
לַעֲרֻגוֹת הַבֹּשֶׂם
לִרְעוֹת בַּגַּנִּים
וְלִלְקֹט שׁוֹשַׁנִּים:

6:2 She knows her lover intended to "go" (same verb as gone, previous verse) to her breasts (see 4:6) but answers in other terms. **My lover has gone down** (not the same verb as "go," previous verse), as one would naturally do from cities, for the houses were built on the heights, the fields being below, **to his garden**, which the Girls hear as directions. She, however, is thinking of something else entirely, their moment of greatest intimacy: "I have come to my garden" (5:1). There are two separate messages in the air — what they hear, and what she says. He has gone down **to the beds of spice**, which grow in the garden and which he plucked (4:14, 5:1). Again, her thoughts and their understanding exist on two different levels. They hear directions while she recalls his cheeks, called a bed of spice (5:13). That picture of his face brings her to describe his purpose as **to pasture**, a word which the Girls must hear as transitive (causing his sheep to pasture) but which the woman means as intransitive (cf. commentary, 2:16), which is for her a term of intimacy (4:5). He went to pasture **in the gardens**, whereby she recalls again their meeting. The plural, "gardens," however, is ominous. Perhaps she is not the only "garden." As in the case of the lilies (2:1f.), she knows there are other women around. She remains worried. He also went **to pick lilies** — another worrisome symbol. Lilies are a symbol of their love (cf. commentary 5:13, where "bed of spice" and "lily" also appear in one verse), but the plural, as in 2:10, might also indicate the presence of other women.

The Girls sought directions. Ostensibly they received them. In fact, they heard words that were only the woman's reminiscence of the love she shared with her lover, and her concerns. Similarly, she had described him (5:12, 13 — see commentary) with terms of her personal appreciation that they could not understand. (**)

6:3　*I am my lover's,*　אֲנִי לְדוֹדִי֮　ג

And my lover is mine —　וְדוֹדִי֮ לִי֒

He who pastures among the lilies.　הָרֹעֶ֖ה בַּשּׁוֹשַׁנִּֽים׃

6:3 I am my lover's, she concludes as a natural, if determined, summary of her own thoughts. The words ward off the Girls of Jerusalem. Continuing the Song's emphasis on mutuality, she adds, **and my lover is mine.** They should have no doubt – he is equally committed, **he who pastures among the lilies,** an indication of location to the Girls who just heard 6:2, but to the woman, it is a recollection of all their intimacy (2:16, 4:5, 5:13) and of the potential threat, in that there are other "lilies."

　　This verse reaffirms and restates 2:16 ("My beloved is mine and I am his…"), but in inverted order. There the two phrases indicated mutuality and equality, and the inverse order here only fortifies those emphases. There the phrase responded to the threat of outsiders as it is here, though then the outsiders were termed symbolically – the little foxes. Here their identity is clear – the Girls of Jerusalem. (✳✳)

XIX. Awesome

6:4　*You are as beautiful, my darling, as Tirzah,*　יָפָ֨ה אַ֤תְּ רַעְיָתִי֙ כְּתִרְצָ֔ה　ד

As comely as Jerusalem,　נָאוָ֖ה כִּירוּשָׁלָ֑͏ִם

As awesome as these visions.　אֲיֻמָּ֖ה כַּנִּדְגָּלֽוֹת׃

6:4 Now that she has praised him (5:10–16) and declared their mutual affection (6:3), he responds, **You are as beautiful, my darling,** recalling her beauty, using terms drawn from his previous praise of her (4:7). (Again, "darling" and "beauty" are paired.) You are as beautiful **as Tirzah,** the first capital of the North of Israel (1 Kings 14:17), late tenth and early ninth centuries BCE, when the kingdom split following Solomon's death. You are

as comely – an adjective which she used for herself, and which he used for her "appearance" and "mouth" (2:14, 4:3). Now, after her declaration of their equality, he also uses it for her entire person – **as Jerusalem**, capital of the South, originally capital of all Israel under David and Solomon. The two cities, evidently, became a standard representation of beauty and power. The comparison to Jerusalem, however, adds a reassuring tone. She originally declared her "comeliness" to the Girls of Jerusalem (1:5), and she has just completed her response to them, warding them off. He confirms her superior beauty in terms they must understand. She is as comely as Jerusalem itself! (This opens the possibility that the word "Tirzah" was meant also to reflect its root, "desire." Some ancient versions translated accordingly: "pleasing one," or the like.)

Indeed, she is **as awesome as these visions** – literally, "things viewed." These capitals, we assume, radiated beauty, and awe-inspiring power. He is overcome by the very sight of her. "Things viewed" recalls his viewing her with love (2:4) and the fact that he was "visible" above the masses (5:10) (identical root, *d-g-l*).

6:5 *Divert your eyes from me,*
   For they overwhelm me.
   Your hair is like a flock of goats,
   Streaming down the Gilead.

ה הָסֵבִּי עֵינַיִךְ מִנֶּגְדִּי
   שֶׁהֵם הִרְהִיבֻנִי
   שַׂעְרֵךְ כְּעֵדֶר הָעִזִּים
   שֶׁגָּלְשׁוּ מִן־הַגִּלְעָד:

6:5 Divert – not an unfair request, for when similarly overcome, she had asked that he "circle" away from her for a while, using the same root (*s-o-v* – 2:17) – **your eyes**, whose effect (4:9) and whose beauty (1:15, 4:1) he has previously recalled. Divert them **from me** – as he pictures her, he feels her seeing him – **for they overwhelm me.** In his previous praise of her beauty, he began with her eyes. Having already mentioned them here, he continues, using terms nearly identical with those he used before. **Your hair is like a flock of goats, streaming down the Gilead.** (See 4:1.)

6:6   *Your teeth are like a flock of ewes,*
      Ascending from the washing,
      All of them properly twinned,
      None of them barren.

ו   שִׁנַּ֙יִךְ֙ כְּעֵ֣דֶר הָֽרְחֵלִ֔ים
שֶׁעָל֖וּ מִן־הָרַחְצָ֑ה
שֶׁכֻּלָּם֙ מַתְאִימ֔וֹת
וְשַׁכֻּלָ֖ה אֵ֥ין בָּהֶֽם:

6:6 He continues his repetition: **Your teeth are like a flock of ewes, ascending from the washing, all of them properly twinned, none of them barren.** (For commentary, see 4:2.) The repetition of the joyful description emphasizes the delight in beauty that is reflected throughout the Song.

6:7   *Like a pomegranate slice is your smile,*
      From behind your veil.

ז   כְּפֶ֤לַח הָרִמּוֹן֙ רַקָּתֵ֔ךְ
מִבַּ֖עַד לְצַמָּתֵֽךְ:

6:7 **Like a pomegranate slice is your smile, from behind your veil.** Again he repeats his words (4:3), now omitting the mouth and lips of the first half of that verse. This is a striking omission, given the centrality granted the mouth in the Song (1:2; 2:3, 14; 4:3, 11; 5:13, 16 — see commentaries, 4:3, 5:16). Is the description meant to be less intimate, less personal? Later the poet will correct that impression. (**)

6:8 *Sixty are they, queens,*
And eighty concubines,
And damsels without number.

שִׁשִּׁים הֵמָּה מְלָכוֹת   ח
וּשְׁמֹנִים פִּילַגְשִׁים
וַעֲלָמוֹת אֵין מִסְפָּר׃

6:8 Sixty are they, the text seems to break off, pursuing a new tack. Having been diverted from his description of the capital cities (verse 4) into a description of her, he now returns to urban imagery. He cites "sixty," the number of warriors around Solomon's litter (3:7). These sixty, however, are **queens, and** with them are **eighty concubines**. The numbers are round, a "full" group. (See notes.) Evidently the mention of royal cities (6:4) brings about a shift to the royal court.

And these capital cities include **damsels without number**. The poet has taken the lover (and the reader) from *the* one to the masses. We know the damsels have found him attractive (1:3). If, indeed, the court and royal cities are implied, then presumably this list is inclusive of the frequently mentioned "Girls of Jerusalem."

The reference is not specifically Solomon's harem (1 Kings 11:3 – seven hundred wives and three hundred concubines). In fact, the mention of the paired cities Tirzah and Jerusalem takes the poem, in its own terms, beyond the time of Solomon, who remains then a symbolic, not a real, figure in the Song.

6:9 *One is she,*
    My dove, my perfect one;
    One is she to her mother,
    Pure to her who bore her.
    Girls see her and they acclaim her,
    Queens and concubines, and they praise her.

ט אַחַת הִיא
יוֹנָתִי תַמָּתִי
אַחַת הִיא לְאִמָּהּ
בָּרָה הִיא לְיוֹלַדְתָּהּ
רָאוּהָ בָנוֹת וַיְאַשְּׁרוּהָ
מְלָכוֹת וּפִילַגְשִׁים וַיְהַלְלוּהָ:

6:9 **One is she**, he declares, in clear contrast to the large numbers cited. (The structure is the same — "sixty are they," "one is she.") If smaller numbers indicate superiority (a finite number of queens and concubines, innumerable damsels), then the smallest number indicates ultimate superiority. She is **my dove**, as stated before (2:14, 5:2), **my perfect one**, the last and broadest of his praises of her (5:2). **One is she**, he repeats, reemphasizing the contrast (just as she contrasted him to all others — 5:10) **to her mother** — i.e., "unique" (scarcely an only child, since she has mentioned her brothers — 1:6), **pure** — implying flawless and chosen — **to her who bore her**. She is unique among children. The phrase "who bore her" recalls her dedication to her mother, "who conceived" her (3:4) and her desire (there) to bring him to her mother's chamber. Is there a subtle reference to the woman's positive association with her mother, and/or a high valuation of marriage and motherhood?

    Girls are now cited, making it probable that the damsels of the previous verse are either identical to, or inclusive of, the Girls of Jerusalem. They **see her**. They had previously set their sight (same root) upon her, which she interpreted as rejection (1:6). He now declares that their gazing is a matter of veneration! Further, the Girls of Zion had been told to "see" Solomon when his mother crowned him at his wedding (3:11). Perhaps they learned the lesson, for now they gaze and praise a "mother's" chosen one. The girls look **and they acclaim her, queens and concubines** (as mentioned in the last verse), **and they praise her**. If these are the Girls of Jerusalem, the lover here repays his beloved. She had told these

girls of his superiority. Now he includes them as those who are her inferiors and admirers. (**)

6:10 *Who is this, shining forth like the dawn,*
    As beautiful as the moon,
    As pure as the sun,
    As awesome as these visions?

י מִי־זֹאת הַנִּשְׁקָפָה כְּמוֹ־שָׁחַר
יָפָה כַלְּבָנָה
בָּרָה כַּחַמָּה
אֲיֻמָּה כַּנִּדְגָּלוֹת:

6:10 Who is this woman? As previously (3:6), this same question is clarified with a description. She is **shining forth**, literally "looking down," **like the dawn**, the first light of day, **as beautiful** – often stated about her (1:15; 2:10, 13; 4:1, 7; 6:4) – **as the moon, as pure** – as her mother sees her (6:9), though here the purity is transferred to light, indicating "shining" or "brilliant" – **as the sun**. The poet builds to the ultimate degree of light. Her splendor is also ironic. She had told the Girls not to look at her, because her black color only indicated temporary sun exposure (1:6 – though a different Hebrew word for sun is used there). Now she proves to be purer than the sun! She is, in fact, **as awesome as these visions**. The lover had so begun his praise for her (6:4). This framing indicates that she is as awesome as any human or natural achievement. (The poet, as often, concludes a specific list with a general item – see appendix.) The ascending order of brightness clarifies in retrospect that 6:4 also ascends – Tirzah, Jerusalem, awesome (general) visions. Indeed, the two verses "ascend," moving from human metaphors (6:4) to heavenly ones (6:10). As before, the speaker is unclear (see commentary, 4:15), either the lover or a quote of the praise of the women of verse 9, possibly indicating both, in agreement.

xx. Disoriented

6:11 *I went down to the nut grove*
To see the fresh growth of the valley,
To see: has the vine flowered,
Have the pomegranates budded?

יא   אֶל־גִּנַּת אֱגוֹז
יָרַדְתִּי לִרְאוֹת בְּאִבֵּי הַנָּחַל
לִרְאוֹת הֲפָרְחָה הַגֶּפֶן
הֵנֵצוּ הָרִמֹּנִים:

6:11 **I went down**, he says. Having completed his description of her (this chapter has included his praise, parallel to her praise in the previous chapter), he returns to a phrase from her last description (6:2 – my lover has "gone down" to his garden), but now he goes down **to the nut grove**, "grove" (*ginah*) being from the same root as "garden" (*gan*). He responds to her metaphoric description with a similar, but not identical metaphor – the nut grove. ("Nut" is not a clear reference, and its implications are similarly unclear – see note.) I went **to see the fresh growth of the valley**, the dry river bed which greens after winter rains bring rushing waters. I went **to see** – perhaps inspired by the Girls who "saw" the woman in all her beauty (6:9): **has the vine flowered?** He has previously been witness to the new, emerging vegetation of spring (2:12–15). He now goes down to a slightly different place, and it is unclear whether he seeks another stage of flowering, signs of spring in this new place, or whether this is a *pro forma* inspection, while he knows full well that all is ready for love. **Have the pomegranates** – an image he has associated with her smile and limbs (4:3, 13; 6:7) – **budded?** He had seen "buds" (2:12).

She had talked of his descent to the garden, which was their moment of lovemaking (6:2). He responds with a slightly different moment – the descent to the grove. He seems to have something new to share. The background to that boldness may be the sexual connection of 5:1, her positive recollection of the same (6:2), the reaffirmation of the mutuality of their love (6:3) or his delight in his love's uniqueness.

6:12 *My soul, disoriented, set me*
Mid the chariots of the nobility.

יב לֹא יָדַעְתִּי נַפְשִׁי שָׂמַתְנִי
מַרְכְּבוֹת עַמִּי נָדִיב:

6:12 My soul, he states, recalling that her soul is the locus of her devotion to him (1:7; 3:1–4; 5:6), was **disoriented** (literally, "I did not know my soul" – see notes). He seems both generally puzzled and specifically out of touch with the center of emotion. The strength of the statement is amplified by previous uses of "soul," all by her. After an initial five uses indicating her devotion, the last use indicated that her "soul went out" (5:6 – see commentary) when he spoke. Now *his* "soul" enters the picture, also on an unsure footing. My soul **set me**, he states. He was not in charge. Something was happening to him. (This reading is based on reading "my soul" twice – see notes.) It set him (just as she was "set" by her brothers, 1:6, also indicating that she was not in control) **mid the chariots of the nobility** – unexpected and unidentifiable images. Clearly the Song has moved to some different plain. Chariots replace the urban and country scenes. The nobility replaces shepherds and city dwellers.

Alternatively, since only she has referred to "my soul" previously, one momentarily assumes that she may be speaking (which might, in turn, call for reconsideration of the speaker of the previous verse). If so, the soul's disorientation continues directly from its loss, 5:6. Since, however, the next verses continue with a description of a woman, with continued reference to the nobility, this and the previous verse were probably spoken by the lover. (**)

Chapter 7

פרק ז

א שׁוּבִי שׁוּבִי הַשּׁוּלַמִּית
שׁוּבִי שׁוּבִי וְנֶחֱזֶה־בָּךְ
מַה־תֶּחֱזוּ בַּשּׁוּלַמִּית
כִּמְחֹלַת הַמַּחֲנָיִם:

7:1 Encore! Encore! O Shulammite.

Encore! Encore! Let us observe you.

What do you observe in the Shulammite

In this Two-Towns Twirl?

7:1 Encore! Encore! The translation anticipates what follows, a dance performed before a group, **O Shulammite** woman. This new term, built on the same three-letter root (*sh-l-m*) as both Solomon and Jerusalem (see notes), has merited many interpretations. Is she related to either? Is she the heroine of the Song, or another? The reader awaits clarification. **Encore! Encore!** they repeat, creating a double echo. The first five words of the sentence are also in assonance in Hebrew. **Let us** – a group speaks – **observe you.** The root (*ch-z-h*) is not the same as those used for "sight" or "view" (*r-'-h*; *d-g-l*) and is therefore translated differently. This verb's implication ranges from general sight to prophetic vision.

What do you – plural, addressed to the group – **observe in the Shulammite, in this Two-Towns Twirl?** Concerning the last phrase: "Two Towns" is a place name in Israel, literally, "Two Camps," and the term "twirl" (translation chosen for assonance with Two Towns) is literally "dance." (See notes.) "Two Towns" could refer to the location of action, a type of dance, or a dance pattern. Whatever specifics are implied, the "double" place name was carefully chosen, and serves as a clue to the entire verse. *Every* basic root word in this verse is repeated (given the echo of "Two Towns" and "Twirl"), and the opening repetition is itself repeated! The verse has four phrases, each with four accents. The verse *itself* dances a two-camp dance, calling for its own repetition (encore, encore)! This is an exceptional achievement. (**)

7:2 *How beautiful are your feet in sandals,*

    O noble girl,

    The turns of your thighs like ornaments,

    The work of an artist's hands.

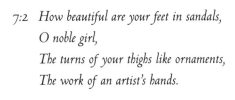

7:2 How beautiful – the same phrase with which he had appreciated her loving (4:10) – **are your feet,** or "steps," and both are implied. The dance has called attention first to her moving feet, **in sandals.** All her descriptions have proceeded from head down (4:1–7; 6:4–7), as did his (5:10–13). That feet, not love, are the referent of "how beautiful," together with the reversal of order, indicate a marked change, scarcely a surprise in that a group is speaking, not the lover (or not he alone). The significance of the change is not yet clear. Similarly, still unclear is the identity of the Shulammite, here called **O noble girl,** clearly a part of that environment (6:12). She is also a "girl," a possible echo to the Girls of Jerusalem. Is she like them in any way?

    The turns – (the same root, *ch-m-k,* as "turned away," 5:6), a term indicating (like "feet/steps" of the first half of the verse) either the curve of the body or its motion in dance, or both – **of your thighs like ornaments, the work of an artist's hands,** they continue, still with terms not used previously. Whatever the specific meaning of the image (attractive shape, smoothness), the implication of beauty is clear.

7:3 *Your navel is a well-curved bowl,*
May the punch never be lacking!
Your belly is a mound of wheat,
Hedged with lilies.

ג שָׁרְרֵךְ אַגַּן הַסַּהַר

אַל־יֶחְסַר הַמָּזֶג

בִּטְנֵךְ עֲרֵמַת חִטִּים

סוּגָה בַּשּׁוֹשַׁנִּים:

7:3 Your navel they continue, ascending, **is a well-curved bowl** — the term may mean "(half-) moon shaped." **May the punch** — literally, admixture, probably a type of wine, which was often prepared by mixing a concentrate with water — **never be lacking!** The imagery and the hope are obscure; the dancer and the observers remain unidentified. Clearly, however, the observers appreciate the Shulammite's body.

Your belly is a mound — a continuing emphasis on curves, a phenomenon well known in descriptions of feminine pulchritude. Here, it is possibly also occasioned by the undulating movements of the dance — **of wheat**, the winnowed grain, piled in hemispheric sheaves, **hedged with lilies.** Suddenly the poet reintroduces a familiar symbol. The lilies have brought the lovers together (cf. commentary 5:13, and 6:2f.). They now decorate the Shulammite. Are they here again a metaphoric reference to part of her body, or an actual decoration? If the former, the description of the woman's breasts as fawns feeding among the lilies comes to mind (4:5). If decorations, the erotic atmosphere sparks, as only sandals and lilies adorn the dancing Shulammite, recalling a flowered belt below the navel found on ancient naked figurines. (**)

7:4 *Your breasts are like two young harts,*
Twins of a gazelle.

ד שְׁנֵי שָׁדַיִךְ כִּשְׁנֵי עֳפָרִים
תָּאֳמֵי צְבִיָּה:

7:4 Your breasts are like two young harts, twins of a gazelle. Surprisingly and suddenly, a description of the woman is repeated verbatim (4:5). Is the Shulammite the beloved?! (The omission of "who pastures among the lilies," 4:5, seems technical, occasioned by the immediate previous reference to lilies.) If the Shulammite is the beloved, why has the description until now been so radically different?

The repetition also places the identity of the speakers in doubt. Until now, an assembled crowd had seemed to react to the Shulammite (7:1–3). However, this verse was previously stated by the lover. Has he been speaking (and if so, since when), or is the description so obvious that any would repeat it (if it is the same woman)? The ambiguity concerning the speaker seems to be a technique (see 4:16, 6:12). (✲✲)

7:5 *Your neck is like an ivory tower,*
Your eyes are pools in Heshbon,
By the gate of Bat Rabbim.
Your nose is like the tower of Lebanon,
Facing toward Damascus.

ה צַוָּארֵךְ כְּמִגְדַּל הַשֵּׁן
עֵינַיִךְ בְּרֵכוֹת בְּחֶשְׁבּוֹן
עַל־שַׁעַר בַּת־רַבִּים
אַפֵּךְ כְּמִגְדַּל הַלְּבָנוֹן צוֹפֶה
פְּנֵי דַמָּשֶׂק:

7:5 Your neck is like an ivory tower, the ascending description continues. The beloved's neck had been compared to David's Tower (4:4). Ivory may indicate smoothness or color, but is surprising as a description of a tower (scarcely constructed of ivory). She has used it to describe his belly, in a description also highly inanimate (5:14). **Your eyes**, which have riveted him and which he has praised (6:5), **are pools in Heshbon**, a city east of the Jordan River and north of the Dead Sea. (An eighth-century BCE water reservoir has been uncovered there.) However, the tone differs again from previous descriptions. Large, inanimate imagery dominates. The pools are **by the gate of Bat Rabbim**, an unknown reference, either the gate of a satellite city or a named gate of Heshbon. Literally, it means the "Daughter of Multitudes." If the name of a gate, it possibly means one used by masses, approximately, "the People's Gate." Possibly, "Daughter of the Multitudes" symbolizes the Shulammite as well, as she dances before a group. It certainly befits the oversized imagery of this description.

Your nose is like the tower of Lebanon, or "the towering Lebanon," which could be a reference to a mountain peak. Again, the image is "larger than life," **facing toward Damascus**. Evidently, the comparison is to the slope. (Damascus is below the mountains.) Heshbon and Damascus further "stretch" the borders of the Song. Places named include Jerusalem, Kedar, Ein Gedi, Sharon, Lebanon, Mount Gilead, Amana, Hermon, Senir, Tirzah, Mahana'im (the Hebrew of "Two Towns," 7:1), Heshbon (Bat Rabbim) and Damascus. (See commentary, 3:6, on the variety of locations.) (**)

7:6 *Your head upon you is like the crimson Carmel,*
And the hair of your head like purple yarn —
A king is captive in the tresses.

ו רֹאשֵׁךְ עָלַיִךְ כַּכַּרְמֶל
וְדַלַּת רֹאשֵׁךְ כָּאַרְגָּמֶן
מֶלֶךְ אָסוּר בָּרְהָטִים:

7:6 Your head upon you is like the crimson Carmel – the last two terms translate one Hebrew word, which can mean either the Carmel mountain in northwest Israel, or, with a slight vowel change, the color crimson. Given the mountains of the last verse and the color of the next phrase, we assume that a double entendre was intended, and we translate both meanings. (See 2:8 for a similar translation.) The large imagery continues.

And the hair of your head like purple yarn – in texture, form, radiance, or all of these. Purple yarn, previously associated with Solomon's litter (3:10), is now "transferred" to the Shulammite. Purple yarn was expensive, and therefore associated with sacred structures and royalty. (A possible alternate translation is "royal purple yarn," reading the next Hebrew word, "king," twice.) In any case, the yarn recalls royalty and therefore **a king** – a term used previously for the lover (1:4, 12) – **is captive in the tresses**, imprisoned in the flowing, or tangled, long hair.

The "king" previously reflected the lover in moments of physical embrace – taking the woman to his chambers (1:4) and lying with her on his couch (1:12). It seems appropriate to the sensual Shulammite dance. The speaker(s) – possibly the lover himself – is/are caught up in desire for the dancing figure. (**)

7:7 *How beautiful you are,*
     How lovely you are,
     O love ecstatic.

מַה־יָּפִית   ז
וּמַה־נָּעַמְתְּ
אַהֲבָה בַּתַּעֲנוּגִים:

7:7 How beautiful you are, almost the identical phrase, "how beautiful," with which the lover praised the beloved's loving (4:10) and the Shulammite's dancing feet (7:2). The reference to "you" would seem to encompass her whole person.

How lovely you are, she is told. It would seem the lover speaks, returning her compliment (1:16 – "indeed you are beautiful...truly lovely"), thus indicating that the beloved is the Shulammite. It is unclear when the lover began speaking. Did he seize the right of response from the very beginning, or did the crowd, while speaking, use some phrase ("lilies," "breasts like young harts," "king"?) that reminded him of his own statements, thereby moving him to speak? As before (cf. commentaries, 2:15, 4:16, 6:10), the poet melds one speaker into another, indicating possible identity of view. The assumption that she is addressed, however, is quickly undone. "You" proves to be not the beloved but you, **O love** – the abstract "love," not an endearing name for the beloved. (The echo of "love" and "lovely" is inadvertent, not present in the Hebrew, which uses different roots altogether.) As before (3:6 – cf. commentary 3:7), the poet surprises the reader by a change of referent. However, there is continuity. It is clear that the vision of the Shulammite has evoked this praise of abstract love, for this is love **ecstatic**, literally, "love with its delights." The dancing Shulammite, with her beautiful body, has brought the lover to a peak of frenzy of his own, here expressed in his praise of love ecstatic.

7:8 *Your risen self resembles a palm-shaft,*
And your breasts, clusters.

ח זֹאת קוֹמָתֵךְ דָּמְתָה לְתָמָר
וְשָׁדַיִךְ לְאַשְׁכֹּלוֹת:

7:8 Your risen self he now recalls, possibly thinking of her rising (3:2, 5:5), finally, to answer his call that she do so (2:10, 13). (Literally, the phrase reads "This, your height," the latter word derived from "rise," Hebrew, *kum*.) It **resembles a palm** – a returned compliment, for she had termed him a cedar (5:15) – **shaft** – not another Hebrew word, but a sound implication of "palm" (*tamar*), which echoes the "shafts" (*timrot*) of smoke while ascending from the desert (3:6). **And your breasts** resemble **clusters** of dates. The oversized imagery continues. These clusters are very large, and can include a thousand dates. A palm can be as high as twenty meters.

7:9 *I said, I will ascend the palm-shaft,*
And I will take hold of its branches.
Let your breasts be like the clusters on the vine,
The fragrance from your nose like the apricots.

ט אָמַרְתִּי אֶעֱלֶה בְתָמָר
אֹחֲזָה בְּסַנְסִנָּיו
יִהְיוּ־נָא שָׁדַיִךְ כְּאֶשְׁכְּלוֹת הַגֶּפֶן
וְרֵיחַ אַפֵּךְ כַּתַּפּוּחִים:

7:9 I said, in determination, **I will ascend** – the root used in the "ascent" from the desert (3:6) a verse including "shafts of smoke" here echoed by **the palm-shaft. And I will take hold** – just as she held him when she

found him after the search (3:4) – **of its branches**, the upper branches among which the clusters of dates grow. As before (4:5f.), mention of her breasts leads to his determination to touch them.

Let (the Hebrew emphasizes the term) **your breasts**, which have so inspired me – and which he now terms "your," moving decisively from the Shulammite image to the beloved. (This great importance of her breasts to him perhaps explains why that detail, taken from his past descriptions of her, forced its way into the description of the Shulammite, in 7:4. That recollection was too strong in his subconscious to be changed.) He hopes her breasts will **be like the clusters** – and here one expects reference to the date clusters above, but instead is offered clusters **on the vine**, the grape vine! A different image is introduced, more delicate and more appropriate in terms of size, recalling the purpose which led to his vision: to see if the "vine" had flowered (6:11). His direct address to her ("your breasts") is thus accompanied by a return to previous, "pre-Shulammite" imagery, softer and more animate. He continues with earlier references: let **the fragrance** – to which she (1:3, 12) and then he (2:13, 4:10f.) have shown great sensitivity. In particular, "vines" recall fragrance (2:13), though here the application changes (as it did with the clusters) from fragrance of the vine to fragrance **from your nose**, i.e., your breath, possibly implying the closeness of a kiss. "Nose" is the last term in this section connected specifically to the Shulammite (7:5). He hopes to find there a fragrance **like the apricots**, which she had requested while lovesick (2:5), presumably because it reflected his kiss (cf. 2:3 and commentary). (******)

7:10 *And your palate like the best wine.*

It goes as it should to my lover,

Stirring the lips of sleepers.

וְחִכֵּךְ כְּיֵין הַטּוֹב י

הוֹלֵךְ לְדוֹדִי לְמֵישָׁרֵים

דּוֹבֵב שִׂפְתֵי יְשֵׁנִים:

7:10 And let **your palate**, he concludes, citing that which tasted the sweetness of the apricots (2:3). (The images have jumped from one to the other, excitedly. Clusters of dates recalled clusters of the vine, which in turn recalled fragrance, which in turn recalled the apricots, which recalled the palate, which will now recall yet another familiar image!) Let it be **like the best wine**, recalling 1:2. Wine has been both the emotion of love (1:2, 4:10) and the enjoyment thereof (5:1). This verse now recalls the kiss, the expression par excellence of their relationship (cf. commentary 5:16).

The centrality of the mouth makes it a fitting conclusion for his awakening. The mouth and its parts are cited constantly in the Song (1:2; 2:3, 14; 4:3, 11; 5:13, 16; here), moving from the opening kiss to the mouth as summation of his person (5:16). Here it is the peak of his final emergence from vision to reality.

It goes as it should, she exults, "as it should" being the same term as "rightly" (1:4), the way the Girls adore him. (Here, too, there is a possible double entendre, the alternate translation reading, "It flows as strong wine.") It goes, just as he intended to "go" (4:6 – "get away"– same root) to her breasts, creating a balancing movement. It goes, flowing, she is overjoyed to report, **to my lover, stirring the lips**, another part of the central mouth (cf. 4:11, 5:13 for relationship to the kiss).

But these are lips **of sleepers**. Who sleeps? Herein lies the understanding of much that has preceded. The last two verses, filled with terminology that "belongs" to the beloved, have led to the conclusion that she and the Shulammite are the same. Prior to that, the reverse order of phrases, the new environment and the newness of the description had seemed to imply the opposite. The stirring of sleepers, however, now recalls the opening of the vision: "My soul, disoriented, placed me…" (6:12). In retrospect, one sees in the Shulammite episode, then, a vision, a daydream, an erotic love fantasy. From it the lover here fully awakes, which he has done by stages, refocusing his desire on his beloved. Explained are the combination of similarities and differences, the gradual change of imagery and the reverse order of the description. This was a symbolic personification of his desires, and only gradually did he identify them with his beloved. At the moment of the kiss, the fantasy finally has dissipated.

Who, then, speaks these final words, "stirring the lips of the sleepers"? Does she declare him awake, does he declare this of himself, or do they both? Again (cf. 6:10) the speaker is unclear, possibly indicating their mutual joy. In fact, the wine kiss may be intended to awaken them both, for she once declared herself half asleep (5:2) and thereby missed an opportunity. It is sleepers' (plural) lips that are stirred. (⁕⁕)

7:11 *I am my lover's*
And it is I whom he desires.

יא אֲנִי לְדוֹדִי
וְעָלַי תְּשׁוּקָתוֹ:

7:11 I am my lover's, she reconfirms, as before (6:3, echoing 2:16). However, the mutuality, so forcefully emphasized in the previous articulations, is now given a new slant. Celebrated is not only mutuality, but also his emergence from his fantasy, as he understands that his beloved is the true object of his passion. Thus she exults: **and it is I whom he desires**. She celebrates his passion being directed toward her, replacing the former phrase "my lover is mine" (2:16) with this delight in his desire.

Indeed, the mutuality is strengthened in another way. In Genesis (3:16), Eve as the mother of all womankind is "cursed" in having her desire directed toward her husband. (That story includes the only other two biblical uses of this term, "desire.") The poet of the Song balances the scale. *His* desire is for *her*. On a biblical level, equality is restored, complementing the equality of the two previous verses in the Song.

XXII. To the field

7:12 *Come, my lover,*

    Let us go out to the field,

    Let us lie among the henna.

יב   לְכָ֤ה דוֹדִי֙

נֵצֵ֣א הַשָּׂדֶ֔ה

נָלִ֖ינָה בַּכְּפָרִֽים׃

7:12 Come, my lover, she seizes the initiative, using the same root (*h-l-ch*) with which he had asked her to "come" away (literally, "go" – 2:10, 13 – and with which the wine had gone to him – 7:10) to the world of nature. Using a similar image, she proposes: **let us go out to the field**, i.e., out in the open. **Let us lie**, literally, "spend the night," the same term she used to describe him as lying between her breasts (1:13), emphasizing the erotic overtones of the present verse. She proposes to lie and spend the night **among the henna**, a spice used to describe, appropriately, both of them (1:14, 4:13). Alternatively, the final term also means "in the villages," a reflection of their desire to escape the city and its values. Both are possibly implied.

7:13 *Let us go early to the vineyards.*

    Let us see:

    Has the vine flowered,

    Have the blossoms opened,

    Have the pomegranates budded?

    There I will give you my loving.

יג   נַשְׁכִּ֙ימָה֙ לַכְּרָמִ֔ים

נִרְאֶ֗ה

אִם־פָּֽרְחָ֤ה הַגֶּ֙פֶן֙

פִּתַּ֣ח הַסְּמָדַ֔ר

הֵנֵ֖צוּ הָרִמּוֹנִ֑ים

שָׁ֛ם אֶתֵּ֥ן אֶת־דֹּדַ֖י לָֽךְ׃

7:13 Let us go early – the term reflects a special effort – **to the vineyards.** "Vineyard" was last mentioned as their vineyard, which needed protection (2:15) because it was in blossom. Again, the vineyard seems symbolic, but its import is not yet quite clear. **Let us see: has the vine flowered?** She proposes to join him in his inspection (6:11 – only there in the Song is "flowered" also used). He has come out of his fantasy. They can act

together, also testing: **have the blossoms opened, have the pomegranates budded?** The second phrase is also taken from his search (6:11), which she joins. The blossoms opening, however, directs attention to his description, 2:10–13, of a world of nature in blossom, ready for love. Indeed, her request that he "come" with her (previous verse) was drawn from that section as well. In fact, then, what is to be inspected is already known. The vines *are* in blossom (2:15). Therefore she knows beforehand what the result of their joint inspection will be.

There – in the vineyards – **I will give you my loving**. Certainly such a place needs protection (2:15). As to the loving she will give him, it has already been described – better than wine! (4:10).

The time of day bears noting. They begin their inspection at dawn. Their loving is to take place while they can see, in the light of day. His accolade that she is greater than the brightest lights comes to mind (6:10). Nighttime, once a time of separation and search (3:1, 5:2), has already become a time for them to lie together (previous verse). Now the day is also open to them. (**)

7:14 *The loving-plant gives forth fragrance,*
And by our entrances: all delicacies,
New – also old –
My lover, I have kept for you.

יד   הַדּוּדָאִ֣ים נָֽתְנוּ־רֵ֗יחַ
וְעַל־פְּתָחֵ֙ינוּ֙ כָּל־מְגָדִ֔ים
חֲדָשִׁ֖ים גַּם־יְשָׁנִ֑ים
דּוֹדִ֖י צָפַ֥נְתִּי לָֽךְ׃

7:14 The loving-plant, the mandrake, known as an aphrodisiac, whose Hebrew name reflects the word "loving," **gives** – a balance to her "giving" her loving in the previous verse – **forth fragrance**, a term which has grown in dimension. First describing her spikenard (while she was on his couch – 1:12), it later described the vines in blossom (2:13), part of nature's readiness for love. Here the very plant of loving gives off fragrance, reaching the crescendo of physical relationship.

And by our entrances – literally, "openings," possibly a double entendre referring to the openings of their houses (1:17) and of their persons – are **all delicacies**, the same words as "delectable" fruits (4:13, 16), which she offers her lover to eat. That previous section of coition, the middle of the poem, is recalled as they are again alone together. At the same time the root of "opening" now changes from failure to success. Her previous attempt to "open" to her lover (5:2, 5, 6) came too late.

These delicacies are **new, also old** – both an expression of whatever is best (according to the delicacy – some foods are better old, some new), and totality. (The poet sometimes uses opposites to create an encompassing phrase – see commentary, 4:16, on "north…south".) **My lover, I have kept** all of this hidden, or stored, **for you.** They are here reunited. She reassures him of her total loyalty between times. The "new" is a renewal of the old.

XXIII. If only

Chapter 8	פרק ח

8:1 *If only you were given me as a brother,*
   Suckling of my mother's breasts.
   I would find you outside,
   I would kiss you,
   Yet no one would scorn me.

א מִי יִתֶּנְךָ כְּאָח לִי
יוֹנֵק שְׁדֵי אִמִּי
אֶמְצָאֲךָ בַחוּץ
אֶשָּׁקְךָ
גַּם לֹא־יָבֻזוּ לִי:

8:1 If only you were given me, a strong contrast to the preceding sense of conclusion, as she "gave" her love to him, while the mandrakes "gave" off fragrance. Longing again dominates, the poet thus signaling a change. She wishes he were **as a brother**, a puzzling wish. Momentarily, one might assume that this term is an epithet for "lover" (as used in ancient literature), consonant with his use of "sister" (4:9), but the continuation clarifies

that the reference is indeed to a **suckling of my mother's breasts**. Questions abound. She has again (as 3:4) recalled her mother in the context of her love relationship, a closeness he has acknowledged (6:9). However, the present association with breasts is highly provocative. By now, such references have become clearly erotic (1:13; 4:5; 7:4, 8, 9). Does she seek to join erotic interests with reproductive ones (motherhood)?

I would find you, "find" having been used only in her searches for him (3:1–4; 5:6–8). The second search (when she did not find him) here reaches its resolution, as she pictures herself finding him **outside**, where she had searched for him before. Those searches were quite public. Does she wish to bring her relationship, already exposed to light of day (7:13f. commentary), out of the fields and into the eye of the public?

I would kiss you. As at the Song's beginning (1:2), the kiss remains the greatest dream, which recently (see 7:10) awoke him from a stupor. **Yet no one would scorn me**, despite the public kissing. Thus one understands the "brother" reference. She seeks the kiss, satisfied if she alone knows its implication (romantic), while others assume it is other (familial), much as she was satisfied recalling physical intimacy to the Girls of Jerusalem while they "heard" only directions (6:2 – commentary).

After this kiss, the mouth is not mentioned again. The frequency of reference is almost matched by the variety of terms – mouth (1:2), lips (4:3, 11; 5:13; 7:10), palate (2:3, 5:16, 7:10), teeth (4:2, 6:6), organ of speech (4:3), smile (4:3, 6:7) and tongue (4:11), plus the mentions of voice. Given the Song's dependence on repeated roots, this variety is exceptional, creating of the kiss an intimate, exploring, intense action. (**)

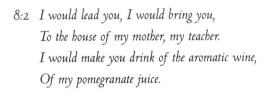

8:2 *I would lead you, I would bring you,*
  To the house of my mother, my teacher.
  I would make you drink of the aromatic wine,
  Of my pomegranate juice.

ב   אֶנְהָגֲךָ אֲבִיאֲךָ
אֶל־בֵּית אִמִּי תְּלַמְּדֵנִי
אַשְׁקְךָ מִיַּיִן הָרֶקַח
מֵעֲסִיס רִמֹּנִי:

8:2 I would lead you, she dreams, still showing the initiative of the end of chapter 7, **I would bring you**, as she said before (3:4), then echoing his "bringing" her to his chambers (1:4) and to the wine house (2:4). As before (3:4), she seeks to bring him **to the house**, which now reads as a contrast to the idyllic tryst of 7:14. That meeting, by light of day, was still private (in nature), and transient ("our entrances"). She now wants to bring him publicly to a single house, that **of my mother** (as 3:4), a renewed hint of marriage and childbearing. Now the mother, however, is called **my teacher**.

Here the poet offers a second and alternate interpretation of 3:4, where her mother was called *horati*, there translated "who conceived me," afterwards reflected in 6:9: "her mother...she who bore her." Here *horati* of 3:4 is reinterpreted, not from the root *h-r-h*, "pregnant," but *y-r-h*, "teach." The double interpretations complement each other. Her mother serves as her teacher, her model, in her aspirations for marriage and childbearing. The association of breasts with mother (previous verse) is thus clarified. She sees the pattern set by her mother as her ideal: physical intimacy leading to marriage and then to childbirth. This term could also be translated "You (the lover) will teach me," as she looks forward to learning love from him. The double entendre is complementary, and both provide a marked contrast to the only other use of "teach" in the Song: Solomon's warriors, trained (literally "taught") in war (3:8).

I would make, or let, **you drink**, in Hebrew (*ashkicha*), a play on words with the previous verse's "I would kiss you" (*eshakcha*). The first mention of kisses (1:2) was in the context of "loving...better than wine," and so, too, here she pictures him drinking **of the aromatic** (as befits him, his

cheeks being "towers of aromatics" – 5:13) **wine**, wine embracing the emotion and enjoyment of love, and recalling the kiss (cf. commentary, 7:10). Since used as one of the images of their lovemaking (5:1), the wine has improved in quality. It has become the "best wine" (7:10) and "aromatic wine" (here). Her desire to bring him to her mother's house and there let him drink wine recasts 2:4, "he brought me to the wine house." Rather than the public bar first envisioned, the wine house can be the intimate context of the mother's house! (The verb "bring" would thus always have reference to places of intimacy.) She would have him drink **of my pomegranate juice** ("juice" is used elsewhere in the Bible for wine). The pomegranate has described her smile (4:3, 6:7), and symbolized her readiness for love (4:13), that they seek to find budding (6:11, 7:13). Here the image reaches completion. It is ripe, processed and ready for the lover as a drink of love.

In these two verses, then, "brother" has undergone an evolution, from sibling to lover. (**)

8:3 *His left hand under my head,*
And his right hand embracing me.

ג שְׂמֹאלוֹ תַּחַת רֹאשִׁי
וִימִינוֹ תְּחַבְּקֵנִי׃

8:3 His left hand under my head, and his right hand embracing me, she repeats (2:6), citing the intimacy at the "wine house," thus confirming the identification of the mother's house, where she gives him wine, with the "wine house." This verse also befits the steady growth of intimacy across the previous two verses. (**)

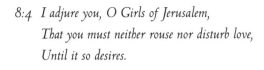

8:4 *I adjure you, O Girls of Jerusalem,*
   That you must neither rouse nor disturb love,
   Until it so desires.

ד   הִשְׁבַּעְתִּי אֶתְכֶם בְּנוֹת יְרוּשָׁלָם
   מַה־תָּעִירוּ | וּמַה־תְּעֹרְרוּ אֶת־הָאַהֲבָה
   עַד שֶׁתֶּחְפָּץ:

8:4 I adjure you, O Girls of Jerusalem, as she did immediately after her previous recollection of this scene (2:6f.) **that you must** – the negative is stronger than before – **neither rouse nor disturb love, until it so desires.** The narrative is cut off at a fevered pitch of excitement with an adjuration of the Girls of Jerusalem. There are, however, two differences from the earlier adjuration: the previous allusion to hinds and gazelles (2:7, 3:5) is omitted, and the adjuration terminology is here stronger.

There are several complementary explanations. First, the stronger negative befits the woman's new assertiveness. Second, the perfect tense (used also in the previous oaths) might here indicate the past, recalling the previous oaths, not making a new one ("I have adjured you"). If so, there is no place for resort to divine names or their replacements.

Third, the stronger oath might, on the other hand, reflect the woman's greater knowledge of the Girls. They have met her, heard her describe her lover and offered to search for him (5:8, 16). If they seem more of a threat, she might be more assertive in warning them off the chase. Fourth, it is possible that the omission of the animals simply reflects their use, after the two previous oaths, as symbols of her breasts (4:5, 7:4), making the poet now reluctant to use them in the oath. It is possible that the poet had one, many or all of these thoughts in mind.

8:5 *Who is this, ascending from the desert,*
     Clinging to her lover?
     Beneath the apricot tree I roused you,
     There your mother became pregnant with you,
     There she became pregnant, she who bore you.

ה מִ֣י זֹ֗את עֹלָה֙ מִן־הַמִּדְבָּ֔ר
מִתְרַפֶּ֖קֶת עַל־דּוֹדָ֑הּ
תַּ֤חַת הַתַּפּ֙וּחַ֙ עֽוֹרַרְתִּ֔יךָ
שָׁ֚מָּה חִבְּלַ֣תְךָ אִמֶּ֔ךָ
שָׁ֖מָּה חִבְּלָ֥ה יְלָדַֽתְךָ׃

8:5 Who is this woman, the Girls ask for a third time (3:6, 6:10), **ascending from the desert**, the same question asked after a similar adjuration (3:5f.). However, "who is this" has appeared again (6:10), the woman there compared to heavenly shining bodies. The now repeated question of ascent from the desert incorporates these heavenly bodies, since they rise in the east — in Jerusalem seemingly rising from the Judean desert, to the city's east. Given the woman's developed assertiveness, the Girls' question here seems as much a challenge as a query — who is this bright, shining, impertinent, presumptuous woman who would tell us what we cannot do? She is **clinging to**, or leaning on (or both!) **her lover**. The question "Who is this?" as in the first two occurrences, is followed by a description of the person, with no direct answer provided. That must be inferred from what follows. As in those previous two occurrences, after the description, the topic seems to change abruptly.

Beneath — an innocent preposition, but one used exclusively in erotic contexts in the Song (see note) — **the apricot tree** — a symbol of his distinction (2:3), fruit that sustains her in love (2:5) and the fragrance of her breath (7:9) — **I roused you.** She has adjured them not to rouse love too early, and she can now state that meanwhile she has succeeded in rousing her lover! (If 8:4–5 are a continuum, then she speaks in the presence of the Girls of Jerusalem. While still holding them off, she succeeds in doing what they were suspected of longing for! She has effectively eliminated the competition, and the Girls are not mentioned again.)

There your mother — she now relates to his mother. (Until now the references were to her mother or Solomon's.) Previously (6:9) he had "accepted" her connection to her mother by citing it, and now she feels free to draw the connection between him and his mother. There **she became pregnant with you; there she became pregnant, she who bore you.** So the woman defines the true import of intimacy under the apricot tree. There conception takes place. Romance is directed toward family and children. (One also recalls that the superiority of the apricot tree to the forest trees is, evidently, its fruit bearing ability – 2:3.) A previous image also now takes on new import – gazelles and hinds, the subject of the earlier oaths (2:6, 3:5), return to the place of birth to bear the next generation.

XXIV. **The seal on your heart**

8:6   *Set me as the seal on your heart,*
      The seal on your arm.
      For love is as mighty as death,
      Jealousy as relentless as the grave.
      Its darts are fire-darts,
      A furious flame.

ו   שִׂימֵ֨נִי כַחוֹתָ֜ם עַל־לִבֶּ֗ךָ
     כַּחוֹתָם֮ עַל־זְרוֹעֶ֒ךָ֒
     כִּי־עַזָּ֤ה כַמָּ֨וֶת֙ אַהֲבָ֔ה
     קָשָׁ֥ה כִשְׁא֖וֹל קִנְאָ֑ה
     רְשָׁפֶ֕יהָ רִשְׁפֵּ֖י אֵ֑שׁ
     שַׁלְהֶבֶתְיָֽה׃

8:6 Set me as the seal, the signet worn either as a necklace or as a ring, one's identifying certification, an item with which one would almost never part, **on your heart**, where the necklace seal would lie externally, but also referring to the center of emotion. In the Song, the heart has been associated with the wedding day (3:11), a subtle and appropriate emphasis, in consideration of the reference to childbearing and motherhood in the previous verse.

She asks to be set also as **the seal on your arm**, i.e., the signet ring. She longs to encircle him. This peak of expression of her hopes leads to an encomium of love in the abstract, carrying the Song to a universal plane: **for love is as mighty** – inescapable and absolute – **as death**. Indeed, **jealousy**, which she knows well from her contacts with the Girls and from her observation of the life of court – is **as relentless as the grave** (*she'ol*, the biblical post-life chaotic nether world). She is overwhelmed by her own passion: **its darts are fire-darts, a furious flame**, literally, a divine flame – a biblical way of expressing a superlative, with possible (but not necessary) overtones of "holiness." (See notes.) "Its darts are fire darts" is onomatopoeic (*rishafeha rishpei eish*).

Here the poet, as the Song nears its conclusion, breaks previous silence to comment directly on love itself. The imagery of this section will remain unique in the Song, as is appropriate to a climactic moment of the poem, and the central statement on love itself. (**)

8:7 *Multitudinous waters cannot quench love*
Nor can rivers sweep it away.
Were a man to give all the wealth of his house for love,
He would be utterly scorned.

ז מַיִם רַבִּים לֹא יוּכְלוּ לְכַבּוֹת אֶת־הָאַהֲבָה
וּנְהָרוֹת לֹא יִשְׁטְפוּהָ
אִם־יִתֵּן אִישׁ אֶת־כָּל־הוֹן בֵּיתוֹ בָּאַהֲבָה
בּוֹז יָבוּזוּ לוֹ:

8:7 Multitudinous waters, a phrase that can range from abundant water, to floods, to the Great Deep (the mythical force which only God can dominate – see notes). Theoretically, they should overcome not only any flame, but also herself, who is but a well of living water (4:15). However, they **cannot quench love**, this furious flame, **nor can rivers** – a term occasionally used for ocean currents – **sweep it away**. She continues to use superlatives. No water can extinguish this fire.

Were a man to give – a contrast to previous romantic uses of "give" (1:12, 2:13, 7:13f., 8:1) – **all the wealth of his house** – another striking contrast, this to the "house" of which she dreams, her mother's house to which she brings her lover (8:2), not something to be used to purchase love – **for love**, not a warning against prostitution, but the ineffectiveness of amassed human wealth in influencing love, parallel to the failure of nature's waters to extinguish it. Were a man so to act, **he**, or it (the wealth), **would be utterly scorned**, precisely the reaction she seeks to avoid in pursuit of her lover (8:1).

XXV. A little sister

8:8 *We have a little sister*
Who has no breasts.
What shall we do with our sister,
On the day when she is spoken for?

אָחוֹת לָנוּ קְטַנָּה ח
וְשָׁדַיִם אֵין לָהּ
מַה־נַּעֲשֶׂה לַאֲחֹתֵנוּ
בַּיּוֹם שֶׁיְּדֻבַּר־בָּהּ:

8:8 We have a little – the only previous use of "little" is to foxes, an ominous image, but this reference is to a **sister**. "Sister" has been used as one of his addresses to her, only in the apex of physical intimacy (4:9–5:2). Its sudden reappearance here is surprising. "Brother" has recently (8:1) been used literally, allowing the reader to posit that in our verse these are true siblings, recalled in light of 8:1–2 (the mention of her mother's house). They call her a sister **who has no breasts**, who is not sexually mature, not ready for motherhood (cf. 8:1). How strikingly different than the lover's description of the woman whose breasts are as two harts (4:5, 7:4), of which he dreams (as clusters – 7:9)! For her, they are the place where he lies (1:13). Could this be the same woman? Can sexual maturity, like beauty, be in the eye of the beholder, leading to such a different evaluation? It would seem so.

They may be thinking only of her welfare, as protective big brothers.
What shall we do with usually translated "do for," possibly "make for" **our sister, on the day when she is spoken for**, the day of her betrothal. How might we help her?

She, on the other hand, may hear a more ominous message:

What shall we do with meaning "do to," act to the detriment of, **our sister, on the day when she is spoken for**, that is, when we must speak against her (see notes)?

They contemplate helping, she hears a threat (much as the Girls of Jerusalem heard one message while she spoke another – 6:1–2)! (The connection of this verse to verse 7 may be, therefore, that both deal with attempted interference with true love.) (**)

8:9 *If she be a rampart,*
  We shall build a silver battlement on her,
  And if she be a door,
  We shall fashion a cedar board on her.

ט אִם־חוֹמָה הִיא
נִבְנֶה עָלֶיהָ טִירַת כָּסֶף
וְאִם־דֶּלֶת הִיא
נָצוּר עָלֶיהָ לוּחַ אָרֶז:

8:9 If they are thinking only of her welfare, as protective big brothers:

If she be a rampart (a protective wall surrounding a city or camp) – on the day when she can protect herself, what would be their role? **We shall build a silver** – a precious investment indeed (cf. 3:10, the silver pillars of Solomon's litter) – **battlement**, also a word for the wall surrounding a camp, evidently implying an extra row ("row" is the meaning of the root), but distinguishing their investment from hers. Her rampart is presumably of stone, theirs of silver. They seem intent to keep guard **on her**, perhaps protecting her virtue until she is properly "spoken for," perhaps guaranteeing that the man be the right one, and perhaps (if the implication of the rampart is that her breasts are still undeveloped) willing to contribute wealth to make her more attractive. "On her" can be translated "on it," referring to the rampart. **And** – the term could mean "but" – **if she be a door**, with three possible alternative implications: (a) undeveloped breasts, (b) well protected (a locked door, parallel to the first part of the verse) or (c) an open door (i.e., promiscuous or careless in guarding her own virtue), **we shall fashion a** strong, beautiful and expensive **cedar board on her**, with three meanings (each one corresponding to the parallel three interpretations of door): either (a) an extra attraction to suitors, (b) extra protection, or (c) an expression of their own intention to protect her virtue despite her.

She, again, may hear a more ominous message:
If she be a rampart, built against them and their determination to be her guardians, **we shall build a silver** – more precious, and superior to her stones – **battlement on her**, here meaning "against" her or "against" it. They will be her adversaries! **And if she be a door**, with the same range of meanings – either closed to them or open to her lover, **we shall fashion a cedar board on her**. If she is open to her lover, they intend to keep him out. If she is resistant to them, they intend to besiege her. ("Besiege" is an alternate meaning of *natsur*, the word which is translated "fashion.") Again, the implication is "against it." There is a beautiful irony in the brothers' proposal that they defend their sister (or imprison her) by using a panel of cedar (8:9). The beauty and strength of the cedar are already hers – in the structure of her abode (1:17) and in the presence of her lover (5:15).

While they continue to worry about her, then, she continues to hear a threat! She also notes their use of materials as strong as her lover (5:15 – he is "singular as the cedars"). In technique, this section is similar to 6:1–2, where the woman has one message in mind, which is heard differently by the Girls of Jerusalem. (**)

8:10 *I am a rampart,*

　　　But my breasts are like towers —

　　　Thus I have appeared, in his eyes,

　　　As finding "shalom."

י　אֲנִי חוֹמָה
וְשָׁדַי כַּמִּגְדָּלוֹת
אָז הָיִיתִי בְעֵינָיו
כְּמוֹצְאֵת שָׁלוֹם:

8:10 I am a rampart, she replies. Their future possibility is her present reality! (In addition, in making this her status, the poet hints that the brothers are possibly identical with the "watchmen of the ramparts" who abused her in her search for her lover, 5:7!) **But**, she clarifies, **my breasts** — so important to her (cf. commentary 8:8) — **are like towers**. She responds in consonance with the multiple levels of the understanding of the previous two verses, in which she saw her brothers opposing her. If the brothers mean that she is ready for neither love nor motherhood, she claims the opposite, in suitable hyperbole. If they feel she needs protection, she reaffirms that she has no need for their battlement — she has towers! Finally, if they threaten to besiege her, she warns them that she can withstand any siege against her. Indeed, her lover has already described her neck as a tower surrounded with shields (4:4).

Thus — a term either temporal ("then") or consequential ("therefore") — **I have appeared**, indicating an unreal impression, the meanings ranging from poetic license to total misconception (see notes), **in his eyes** — a central image of her beauty and effect on him (cf. commentary 6:5). His eyes have been mentioned but once (5:12), there compared to doves. She is often called his dove (2:14, 5:2, 6:9). By simile, then, she in fact appears in his eyes. She appeared **as finding**, a most appropriate description for her who has dreamed of, and envisioned "finding" her lover (3:1–4; 5:6–8; 8:1). "Finding" (*mots'et* from the root *m-ts-'*), however, if construed from a different root (*y-ts-'*) would mean "producing," granting the woman a still more active role in terms of the object of the verb: "**shalom**," literally, "peace" or "well being."

Many have been the interpretations of this unique phrase, "finding shalom." (It here would seem to pun a familiar Hebrew phrase, a woman "finding favor" in a man's eyes.) As so often, the key lies in the repeated use of a three letter root, *sh-l-m*, as found in "Solomon," "Shulammite" and "Jerusalem." (See introduction, on the theme of the Song.) Two alternatives suggest themselves. First she might recall the lover's waking from the vision of the Shulammite, when the breasts were among the specifics that led to his realization that his beloved was the true object of desire. She would be recalling that he understood her to be the cause of, the "producer" of, the Shulammite vision. Alternatively, since the *sh-l-m* view of love is rejected only because of what it lacks, not because of its emphasis on physical delight, she could celebrate the incorporation of that physical element in their love, as reflected in her invitation to him (after the Shulammite fantasy) to sleep with her in the fields (7:12f.).

The direct, nonsymbolic meaning also remains relevant. For a brief moment, it seemed to him that she had produced peace — final well being, fortune and contentment. Their togetherness ultimately proved to be fleeting, and they look forward to reunion, but so she had briefly "appeared." (**)

XXVI. My very own vineyard

8:11 *Solomon had a vineyard in Ba'al Hamon.*
   He gave the vineyard to the guards —
   A man would bring for its fruit
   A thousand pieces of silver.

יא כֶּרֶם הָיָה לִשְׁלֹמֹה בְּבַעַל הָמוֹן
נָתַן אֶת־הַכֶּרֶם לַנֹּטְרִים
אִישׁ יָבִא בְּפִרְיוֹ
אֶלֶף כָּסֶף:

8:11 Solomon suddenly reappears, an indication that the previous verse in fact emphasized the root *sh-l-m*, the same as that of "Solomon." Solomon was last cited in 3:7–11, where his lifestyle was held to be less impressive than his true glory, his wedding day.

Solomon **had a vineyard**, a second connection to the preceding section, for her brothers were connected to vineyards: they had forced her to guard vineyards, while she had not guarded her own (1:6). The vineyard has also appeared as that which surrounds her lover (1:14), the lovers' threatened possession (2:15) and the context of physical loving (7:13). Anticipating the next verse here, "vineyard" would seem to symbolize the love relationship itself, and if so, the appearance of Solomon's vineyard allows for another comparison, in consonance with the tone of the chapter. The vineyard was **in Ba'al Hamon**, an otherwise unknown location. The term, however, means "master (or owner) of a (vast) host," possibly reflecting many marriages, or the opulence of the court and harem. As such, the contrast with the two lovers is stark. (One also notes the only other unidentified location in the Song – Bat Rabbim, 7:5, used in reference to the Shulammite [same root as Solomon]. It means "Daughter of Multitudes." This is another indication that these two images, Solomon and the Shulammite, related by letters, are also intended to be related as symbols.) On an added level, *hamon* ("multitudes") can mean "wealth," a reflection of the value of the vineyard.

The contrast is emphasized through use of other terms drawn from earlier in the Song. **He gave the vineyard** – "gave" is a literal translation, implying transfer of property for financial consideration. Nevertheless, the use of the term implies another contrast. If vineyards symbolize love relationships, they are not to be "given" away. The *lovers* only "give" in the context of love, already contrasted with those who would "give" money to buy love (7:13, commentary). He gave it **to the guards,** evidently, tenant farmers. *She* had rejected the role of guarding, but had been forced into it (1:6). Now she feels free and independent, and relationships are her own. **A man** – a word with negative association in the Song: heroes fearful at night (3:8) and one who would buy love (8:7). This man, too, is willing to pay for a "vineyard" and **would bring** – as opposed to *the couple's* use of "bringing" to places of love (1:4, 2:4) and to her mother's house (3:4, 8:2) – **for its fruit** – evidently for sale, while *for the lovers* "fruit" has symbolized the kiss (2:3) and intimacy (4:13, 16) – **a thousand** – the only other thousand are the shields which form her necklace (4:4) – **pieces of silver**, a precious metal associated with Solomon's litter (3:10) and her brother's threats (8:9), but which the lover would use as decorations for her jewelry (1:11).

8:12 *My very own vineyard is before me.*
The thousand is yours, O Solomon,
And two hundred to the guards of its fruit.

יב כַּרְמִי שֶׁלִּי לְפָנָי
הָאֶלֶף לְךָ שְׁלֹמֹה
וּמָאתַיִם לְנֹטְרִים אֶת־פִּרְיוֹ:

8:12 My very own – the Hebrew emphasizes her ownership – **vineyard**, she cites, confirming the comparison to Solomon and the symbolic value of the term, here drawn directly from 1:6, "my very own vineyard I did not guard." There the contrast was to the brothers, here to Solomon. The vineyard **is before me**, in her presence, possession and control. In fact, the vineyard seems to be the love relationship. Early on, perhaps, she had not guarded it properly. The mistake is not to be repeated. She holds fast, and he is with her.

The thousand is yours, for she will not sell her vineyard, even for that sort of price! Given the symbolic value of the vineyard, however, there would seem to be (as many have noted) a reference here to Solomon's thousand wives as well (1 Kings 11:3). Her one love is not only sufficient — it is superior to his thousand loves! Her only "thousand" is the pieces of her necklace, described by her lover as a thousand shields (4:4 – significantly these "shields" are of "warriors," elsewhere named as Solomon's entourage – 3:7). The statement is addressed: **O Solomon**, though he is scarcely present. He is cited to be rejected, the clearest clue to the use of the root *sh-l-m* throughout the Song. Rejected is the world of Solomon (of a thousand loves), of the Girls of Jerusalem (experts in the city world of loving) and of the Shulammite (the sexual fantasy). By no means a rejection of physical loving, which is celebrated in the Song, this is a rejection of the partiality of such relationships, which are properly enjoyed within the contexts of devotion, exclusivity and commitment, with associated dreams of marriage and parenthood. She rejects all multiples connected to the vineyards, Solomon's thousand **and the two hundred** pieces of silver due **to the guards of its**, or "his," Solomon's, **fruit** (a symbol of love – 8:11). The "thousand," the second largest biblical number, recalls "ten thousand" (5:10), the largest number — the lover stands out above this number of men. These numbers are paired elsewhere in the Bible to indicate a superlative amount. (See notes.) Did the poet mean for the reader to pair the two numbers, deepening the rejection of all plural relationships? (**)

XXVII. Be swift, my lover

8:13 *O you who linger in the gardens*
   Fellows are listening for your voice.
   Let me hear...

הַיּוֹשֶׁבֶת בַּגַּנִּים   יג
חֲבֵרִים מַקְשִׁיבִים לְקוֹלֵךְ
הַשְׁמִיעִנִי׃

8:13 O you who linger, he calls to her — as before she delighted to "linger" in his (the apricot tree's) shade (2:3), now she lingers **in the gardens.** "Garden" has been used for her (4:12, 15ff.; 6:2, 11) and for her location. The plural might refer to two locations — the garden of spices (4:5–5:1) and the nut grove (6:11), combining the tenderness of the first with the passion of the second. In any case, she is now tranquilly settled there, the translation's present tense ("linger") reflecting the Hebrew participle ("she who lingers," "dweller"). ("Fruit" of 8:11 had been previously associated with "garden" — 4:16 — and with lingering — 2:3. These are two possible bridges from the previous section to this.) **Fellows,** possibly those among whom she might have to wander in searching for her lover (1:7), **are listening for your voice.** They seek to hear her, just as he did (2:14). He, too, seems to have competition.

Let me hear... he states, accentuating the competition and repeating his previous request to hear her voice (2:14). He wants her for himself. (His presence among others is no surprise — she has praised him as superior to those around him — 2:3, 5:10.) Lacking is an object for "let me hear." Evidently, the woman cuts off the lover in mid-statement. He asserts himself by declaring his desire that they be together, and she responds before he can even finish his sentence! Thus their total commitment is indicated, and the competitors are summarily dismissed. (However, the object of "let me hear" could be provided either by a double reading of "for your voice" or by breaking the verse after listening — "Fellows are listening. For [or 'to'] your voice let me hear.") (**)

8:14 *Be swift, my lover,*
   And make yourself like a gazelle or a young hart
   On mountains of spices.

יד בְּרַח | דּוֹדִי
וּדְמֵה־לְךָ לִצְבִי אוֹ לְעֹפֶר הָאַיָּלִים
עַל הָרֵי בְשָׂמִים:

8:14 Be swift, i.e., flee, either to her or away from the fellows, **my lover**, she replies, almost repeating her previous request to him (2:17), while omitting phrases implying delay ("until the day breathes…" and "circle about") in favor of direct movement. Be swift, **and make yourself like a gazelle or a young hart**, as in 2:17, now approaching me quickly – this reemphasis on speed and agility make these animals ever more appropriate, in retrospect, as a referent for her oaths (2:7, 3:5) – **on mountains** – again, as 2:17 – **of spices** – totally unlike the previous call, to the "cleft" mountains, a symbol of their separation. Subsequently, mountains took on new meaning – he identified her breasts as the mountain of myrrh and the hill of frankincense, to which he aspired (4:6). Here, in further describing those mountains by spices, she incorporates the description of their greatest moment of intimacy (4:13–5:1). The previous request (2:17) had been a call for caution, for either patience or discretion. This call is radically other, an open invitation to love, as befits the end of the Song. Appropriately, it balances and echoes the Song's beginning as well: "Draw me after you" (1:4).

A complementary level of interpretation is also possible. Perhaps the object of the previous verse's "let me hear" is none other than this sentence as a whole, a quote of that which the lover wants to hear from his beloved ("Let me hear: 'Be swift…'"). As often in the Song, both levels of meaning are possibly meant, implying that the two of them are speaking the same phrase, thinking the same thought. (For similar effects, cf. 2:15, 6:10; and see appendix.) This literary reflection of their mutuality is a prodigious poetic achievement, and a most appropriate finale to the Song. (*******)

Rereading the Song of Songs

While we have, in the commentary, occasionally looked forward to a parallel usage or development, we have scarcely done justice to the complex rereading necessary as each section retrospectively adds new implications to what was said before. We here continue with central rereadings, new understandings of verses that can only be accomplished after having concluded the first full reading.

1:4 The king has brought me to his chambers…. 1:12 While the king was on his couch
Clearly the Song differentiates Solomon from the two lovers. Context would then seem to indicate that the poet uses "king" for the lover when he approximates most closely the physical, erotic "Solomonic" love, with an overtone of reference to marriage (see 3:11). In these verses, they embrace alone.

1:6 Do not set your sight on me…. My mother's sons waxed hot in anger at me. They set me as guard to the vineyards. My very own vineyard I did not guard.
After 6:9, "Girls see her and praise her," one might question whether she initially misunderstood the staring of the girls. Perhaps originally their attention was also a matter of envy, not scorn.

The vineyard, not apparently a symbol at first, came to symbolize the love relationship itself (8:11f.). The verse 1:6 then can be reread. Are the brothers angry because she was being too careless about her "vineyard"? Were they in fact wroth at the growing, "unguarded" relationship with her lover? Or is their care more general – do they feel she is not ready for love, and therefore force her to guard what she neglected? In yet another level of meaning, she regrets that she has not guarded, held on to, their love. Her lover is not with her. Other vineyard references now also bear rereading. She wishes to awake in a vineyard (7:13) and she seeks to protect a vineyard (2:15).

Here her brothers are called her "mother's sons." That accepted usage now appears quite purposeful and ironic. She sees her mother as model and teacher, of love, sex and childbearing. Her brothers do not understand this.

1:7 Tell me, you whom my soul loves: Where do you pasture, where do you lie down at noon? Lest I be as one who wanders beside the flocks of your fellows.
The continuation of the Song allows the reader to reread that she asks the lover, "where do you

pasture" not only as shepherd, but also as he who feeds among the lilies (2:16). (As previously noted on 2:16, the Hebrew "pasture," like the English "feed," can be either active or causative.) For the shepherd she longs; but about him "who feeds among the lilies" she is worried: where do you pasture now (carrying out the image, to whom is your mouth drawn?) while you are away from me, your true lily (2:2)? The damsels of 1:2 are now cast in a more ominous light, as potential competitors.

Is her wandering among his fellows, then, a veiled counter-threat? Indeed, at the end of the Song, we find that the "fellows" are seeking her voice (8:13). One would not want her wandering among them! Such a reading allows for another double entendre, for "where" can also be translated "how" (see note). How could you be pasturing out there, thus allowing me to wander near these fellows!

1:8 If you do not know, O most beautiful of women, then follow the tracks of the sheep and pasture your kids next to the shepherds' huts.

This verse had seemed to be the man's response — but subsequently only others use the phrase, "O most beautiful of women" (5:9, 6:1), allowing for an alternate, or additional, interpretation. The respondents of this verse could be the shepherds, who taunt her: if you do not

know where he is, why not join us — just follow the tracks of the sheep to our huts. If so, 1:15, where the lover affirms her beauty, can be seen as a stinging response to their taunts. "Shepherds" (literally, "those who pasture") is now also a double entendre. For just as he was both shepherd and lover (he who feeds among the lilies) so, too, these shepherds apparently fancy such a dual role. "Join us," they say, "you who consider yourself so beautiful. We, too, would 'feed among lilies.'"

Their mocking of her supposed beauty is ultimately turned back at them. Her outstanding beauty will be confirmed. The lover finds her more beautiful than other women, and these women in fact join in praising her (6:9, 10).

1:11 Circlets of gold we shall make for you with spangles of silver.

The verse may purposely contrast other uses of silver and gold. By implication, the verse rejects the other uses of the special metals in the Song: for the battlement (8:8 — that verse also uses "we shall make," there translated "we shall do"), for decorating Solomon's litter (cf. 3:10 and commentary there) or for "payment" for the fruits of the vineyards (Solomon's guards — 8:11). Silver is best used as her jewelry. Similarly, 1:17 uses cedars as support beams of their house of love, the very cedars that her brothers propose to use as a door to lock her in (8:8f.).

1:13 A bag of myrrh is my lover to me, lying between my breasts.

Her brothers, perhaps protecting their "kid sister," saw her breasts as unready for love (8:8), but she thinks the opposite (8:10). Indeed they are a focal point of his physical adoration (4:5; 7:4, 9, 10). It is these attractive breasts, symbol of her maturity, which beckon him here, as the place where he is to lie, or spend the night.

The words here translated "is my lover to me" later form a statement, "My lover is mine!" (2:16, 6:3), allowing for a complementary reading of this verse, using a double reading of one word (see appendix): "A bag of myrrh is my beloved. My beloved is mine: he lies between my breasts." This additional understanding does not alter the meaning of the verse, but lends depth thereto. The verse 1:14 also now allows the same complementary reading: "A cluster of henna is my lover. My lover is mine – [but he is far away,] in the vineyards of Ein Gedi," as does 1:15, "Indeed you are beautiful my darling. My darling you are! Indeed you are beautiful..."

In turn, this calls attention to the tense (imperfect) of the verb "to lie," here translated "lying," but also possibly "he will lie," an anticipation of reunification. The Song supports both understandings, moving between fulfillment and separation. The lingering tone toward the end of the Song is one of determination, as she invites him to "lie" with her (7:12).

1:16 Indeed you are beautiful, my lover, truly lovely; truly our pallet is verdant.

Only here does the woman call her lover "beautiful." She is taken with his physical appearance (5:10–16), but she seems to prefer simile and metaphor. He, on the other hand, uses "beautiful" often. Is the difference one of temperament, gender differentiation or other?

The terms "beautiful" and "lovely" are used in sequence one other time in the Song (7:7), in his sexual fantasy of the dancing Shulammite, praising physical love. It is therefore most appropriate that the parallel use occurs in our verse, which recalls their "pallet."

At first, one assumes that she continues speaking: "Truly our pallet..." However, the Song includes several instances of unclear transfer of speaker from one party to another, including possible overlapping meanings (cf. commentaries, 3:10, 4:15, 7:7 and appendix). It is therefore reasonable to read the two lovers joining now in this statement, continuing with verse 17.

2:2 As a lily among the brambles, such is my darling among the girls.

Despite this declaration of her uniqueness, it will take her some time to accept that he is committed to her alone. She will yet describe him as feeding among the lilies (plural – 2:16), the poem marked by fear of competition until the

very end. In rereading, the reader is left to ponder which of the two, the man or the woman, had a more realistic evaluation of the potential competition from other women.

Two additional understandings of the "lily among the brambles" suggest themselves on re-reading. (A) Might this also symbolize her inaccessibility? Elsewhere he cites her covert location (2:14f.). This valley-lily, set among thorns, it is hard to reach. (B) Medieval commentators often saw the thorns as a threat to the lily, lest the fragile plant be overgrown by the weeds. Might they, then, secondarily also symbolize the ominous competition of the other girls, weeds that might swallow her up.

2:3 As an apricot among the trees of the forest, such is my lover among the boys. I delight to linger in that shadow, and that fruit is sweet to my palate.

Many details in this first declaration of her appreciation of his uniqueness become central images of the Song, and are redefined in the process. The "apricot" tree evolves into longing for intimacy, marriage and fertility (2:5, 7:9, 8:5). "Palate," seen as a kiss from the beginning, takes on great physical intimacy (5:16, 7:10). "Palate," "sweet" and "delight" reappear together in 5:16, summarizing his superiority, and therefore verifying the strong sense of comparison felt in this verse. "Fruit" will both mark

their mutuality (4:13, 16) and differentiate them from others (8:11). Even the "shadow" continues to bind them (2:17, 4:6). The poet's genius shines through — images so natural in the context of the first reading later move far beyond themselves.

2:4 He brought me to the wine house, and he viewed me with love.

The "wine house" of this verse must be reinterpreted. "Wine" has become a symbol for physical love (5:1), and she dreams of giving him spiced wine (8:2). Concerning "house," she seeks to "bring" (the verb used here) him to her mother's house (3:4, 8:2), and there she seeks to give him spiced wine (8:2)! Read in that light, our verse is the exact opposite of a bar or public house — it is the envisioned intimacy of her mother's house, the marriage house, the house where she will give him "wine."

2:5 Sustain me with cakes, cushion me with apricots, because I am lovesick.

Later reference to lovesickness challenges the original interpretation. In 5:8 the woman explains that she is lovesick, and its apparent cause is his *absence*, not his presence. If the two love-sicknesses are the same, this scene must be a vision, a view of the "past" that is both symbolic and hopeful — his absence eliciting a vivid dream of his presence. (If a dream, it also better explains the new subject in 2:8. Having fantasized, she longs to have her lover come near her.)

Is her love sickness then a weakness of body (Saadia Gaon translated a "weakening" love) or is she concerned lest love itself grow weaker due to his absence? Might we not read both? In the vision, she would be overwhelmed with passion; in reality, she would fear that absence would weaken love.

The confusion of time, past, present and future, takes on a value of its own in the Song. Is the poet intimating thereby a statement on the relative powers of time and love? Such a conjecture might seem improbable, were it not for the poet's willingness to reflect of love's strength in the abstract, and in the strongest of terms (8:7).

2:10 My lover responded, saying to me: rise up, my darling, my beauty, come away.
Understanding that others, not he, mockingly designated her "the most beautiful of women" (1:8, as reread), we can guess that the linkage of "my darling" to "my beauty" indicates that it is their relationship that allows the lover to see all that beauty.

His request that she "rise" (here and 2:13) becomes a poignant irony. Twice she has risen (3:2, 5:5f.), both times too late. (Indeed, in 5:6 her late rising results in there being no "response.")

As in all good love stories, too often when he is ready, she is not, and the opposite.

2:12 The buds are seen in the land, the time of singing has arrived, and the voice of the turtledove is heard in our land.
While the turtledove's voice is actually heard, her voice is sought (2:14, 8:13). Nature is ready, and she is invited to join. In fact the woman speaks most often in the Song, but it is appropriate that she responds to a request to be "heard" only in the last verse of the poem.

"Our" land – the Song encompasses locations across Israel (commentary, 7:5). The frequent references to nature grant ownership to the physical land.

The lovers' later searches – his (6:11) and theirs (7:13) – to see if the vines are in blossom are set against this verse's assurance that the world of nature is in fact ready, and awaits them and their decisions.

2:14 My dove...let me hear your voice.... 2:17 Until the day breathes..., make yourself like a gazelle, or a young hart, on the cleft mountains.
Verses 14 and 17 now are seen to have anticipated the last two verses of the Song, which to some degree resolve chapter 2. In retrospect, this echo calls attention to the two verses between (15 and

16), which summarize the condition in which the two find themselves as the Song is written.

2:15 Hold off foxes for us! Little foxes that ruin vineyards, and our vineyard is in blossom.

The vineyard has been redefined (see above, 1:6) as their love relationship: it is ripe, but exposed to potential harm. The act of "holding" has a direct effect. The foxes are "held off" so that she might "hold" him (3:4) and he might "hold" her, the palm tree (7:9). The later use of "little" by the brothers (8:8), referring to her, reflects a difference in perception. For them, "little" means unready and fragile; but for her, "little" can be powerful and effective.

2:17 Until the day breathes, and the shadows flee, circle about, my lover, make yourself like a gazelle or a young hart on the cleft mountains.

From 2:17, the image "mountains" is developed — the split mountains become a myrrh mountain and a hill of spice, symbols of her breasts (4:6), a direct response to this verse. The myrrh then becomes one of the metaphors for their lovemaking (5:1). Therefore, the invitation at the end of the Song to the "mountains of spices" (8:14), a partial echo of 2:17, is an invitation to intimacy.

While the cleft mountains here retain their primary implication of separation and waiting, other levels of meaning, both contradictory and complementary, are added. Cleft mountains can also be her breasts, with their cleavage. Reading thus, he might be invited to stay *until morning* (they lie down at night – 7:12). He is to fondle her breasts, she stated (1:13), "[he is] lying between my breasts" ("lying" being the same word as "spend the night" in 7:12). Alternatively, he is told to bound across the (nonmetaphorical) mountains, *waiting until evening* to return. The two alternatives (stay the night, come back at night) are complementary, and can both be read. Both also increase the irony of the next verse, 3:1, for her inability there to find him would come against a background of her having told him to stay, or return. Both new readings coexist with the first, still valid meaning of a call to bide his time altogether. All are aspects of their relationship.

Apart from the repetition of this phrase "until the day breathes" (4:6), the only other uses of "day" in the Song are to a wedding day (3:11, 8:8). Is she subtly also calling on him to look forward to that day?

3:1–4 On my bed at night, I sought him whom my soul loves. I sought him, but found him not…. The watchmen…found me. Scarcely had I passed them by, when I found him whom my soul loves. I held him and shall not let him go until I have brought him to the house of

my mother, to the chamber of her who conceived me.

This nighttime sequence anticipates the longer, slightly different tale of chapter 5. If this scene is a dream, then perhaps its inclusion of finding him is wish fulfillment, as opposed to the reality of chapter 5. The reinterpretation of 2:5–7 as possibly reflecting a dream (above, on 2:5) might support the view that 3:1–5 (which ends identically, adjuring the Girls of Jerusalem to noninterference) is also all a dream. However, the dream understanding of 2:5–7 is not certain. In the end, the gray line between dream and reality remains.

The absence of her circling through the city in chapter 5 focuses attention on the motion here. All seems in a swirl. Perhaps the absence here of the physical conflict with the watchman is purposeful, to focus on the woman's search. What concerns her here is finding her lover – any other detail is irrelevant. Indeed, the brevity of this moment of discovery and togetherness is ever the more poignant as the Song, with its recurring motifs of search and longing, is reread.

The "mother's house" later proves to be an appropriate parallel term for the (intimate) "chamber." In that house she longs to have him drink "spiced wine" (8:2) and it is in that wine house that she has envisioned one of their intimate scenes (see 2:4, as reread above). That scene and this one end identically, with an adjuration that the Girls of Jerusalem not interfere (2:7, 3:5), confirming that they are aspects of the same "reality," their intimacy.

3:6 Who is this, ascending from the desert… with all the peddler's powder?

The "who" is not identified in context. The next verse describes Solomon's bed, scarcely a "who." However, the poet repeats the question (8:5), adding the phrase "clinging to her lover." That this is the woman ascending seems clear. An additional retrospective indication that this is the woman is the form of the description – "myrrh and frankincense *with all…powder.*" This is parallel to the use of "with" and "with all" in 4:13–14, his description of her as an orchard of spices. One guesses (in light of 3:11, which describes Solomon's wedding) that the ascending woman is the woman as bride, perfumed for the wedding day. If so, his desire in 4:6 to join her in ascent can also be seen as looking forward to the wedding. In any case, our verse establishes the presence of the woman, which is set in sharp contrast to the description of Solomon, which follows.

The poetic structure is less clear. Three times the poet asks, "Who is this…?" (also 6:10) without providing a direct answer. In each case, the "this" is described, but the full answer to the question "who is this" can only be deduced from the texts that follow (and not necessarily immediately). In part, the question seems rhetorical, and in part, a purposeful sense of mystery established by the poet.

3:7–8 Behold – the bed, Solomon's own. Encircling it are sixty warriors of Israel's warriors. All of them held fast to their swords, trained for war, each man with his sword on his thigh because of the terror at night.

Solomon's warriors come off poorly. Beyond the immediately obvious comparisons (the contrasts of "circling," "hold" and "at night"), warriors appear only once more, warriors' shields becoming mere decorations on the woman's necklace (4:4). Even more subtly, the lover's heart is stolen (4:9) by even *one* jewel of that necklace – her "one" is superior to their sixty! They thus join another one-superior-to-sixty comparison – she is the single one, greater than "sixty" queens, who praise her (6:8f.). Further, while here the warriors are taught (trained) for war, in 8:2, she is "taught" (the only other use of that verb in Song) lessons of love and relationship by her mother. The warriors, bold national heroes, fade in comparison to this woman.

Some commentators read these verses, and those that here follow (i.e., 3:7–10) as part of Solomon's wedding day, 3:11. However, the tone of these verses is definitely negative, the tone of 3:11 all positive. Solomon's bed (here) and litter (next two verses), "inlaid with love," are the antithesis of the marriage day. We here see Solomon not in his glory, but in the glittering emptiness of wealth (following verses) and military display. Verse 3:11 will point out his true glory.

3:9–10 A litter he made for himself, the king, Solomon, of wood from Lebanon. Its pillars he made of silver, its cushioning of gold, its seat of purple yarn, its interior inlaid with love by the Girls of Jerusalem.

In retrospect, these are verses of great transition and comparison. Solomon's involvement with many women is reflected by the presence of the Girls of Jerusalem and their expertise. Only here are the Girls of Jerusalem mentioned but not addressed. Their actions are thereby highlighted, a clue to their very nature (see commentaries on 7:1; 8:4, 12).

The connection of the term "king" to "Solomon" grants the former sexual connotation it would not otherwise have, appropriate to its former uses. This will soon be complicated in verse 11 by the internal word game wherein "king" moves to mean "groom." The uses of the term "king" for the lover elsewhere in the Song would seem to straddle both meanings.

A series of terms is used to compare Solomon to others. "Lebanon," wood for his litter, is a term of beauty for the lovers (5:15, 7:5) and the locality from which they emerge (4:8). Terms used here for Solomon are later used to describe the lover (Lebanon, pillars, gold – even Girls of Jerusalem – 5:14–16). The purple yarn later describes the woman's hair, and it, in turn, holds *her* king captive (7:6).

That "love" (Hebrew, *ahavah*), which generally indicates the emotion of love, can encompass physical lovemaking has been confirmed by 7:7, "love with all its delights."

Since she – never he – uses "Girls of Jerusalem" elsewhere, one guesses that here she speaks. Verse 3:6 was clearly said by him. She has begun to speak either in verse 7 or 9. The very uncertainty is testimony to the Song's success in presenting the two lovers as being of similar mind and heart.

4:5 Your breasts are like two young harts, twins of a gazelle, who pasture among the lilies.
The lilies are a symbol that helps carry the Song (2:1, 2, 16; here; 5:13; 6:2, 3; 7:3), bringing the lovers ever closer physically. The conjecture of a reference here to the nipples is supported by 5:13, "lilies" as lips (5:13), the appropriate coloration.

That breasts are a symbol of sexual readiness is confirmed by the inclusion of the present verse in the description of the Shulammite (7:4). In fact, that reference is the first hint there to the lover that his sexual fantasy is properly

to be directed to his beloved. The importance of her breasts is reconfirmed in 7:9f. where the mention of her breasts moves him to want to touch her body. Our verse also provides, in anticipation, a response to the brothers, who claim that their sister has not yet developed breasts (8:8f.).

4:8 With me from Lebanon – O bride, come with me from Lebanon. Trip down from atop Amana, from atop Senir and Hermon, from the lions' dens, from the leopards' mountains.
"Bride" will be used six times in Song, all in this section, which ends with full sexual union (5:1). It is the most intense moment of togetherness in Song, and therefore an appropriate context for the dream of future marriage. Once 4:6 is seen as desire to join the wedding (3:6, above), we understand the poet's transition here to "bride."

Lebanon – later in this section (4:16), the lover will equate his darling to water flowing from Lebanon, thus making the descent even easier. Her locale in Lebanon is "transformed" via echoing words in the coming verses. As she descends to him, Lebanon becomes "incense" (*levonah* – verse 14); "atop" becomes "top" spices (4:14); lions (*arayot*) become "I gathered" (*ariti* – 5:1); "leopards" (*nemarim*) become myrrh (*mor* – 4:14, 5:1); and "dens" (*m'onot*) become a well (*ma'ayan* – 4:12, 15). Indeed, the metaphors in the coming section also prove to be rapidly

changing – the garden changes from inaccessible to accessible; she changes from the orchard to the waters which irrigate it. The rapid change befits this concentrated section, as it moves toward the moment of sexual coition.

4:9 You have stolen my heart, my sister-bride, you have stolen my heart with one of your eyes, with one jewel of your necklace.

Her eyes will continue to overwhelm him (6:5). The heart reference is framed by two uses, both – 3:11 ("the day of his heart's delight" – his wedding) and 8:6 ("place me as seal upon your heart," implying binding commitment) – reinforce the undertone of marriage here (see previous verse, "bride"). (For the other use of heart, see 5:2.)

The emphasis on "one" is echoed in the only other use of that number (6:9), one beloved as opposed to sixty queens. We recall that the necklace is a thousand pieces consisting of shields (4:4), the shields representative of sixty warriors (3:7). Again, "one" is what wins his heart. Apart from paired body parts, in fact, all multiple numbers in the Song are negative! The poet emphasizes commitment and the exclusive relationship, to the point of (absurdly) praising but a single eye.

The range of meanings of "sister" allows for multiple comparisons. Her brothers seek to protect their "sister" (1:6, 8:8f.) while the lover already uses "sister" in conjunction with "bride"!

4:10 How beautiful is your loving, my sister-bride, how much better is your loving than wine, the fragrance of your oils than all spices.

Wine, used for comparison here (as 1:2, 4) is subsequently used to symbolize their love (5:1, 7:10, 8:2). This legitimizes a complementary translation – "for your loving, made of wine, is good" (which does not change the essence of the phrase).

One now appreciates how this verse prepares for 5:1 (that celebrates sexual coition), combining and emphasizing several of its basic terms ("wine," "spice," "loving").

"How beautiful" is used here with "loving," the physical side of love. It is therefore appropriate that the only other use of "how beautiful" is to the feet of the Shulammite. The connection to that sexual fantasy befits the emphasis on physical love.

The connection to the next verse is better understood from 7:10, "your palate, like good wine." Wine recalls the mouth, which is explored in the coming verse.

4:12 A locked garden, my sister-bride, a locked cistern, a sealed spring.

The terms of separation here are later

transformed to terms of opening and attachment. In 5:5 she extends her hand to the "handles of the lock" (same root as "locked" here) to reach her lover. In 8:6 she asks that he set her "as a seal [same root as "sealed" here] on your heart." These reinforce the temporary nature of the locking and sealing, a transformation soon obvious in the verses that here follow.

The garden will become a central image (6:2, 11; 8:13), a vibrant symbol both of her and her place, of what they experienced and also of the circumstances that keep them separated. Still, the "locked garden" remains a living image even as the Song is over. Though he has visited the garden, they are still apart.

5:1 Eat friends, drink, be drunk with loving.
Concerning the radical rereading wherein the audience both speaks ("Eat, darlings; drink, be drunk, lovers, on love") and is addressed at the same time: the possible double reading of a single term (here, *dodim* read as both "loving" and "lovers") is used elsewhere in the Song – 5:2, 6:12 (and see on 1:13, above). Reinforcing the idea that they are addressed as "darlings," we note that while until this point only *she* had been termed "darling," *he* also is so addressed in 5:16. As the centrality of this verse becomes clear, its exceptional technique becomes more understandable. From the "outside" the readers encourage the lovers to enjoy what they have.

From the "inside," the lovers can only wish that the outsiders might have similar good fortune.

5:2 I was asleep, but my heart was aroused….
Her "aroused" heart will find its fulfillment in her success in "rousing" her lover, 8:5.

Clearly the poet begins here a reprise of the night search (3:1–4), with significant differences. The blurred line between dream and reality in the earlier section only enhances the same ambiguity here. There are many possible relations between the two stories. Perhaps the first search story was her fantasy, her dream, engendered by the reality reflected in this longer (and perhaps more "factual") version, which does not end with her actually finding her lover. Among the differences is the assertive role played here by the lover, who is absent from the first version altogether until he is "found." This mutual involvement is more appropriate after the change of 5:1.

5:5 I did rise to open for my lover. My hands dripped myrrh, my fingers, passing myrrh upon the handles of the lock.
Her hands "dripping myrrh" now recall the ascent "from the desert…perfumed by myrrh" (3:6), for we have concluded (above on 3:6) that this was in fact the beloved. The "passing" myrrh is an ironic usage, for in the next verse, he has "passed" by. Eventually this liquid

myrrh is attributed to him, another symbol of mutuality (5:13).

The use of the emphatic – "I did rise" – is better understood in light of the discovery of the next verse that she arose too late. It reveals a sense of guilt.

5:6 I did open for my lover, but my lover had turned away and passed on by.... I called him, but he did not respond to me.

The frustration of this verse finds its resolution in the final verse of the Song, when his unfinished request, "Let me hear…" receives immediate response from her.

5:7 The watchmen, circling through the city, found me. They struck me, they bruised me, they stripped off my mantle, the watchmen of the ramparts.

Notably missing from this retold account of search is the moment of discovery (3:4) – the finding, and the desire to bring him to her mother's house. Again, the explanation seems to lie in its coming after 5:1. Subsequent to that moment of coition, the poet will recall former sections, but not complete them, leaving a vital element in suspension, as it were, until resolved by a later inclusion. The "discovery" surfaces in 8:1, the mother's house in 8:2. Similarly the absence of breast and mouth from the description in chapter 6 will be resolved by later inclusions (see below on 6:7).

If 5:2–6:3 can be considered one continuum, then this brutal confrontation sets a tone for that which follows. Having confronted the watchmen, she then dialogues with the Girls, in a tone of competition. That dialogue concentrates on contrasting her lover to others. At the end of the section, however, beyond all confrontations, only the two of them remain – "I am my lover's and my lover is mine" (6:3).

The watchmen of 3:3 here become the watchmen "of the ramparts." At the end of the Song, her brothers seek to protect her by erecting a "rampart" (8:9). Is that verse here anticipated? Are the watchmen the brothers?

5:8 I adjure you, O Girls of Jerusalem: If you find my lover....

The commentary notes a secondary meaning, "that you not find my lover." Section 6:1–3, which "directs" the Girls of Jerusalem to her lover in places they will not find him, ending in a declaration of the exclusivity of their relationship, reinforces that subtle negative message. Indeed, the Song's composite picture of the Girls of Jerusalem as competitors does the same. Finding him remains her province exclusively (see 8:4, 10).

5:13 His cheeks are like the bed of spice, towers of aromatics; his lips are lilies, they drip passing myrrh.

Appropriate to a verse concentrated on the mouth, so important to their relationship (see 8:1), central images abound. Myrrh, having been singled out as a symbol of all spices (5:1) and elevated in quality ("flowing myrrh" – 5:5), is here shared with the lover. In 5:5 it was hers; now it is also his. It is used here for the last time.

Several symbols anticipate further developments. In the end, she will invite him to mountains of *spices* – and perhaps the description here is then reassuring that he will accept the invitation. The *lily* will continue to bind the lovers ever closer, the present attribution to his lips central to that process (cf. 6:2f., 7:3). His *lips* become the means of his awakening to his lover's presence and his own desire for her (7:10). The term *towers* will brings his cheeks close to her neck (4:4), nose (7:5) and breasts (8:10). The *bed of spice* becomes part of the garden of lovemaking (see 6:2). The *aromatic* cheeks will be reflected in her dream of giving him "aromatic" wine (8:2).

5:16 His palate is sweetness....

The commentary postulates that the palate appears here not as one body part, but as that part which can best symbolize all of him. Indeed, the centrality of the mouth is further confirmed by use of "palate" and "lips" to awaken the lover from his fantasy (7:10). The association of the palate with good wine (see the kiss image, 1:2,

and the awakening, 7:10) confirms the association of the parts of the mouth with the kiss.

6:2 My lover has gone down to his garden, to the beds of spice, to pasture in the gardens, to pick lilies.

In 8:13, "gardens" also becomes her place, so in our reread verse he goes both to her person and to her place (supplementing, not replacing, the implication of the presence of other women). A third level of meaning is also possible. If no time barriers are implied by the order of verses, then perhaps the "gardens" refer to the two types of love moments which they experience – the tender love of the spice garden (4:12–5:1) and the more intense love of the nut grove (a root associated with "garden," 6:11).

6:3 I am my lover's, and my lover is mine – he who pastures among the lilies.

The phrase "I am my lover's" will be repeated once more (7:11), the parallel statement there being, "and his desire is for me," replacing this verse's "and my lover is mine, he who pastures among the lilies." That substitution verifies that the woman understands "he who pastures among the lilies" erotically.

6:7 Like a pomegranate slice is your smile, from behind your veil.

Far from signaling a lack of intimacy, the

omission of the mouth from this description now appears to be a carefully structured poetic device of leaving a former description incomplete, and creating thereby a sense of tension at the absence, until the element reappears later. (This was done in the search for the lover – see above on 5:7.) Here the resolution will come in 7:10, when the palate and lips awaken the lover to the fact that his sexual desire is really directed to his beloved. Similarly, the absence of breasts from this description will be resolved in 7:4, 9; 8:8–10.

6:9 One is she, my dove, my perfect one; one is she to her mother, pure to her who bore her. Girls see her and they acclaim her, queens and concubines, and they praise her.

In retrospect, this verse is an additional link in the chain of affirming her connection to motherhood, which she will apply to him (8:5).

The comparison of one to many (see above, 4:9) will be further reinforced, 8:11f., as she rejects his "thousand."

As an object of others' gazes, her position will be clarified by the next verse. She is as pure as the sun. Humans cannot stare directly at the sun, but only be overwhelmed by it.

6:12 My soul, disoriented, set me mid the chariots of the nobility.

Given the nature of the scene that follows, the "loss of contact with the soul" here prefigures a fantasy. The terms "dream" or "day dream" would also be accurate, as the lover eventually is stirred from his sleep (7:10). The nobility image can be seen, in light of what follows, as representing a "world apart." That image, like the body description that proceeds in reverse order (bottom to top) and the large number of new metaphors and similes, is a literary technique reinforcing the message of the text itself, that something out of the ordinary is happening.

"My soul" is indeed repeated seven times in the Song (1:7; 3:1, 2, 3, 4; 5:6; here), sharing this highlighted pattern with the central terms "Solomon," "Girls of Jerusalem" and "mother." The contrast of its first five appearances (emphasis – "he whom my soul loves") and the last two (lost or disoriented soul) mirror two major themes of the Song: devotion, and the frustration at circumstances that keep them apart.

7:1 Encore! Encore! O Shulammite. Encore! Encore! Let us observe you. What do you observe in the Shulammite in this Two-Towns Twirl?

In retrospect one sees a hint that the coming verses will to be a sexual dance fantasy: related to "Solomon" and "Jerusalem," the "Shulammite" is the woman of the root *sh-l-m*, with its consistent implication in Song of raw eroticism, devoid of the loyalty, exclusivity and commitment that make love complete. The doubling nature of the verse is also possibly an early hint that this is only a reflection of the beloved, some sort of mirror image, rather than reality.

While the fantasy is a section apart, the four-time repetition of "return" (here, "encore") echoes with a call for the poem as a whole. The poem is written after they have been together, are now apart, and look forward to recapturing their union. How sharp the call "Return! Return!" seems.

The use of the verb "observe," with its undertone of apparition, may have been purposeful, given the nature of the event.

7:3 Your belly is a mound of wheat, hedged with lilies.

In light of the later understanding that the Shulammite is a fantasy that the man eventually applies to his beloved, the inclusion of lilies (in a different role than previous uses) serves to indicate both the identity and the difference. If this is a low-hanging belt of flowers, the erotic imagery of lilies is intensified. Previously the use of this term had brought his lips close to her breasts. Afterwards, he is confirmed to be the one "who pastures among the lilies," and here they are placed below her navel!

The Shulammite fantasy remains isolated in the Song, and its internal imagery is never clarified. One might consider some connection to fertility of the navel and the belly (the word "belly" also means "womb"), but this remains only conjecture.

7:4 Your breasts are like two young harts, twins of a gazelle.

On the implication of the imagery after full reading of this verse, see above on 4:5. The final reference to the breasts, as a symbol of her readiness for love (8:10), is most helpful in understanding why specifically the breasts in the sexual fantasy of the Shulammite are described exactly as previously.

The identity of the Shulammite – the beloved, but only by way of the man's fantasy – accords well with the inclusion both of radical differences and of some similarities. The most important images of the past – the lilies, the breasts and the mouth – eventually bring the lover to realize this shared identity.

7:5 Your neck is like an ivory tower, your eyes are pools in Heshbon, by the gate of Bat Rabbim. Your nose is like the tower of Lebanon, facing toward Damascus.

One now suspects that the hyperbolic imagery of this section (e.g., the eyes, previously described in terms that bind the two, here become simply big and reflective) is not so much inappropriate as it is an indication of the fantasy element.

The connection of the Shulammite to Solomon (see 7:1 above) explains the choice of locale. Her eyes are associated with "Bat Rabbim" (literally, "Daughter of Multitudes"); he owns a vineyard in "Baal Hamon" (8:11 – literally, "Master of a [vast] host") – the one other unidentified location in the Song. Both terms hint at the plural love relationships that the Song rejects.

To the places already noted, the Song will add Carmel (7:6) and Ba'al Hamon (8:11).

7:6 Your head upon you is like the crimson Carmel, and the hair of your head like purple yarn – a king is captive in the tresses.
"King" was used twice of Solomon (3:9, 11) and thrice of the lover (here; 1:4, 12). It would seem to hint of that world which Solomon represents – love in its aspect of eros, physical passion, which is seen in the Song as an *insufficient* picture of love. Physical love, *in the context of devotion and exclusivity,* is celebrated. In the composite picture, her lover is thus partially "the king," particularly in the contexts of his chambers (1:4), his couch (1:12) and his sexual fantasy (here).

The insertion of a personal comment in the midst of a description of the body is a departure from the other descriptions. The fact of the exception is perhaps another hint that the Shulammite vision somehow differs from the beloved, at least in part.

7:9–10 I said, I will ascend the palm-shaft, and I will take hold of its branches. Let your breasts be like the clusters on the vine, the fragrance from your nose like the apricots, and your palate like the best wine…stirring the lips of sleepers.
These verses now read cumulatively. His determination to climb toward her breasts is followed by a series of staccato phrases all drawn from past experience, which, through their disconnected form, reflect his excited state.

Since this verse already begins the emergence from the Shulammite vision, its central terms will be echoed and further clarified (unlike the terms describing just the Shulammite, which remain isolated). The breasts' centrality will be confirmed and clarified (8:1, 8, 10). The vine reappears, jointly investigated (7:13). "Fragrance" will reemerge from yet another source (7:14), and the apricot tree will again be cited (8:5).

She too desires to have him drink the wine (8:2). While the mouth and its component parts are not mentioned again, the kiss is (8:1). (All mentions of the mouth are framed by the two references to the kiss, further clarifying the mouth's import.)

7:13 Let us go early to the vineyards. Let us see: has the vine flowered, have the blossoms opened, have the pomegranates budded? There I will give you my loving.

The vineyard proves to be a symbol of their love relationship (1:6, above). This verse bears this meaning beautifully.

The progression from pomegranate to loving makes sense in light of 8:2, pomegranate juice as aromatic wine. Previously, "loving" has been used exclusively in contexts of wine (1:2, 4; 4:10; 5:1). Here the pomegranate assumes the "wine" role.

8:1 If only you were given me as a brother, suckling of my mother's breasts. I would find you outside, I would kiss you, yet no one would scorn me.

The kiss recalls the Song's beginning, and with that signals a return to the staccato style of the opening. That style and final clarification of images dominate chapter 8.

The connection of breasts to motherhood will be strengthened by further references to motherhood (8:2, 5) and breasts as a symbol of readiness for love (8:8, 10).

The desired lack of scorn at their kiss will be compared to the "scorn" which all bear for cheap love, bought with money (8:7). Their relationship is other.

While the play on the word "brother" is developed immediately in the next verse, with erotic emphasis, the sibling image is also developed through a later comparison with her true brothers, with whom she is in conflict (8:8–10, and one recalls her conflict with her "mother's sons," 1:6). She prefers him to them as a companion.

8:2 I would lead you, I would bring you, to the house of my mother, my teacher. I would make you drink of the aromatic wine, of my pomegranate juice.

The woman's initiative sets the tone we have seen throughout chapter 8. She is now very assertive, declaring her worth, rejecting the values of others. Gone are her coy reluctance to rise to his call (5:13), her failure to join him (2:10–13), her hiding in the rocks (2:14). His slightest call elicits a rapid response (8:14). Now a fully self-assured, confident woman speaks.

The hinted comparison here to the warriors (commentary on "teacher"), is reinforced by later, other comparisons. The lovers' positive "house" is set against a "house" whose wealth is used to buy love (8:7). Their intimate acts of bringing are set against "bringing" money to buy the fruit of the metaphorical vineyard (8:11).

8:6 Set me as the seal on your heart, the seal on your arm.

The coming verses will note conflict with her brothers (8:8–10). In light of previous comparisons (above, 8:1), possibly another is implied in the term "set." The brothers (1:6) "set" her as

guard over vineyards. The lover is here asked to "set" her as a seal on his heart.

8:8–9 We have a little sister who has no breasts. What shall we do with our sister on the day when she is spoken for? If she be a rampart, we shall build a silver battlement on her, and if she be a door, we shall fashion a cedar board on her.

The woman's response (8:10, commentary) reinforces the understanding that she is in conflict with her brothers. Chapter 8 is dominated by comparison – to the Girls, to those who would buy love, to the brothers and to Solomon. Despite sharp changes of subjects, the motif is indeed unified.

Given this tone of comparison, and the approaching rejection of Solomon (8:11–12), we note a possible implied connection of the brothers to Solomon. They intend to use silver and cedar, as did Solomon in his litter (3:10). To the opposite effect, the lover is compared to the cedars (5:15) and has better use for silver – to make jewelry for his beloved (1:11)!

8:10 I am a rampart, but my breasts are like towers – thus I have appeared, in his eyes, as finding "shalom."

The next two verses clarify the rejection of the world of sh-l-m, and the preference of the two lovers for an exclusive one-to-one relationship, thus confirming the importance of the root here. In light of that rejection, the phrase here could be restated as the lover's temporary and unreal understanding of his passion as belonging to the world of sh-l-m, the fantasy from which he awoke.

8:12 My very own vineyard is before me. The thousand is yours, O Solomon, and two hundred to the guards of its fruit.

In retrospect, the vineyard must indeed be symbolic. Otherwise, 8:11–12, a unit apart, would be irrelevant to a love poem.

The centrality of this verse, confirmed by the full reading of Song and the import of the root sh-l-m, makes it an example of the rhetorical technique known as antiphrasis – the use of a word in a sense opposite to its proper meaning. Sh-l-m serves as a symbol of incomplete picture of love, whereas the core meaning of sh-l-m is "complete." (See note.)

The possible reference to the thousand wives also directs the reader to the biblical section that may have inspired this major literary theme, including the antiphrastic use of sh-l-m. 1 Kings 11 negatively recalls not only the thousand wives whom he "loved," but also how Solomon's foreign wives corrupted him in Jerusalem. Indeed, the antiphrasis implied in Song is emphasized there – Solomon's (*Shlomo*) heart was not *shalem*, was not complete and full, with the Lord his God (1 Kings 11:4).

(In fact, 1 Kings 11:4 compares him unfavorably in that regard with his father David, whose name is echoed in the term "lover" [*dod*] in Song! Interestingly enough, *dod* appears thirty-three times in the Song, which is precisely the number of years David ruled in Jerusalem [1 Kings 2:11]. While this gives one reason to ponder, the connection to David is not clear enough for one to conclude that the author had it in mind.)

8:13 O you who linger in the gardens, fellows are listening for your voice.

In 1:8, above, we saw that the fellows previously called her to join them, now verifying the understanding of competition.

8:14 Be swift, my lover, and make yourself like a gazelle or a young hart on mountains of spices.

Repeated readings of the Song only strengthen the sense of completion at its end. The contrasts between the lovers and all that surrounds them – the brothers, Solomon, the Girls of Jerusalem, the crowd observing the Shulammite, the Shulammite herself, etc. – all lend added weight to the call to flee, to "be swift." They are each other's alone. This is reinforced by the recognition (above, 1:2) that the opening of the Song invites the audience in as a close observer. Here at the end, the audience is dismissed. Others ask to hear her, but the couple clarifies that the time has come for them to be alone.

This closure, however, even in the Song's own terms is not complete. As the Song ends, they are fully committed to one another, having fended off all competition – but there is a lingering degree of separation. Even this last verse continues to incorporate the echo of 2:17, which so emphasized caution. The Song ends frozen in expectation, love ever moving in its upward cycle. If much has been told and done, the future – as hope, dream and invitation – still remains, love's ultimate domain.

Notes

*F*ootnotes are included: (1) to explain a new or unusual commentary or translation; (2) to cite parallel uses elsewhere in the Bible; (3) to clarify that a choice has
been made among interpretations, or to justify that choice; or (4) to enlighten on
matters of general interest.

Earlier interpreters and commentators are cited: (1) to give credit where it is
due, particularly for striking or original interpretations; (2) to refer to more comprehensive overviews of particular issues (since we seek to avoid repetition); or
(3) to buttress our claim of a pattern by citing isolated instances previously noted
by others.

These notes are not exhaustive. Prior commentaries have done excellent work
in that regard. Even when we choose between well-attested alternatives, we comment only if the choice seems controversial. We shall not cite or evaluate all previous interpretations.

We shall proceed by verse order. **Notes applicable only to the chapter "Rereading the Song of Songs" appear at the end of the relevant verses, marked
with an asterisk (*).**

Bibliographic references with just the author's name refer to the volumes listed
in the "Selected Bibliography." All other bibliographic references are detailed. If
no page reference is listed, the citation is taken from the commentary on the verse
under consideration.

1:1 "Of" – For support for understanding the Hebrew letter *lamed* to mean "concerning" as per the Ugaritic, see Pope, p. 295f. Murphy cites 1 Chron. 24:20 in this sense. Rashi, interpreting allegorically (Solomon as a symbol for God) reads "a song written for Solomon."

1:2 While change of person (enallage) occurs frequently without implication in biblical poetry (see Pope, p. 297), the author's careful use of person and sensitivity to language warrant attributing meaning to the changes in this verse.

"Loving" – The Hebrew *dodim* always refers to physical love. We therefore translate "loving." ("Love" is the translation of the more general, and usually more emotional, *ahavah*.) See Zakovitch, p. 47; Bloch, pp. 3, 137; and Fox, p. 97. See Overview, III c, "On Translating and Interpreting the Song of Songs."

1:3 "Excellent" – Hebrew *turak*, of uncertain meaning, variously interpreted as a place name (oil of Turaq – Fox), "wafted about" (Gordis), "flowing" (Murphy). We have adopted "excellent," following NJPS's "finest" (with footnote – "meaning uncertain") as the implication of the context.

"Oils…known" – The play on words, *shem* and *shemen*, together with the term "good" is found also in Eccl. 7:1.

"Love" – *Ahavah* can include physical, lustful feeling, as II Sam 13:4, 15 (so Bloch, p. 138).

1:4 "After you" (as read twice) – This word is integral both to what precedes it and what follows. Most connect it with the former ("draw me after you"), as do the accents, while the LXX and Luther connect it to "we shall run." There are several double readings in the Song. (See appendix.)

"King" – As per most commentators, the term is to be taken neither as a literal king, nor as King Solomon. Bloch refers to this phrase as a "courtly epithet for her lover" (p. 139), Murphy as a "literary fiction." ("In her ardor, the woman sees her lover in the guise of a king" – p. 83.) The reference may be a by-product of grooms wearing crowns or garlands at weddings (see note, 3:11). Fox feels that the reference is not drawn from marriage, but reflects accepted use of royal imagery as a love term, as in the case of "prince" in Egyptian love poetry (p. 98) (not unlike modern English "prince" and "princess!").

"Chambers" – as a place of intimacy, see Judges 15:1, Joel 2:16.

"Savor," complementarily, "celebrate," an alternate understanding of the same term. Hakham suggests the double entendre. For *nazkirah* as "inhale," see Gordis, p. 78 (citing Lev. 24:7, Isa. 66:3, et al.) and for the root meaning "praise," cf. Isa. 12:4, 1 Ch. 16:4. Pope suggests different pre-Hebrew Semitic roots.

"Rightly," alternatively, "strong wine" – the latter translation as per Ibn Ezra, and cf. Gordis, p. 78f., and Fox, pp. 98ff.

Verses 1:2–4 form a unit as an opening, the end of verse four echoing the endings of the two previous verses ("loving…wine"/"have they loved you").

1:5 "But also" – Most translations choose between the two meanings "and" or "but," the latter often preferred because of the next verse, which has others staring at her blackness. That point is well made, but the blackness is not seen as opposed to beauty (as Falk points out) – one can be black and beautiful, like the items noted. Our translation "but also" takes both concerns into account.

"Kedar" – the proper name of a nomadic tribe in the Arabian desert, mentioned several times in the Bible. (Kedar is listed as a son of Ishmael – Gen. 25:13.) Presumably, these Bedouin tents were dark. However, the root *k-d-r* itself also means "dark" and the pun ("tents of darkness") is probably intentional.

"Pavilions" – Pavilions are included in the booty from Kedar, Jer. 49:28f. Pavilions are tent-like structures in biblical Hebrew.

1:6 "Set sight on" – implying "look" – translation maintains uniformity of root application throughout the Song, here the root *r-'-h*.

"Glared" – The root *sh-z-f* means "see" in other biblical appearances – Job 20:9, 28:7.

"Blackish" – The form could indicate either dark black (so Hakham) or light black (so Zakovitch).

The third through sixth words are in alliteration. The phrase "I am blackish" reverses the order of the opening of verse five (literally, "black am I") and the last part of this verse is chiastic (guard-vineyard-vineyard-guard).

The interpretation reflected in the initial commentary is that of Ibn Ezra.

"Mother's sons" – an accepted parallel to "brothers" – cf. Gen. 27:29, Ps. 50:20.

Brothers were responsible for their younger sisters in antiquity. Note Gen. 24:29, 34:11.

1:7 "Pasture" (your sheep) – implies ellipsis. Shepherding is considered a particularly good background. Moses, David and Amos were all shepherds.

"Lest I be" – this may be a veiled reference to Solomon. The Hebrew consonants are identical to his name. Given the implication of Solomon in the Song (see 8:11–12, and Overview, II B, on Solomon as the antihero of the Song), implied would be that she will find herself the subject of sexual attention of these fellows, an implication which befits the verse.

"Wanders" – a difficult term. Various suggestions have been offered for the Hebrew *'otyah* (literally, as Fox, "one who wraps herself up," which he presents in quotation marks), often taken to indicate prostitution (see Fox, commentary). The implications of being "wrapped" (often presumed to indicate a veil), however, are less than clear. In II Sam. 15:30, all cover their heads in mourning. Zakovitch understands it to be a sign of modesty, Murphy as an attempted disguise. We assume either metathesis or a scribal error, from the root *t-'-h* (so Gordis) and translate "one who wanders."

* "Where," alternatively "how" – "how" is the accepted meaning of the term in biblical Hebrew. "Where" is based on an Akkadian cognate, and is accepted by most translations. Note use of a parallel term (same consonants, different vowels), II Kings 6:13.

1:9 "A mare" – a feminine form with an archaizing suffix. Egyptian horses enjoyed a reputation of preeminence – see II Chron. 9:28. The emphasis on a female among males is as discerned by Pope, p. 338f.

1:10 "Circlets…beads" – See Pritchard, James, *Ancient Near Eastern Texts with Pictures* (Princeton: Princeton University Press, 1954), pp. 22f., for the style of twisted hair, and rows of beads as a necklace, respectively. However, the horse is also described at the same time: "the cheeks and necks of royal horses were always decorated with particular care" (Keel, p. 56, with illustrations, pp. 57, 61).

1:13 The double entendre (it/he lying between her breasts) is noted by Zakovitch.

"Between my breasts" – For illustrations of cloths bags as amulets, see Keel, p. 65f.

1:14 The alternative interpretation in the first commentary is as per Ibn Ezra.

"In the vineyards" – Since henna does not

grow on vines, it is a foreign body in the vineyard, an apt parallel to the myrrh between her breasts in the previous verse. Fox (p. 106) considers this an exact parallel through metaphor, Ein Gedi being in a ravine (= cleavage). Gordis cites Ein Gedi's fame for vineyards as noted in Pliny, *Historia Naturalis*, XII, 14, 24. It boasted well-tended royal gardens from the seventh century on.

1:15 "Doves" — We list the image's possible implications so as not to reduce its power. Various commentaries err in seeking the one, single implication. Several commentators have noted the drawings of eyes in the shape of doves. (For a dove shaped like an eye on pottery, early biblical era, see Hakham, p. 12.) The dove appears as a symbol of love in many Mediterranean countries from the mid-second millennium BCE.

1:17 "House" — On the late (Mishnaic) form of the Hebrew that allows the singular reading "house," see Gordis.

2:1 "Rose…lily" — Given that there is no agreement on the identity of the flowers, we have maintained traditional translations. The "rose" is probably not the plant so identified today, which apparently arrived in the region (from Armenia) later. The lily here must be a pink-to-red plant, given the later implications to such body parts (lips, nipples) — see particularly 5:13 (so several commentators, including Pope, p. 368). A possible reference is to red anemones, which bloom plentifully in Israel, in March and April. Lacking certainty, however, we follow the traditional translations. The widespread appearance of these two flowers makes them available as prophetic similes for the return to Zion (Is. 35:1–2, Hos. 14:6–8), as noted by Bloch, p. 148.

2:2 * "Lily among the brambles" as "inaccessible" — as Ibn Ezra.

2:3 "Apricot" is the preferred modern translation, given that edible apples (the implication of the term in modern Hebrew) were not then found in that region — see Fox, Bloch.

2:4 "Viewed" — from Acadian root *dagalu*, as per many commentators (Pope, Fox, Zakovitch). "Viewed" was chosen rather than other terms in consideration of other uses of the root, as reflected in the last paragraph of the commentary on this verse.

   * "Wine house" as mother's house — Keel, p. 55, sensed the need for a private area here: "The term [wine house] can probably also refer to a private home where for a time…wine is publicly served."

2:5 "Sustain" — as Genesis 27:37 (contra Fox).

   "Cakes" — as associated with fertility cults; see Hosea 3:1.

2:7 "By the gazelles and by the hinds of the field" — For the use of the animals' names for oaths referring to God, see Gordis, pp. 26ff. The two animals are paired frequently in the Bible — cf. Deut. 12:22, 14:5, 15:22.

   "Rouse…disturb" — The two terms, variations of a single core root, need not have separate implications. The form could be a matter of emphasis (so Zakovitch). The double implication holds nevertheless, a product of the inherent range of meaning, as much as the appearance of two terms.

2:8 "Hark, the voice" — most translations prefer "hark" (e.g., Fox). Bloch recognizes both possibilities.

2:9 "He stands" (referring to lover or animal) — as Alter, 1985: "The figure at the lattice is simultaneously stag and lover" (p. 194).

   "Peers" — The translation, well accepted, is based on a Mishnaic usage (*Hagigah* XIII:2). biblical meanings are "sprout" (Ps. 90:6) and "shine"

(Ps. 132:18). The poet possibly meant these as secondary implications, a technique used often in the Song.

2:10 "Responded, saying" – For these two roots implying "begin to speak," cf. Job 3:2.

2:12 "Are seen" – meaning "appeared." The literal translation is chosen to reflect the other appearances of the root.

"Singing" – not the same root as "song" in the title of the poem.

"Singing" – alternatively "pruning." "Pruning" is doubtful, as it does not take place in spring (so Gordis, p. 67, based on earlier studies, and pointing out that this root is applied to the second pruning of the season, in June/July). Others, however, feel it can be applied to other agricultural activities, even in the spring, and suggest the double entendre (Pope). If so, "pruning" echoes the preceding phrase (budding), "singing" the following phrase (voice of the turtledove) – see Fox.

2:13 "Puts forth" – ch-n-t is used for embalming (Gen. 50:2, 3, 26). Fox and Bloch connect this to aromatic spices, and associate this verse with "sweetening" (as Ibn Ezra). Murphy relates the term to change of color. The translation allows for either understanding.

2:14 "My dove" – The dove's qualities made it an international model of perfection of a loved one. See Pope, p. 399f.

2:15 "Hold off" – a literal translation, used to emphasize the other uses of the root. The root can indicate "catch" – see II Sam. 2:21.

"Foxes" – there have been many attempts to identify the symbolic meaning of the foxes. However, terms important to this poet are precisely those that are repeated, not those appearing in only one context, such as the fox. The fox was known in popular folklore as an enemy of the vineyard (see Pope, 403; Keel, p. 77), which indeed it was, and the vineyard is a symbol of import, including its being threatened here. That need is a sufficient explanation for the mention of foxes, and no other symbolism is implied.

2:16 Zakovitch notes a parallel structure, Jer. 7:23 – "I shall be your God, and you shall be My people."

2:17 "Until the day breathes…" Commentators have spent much effort in determining whether morning or evening is implied. In fact, the words can imply either, allowing for the wonderful range of meanings of the verse.

"Cleft" – For the range of interpretations of this unique usage, see Fox, p. 116. There is no necessity, however, to move beyond the root definition (cleave, divide), which fits perfectly.

3:1 "At night" – For use of the plural in this sense, see Ps. 16:7, 92:3, 134:1.

"I sought" – B-k-sh can imply "to desire" (Fox), as Exod. 10:11 and 1 Chron. 21:3. This helps allow for the possibility that a dream is described.

3:2 "Watchmen" – not the same term as "guard," 1:6.

3:4 * "The house of my mother" – The unmarried woman is seen as belonging specifically to her mother's house – Gen. 24:28, Ruth 1:8. See Carol Meyers, "To Her Mother's House" in Jobling, Day and Shepphard, *The Bible and the Politics of Exegesis* (Cleveland: Pilgrim Press, 1991) for the interesting, but not proven, contention that "mother's house" is a feminine perspective of the institution known otherwise as "father's house." Edward F. Campbell Jr., *Ruth* (Garden City: Doubleday, 1975) sees a connection to marriage: "I propose that in some circle of custom…the 'mother's house' was the locus for matters pertinent to marriage, especially for discussion and planning for marriage" (p. 64).

3:5 See notes, 2:7.

3:6 "Who is this" – not "What is this" (*contra* Murphy). The term is a "stylized formula of dramatization" (Bloch, citing Isa. 60:8, 63:1; Jer. 46:7; Job 38:2), always referring to people, the usual implication of the Hebrew term.

"Shafts of smoke" – The translation is chosen to allow comparison to the palm (shaft), 7:9. Zakovitch notes the relation between the terms.

3:7 * Ibn Ezra already understood that the description of Solomon in this section (3:7 and on) is intended as a foil, praising the woman by comparing her simplicity and lack of fear at nights to the description of Solomon.

3:8 "Held fast to their swords" – as "skilled soldiers": note NJPS ("trained in warfare") and see Pope, p. 434f.

3:9 "Litter" – Most commentators take the litter as a portable structure, though some are insistent that it is not (e.g., Ibn Ezra among medieval commentators, Bloch among moderns).

3:10 "Inlaid with love" – For the possibility of pictures or statements, see Pope, p. 445. The implication of "acts of love" is secondary, drawn from the use of such pictures to stimulate, as on a love couch (see Pope for the couch decoration). In the Babylonian Talmud (*Sanhedrin* 39b), Rava (third century CE) states that (biblical) Queen Jezebel had pictures of prostitutes engraved in King Ahab's chariot, to excite him.

3:11 "Go out and see" – a hendiadys (two verbs indicating a single action), translated by separate terms to allow appreciation of other appearances of the roots.

"Girls of Zion" – Michael D. Goulder, *The Song of Fourteen Songs* (Sheffield: JTOS Press, 1986), p. 30, notes the differentiation: "There may be a distinction between the 'Daughters of Zion' here

(only), perhaps the female inhabitants of the capital and the 'Daughters of Jerusalem' of verse 10 (and often), viz. Solomon's own women."

"Crown...on his wedding day" – For reference to an honorific turban crowning the groom, see Isa. 61:10. The Talmud notes that brides and grooms ceased donning crowns after the Temple's destruction (*Sotah* 49a). Note also the rabbinic saying: "A groom is similar to a king" (*Pirke deRabbi Eliezer*, ch. 16; edited eighth century CE).

4:1 "Doves" – Some commentators emend to "as doves," to conform to the rest of the list. The poet, however, wishes to emphasize the continuation from 1:15, which is purposely quoted verbatim.

"Veil" – Its import for modesty is obvious. See Gen. 24:65. As a sign of prostitution, see Gen. 38:14. (Neither case uses the same term used here.) (For *tsamah* as "veil" see Fox, *contra* Bloch, "tresses.")

4:2 "Woolly ewes" – The root meaning of *k-ts-v* is "cut," and the word is probably a synonym for "ewes," the term used in 6:6. While we see no implication to the change, we translate the terms separately to allow for further thought. "Shorn ewes" (LXX) makes little sense, for they are washed before shearing. The association with the root possibly implies "about to be sheared" (so Gordis, citing Ehrlich) or "wool-giving animals."

4:3 "And your mouth is lovely" – Fox, p. 130, finds a complementary meaning, "(even) your wilderness is an oasis." This, however, is an aural double entendre (the written letters could not be so understood), and it is difficult to imagine the lover attributing desert status, even as a first impression, to any part of her body.

"Smile" – a difficult term. It appears also in Jud. 4:21f., 5:26, there often taken to mean "temple," by context. "Cheek" is often proposed here, in consideration of the external shape of the pomegranate and its reddish hue. We translate "smile" in consideration of the following. (A) The descending order of the description requires a body part no higher than the mouth. (B) Indeed, the poet makes an attempt to include in the Song every possible term for the mouth and its parts (see commentary here). (C) A pomegranate sliced in half would resemble nothing more closely than a smile, the red skin resembling lips around the exposed seeds, resembling teeth. (D) *Rakta*, an Aramaic form of this word, appears in rabbinic literature as banks of a river (e.g., *Baba Metzia* 23b, 108a; *Megillah* 6a). The Hebrew term *safah*, "lip," also takes on the secondary meaning bank of a river (as Gen. 41:3, 17), and this might be a borrowed application or a parallel development. (E) The later use of pomegranate (8:2) fits best with a reference here to the mouth. (F) As Keel notes, the form indicates a single, not doubled, part of the face. We therefore conclude that the reference was to an otherwise unknown term, referring to a section of the mouth, approximating our "smile."

4:4 "Tower of David" – an otherwise unknown and unidentified structure.

"Row by row" – a *hapax legomenon* (a term which appears only once in the Bible), here translated as by many moderns, based on A.M. Honeyman, "Two Contributions to Canaanite Toponymy," in *Journal of Theological Studies* 50 (1949), pp. 50–52.

"Hung thereon" – Note that warriors would hang their shields on city walls – cf. Ezekiel 27:10f.

4:6 "Locked…sealed" – Cook, p.140, notes the later "transformation" of these two terms.

4:8 "Lebanon" – The Hebrew (*Levanon*) also echoes "frankincense" (*levonah*) of verse 6.

"Bride" – *Kalah* is used here for the first of six times in the coming verses, and echoes "you are totally" (*kulach*) of the previous verse. The context dictates the conclusion that the implication is not literally marriage, even though the term appears exclusively so elsewhere. Note the following comments: "*Kalah* need not imply marriage here…it is used in anticipation, as a love term" (Murphy). "'Bride' is not to be taken literally as implying a wedding ceremony" (Bloch). "This affectionate epithet does not show that the Song, or even this unit in itself, is a wedding song" (Fox). See Overview, II c-6, "The Horizon of Marriage," for our understanding for the poet's unique use of this term.

"Trip down" – as NJPS. Gordis translates "leap" (citing *ashur* in Hosea 13:7). Pope translates "come" (from "travel," based on Arabic cognate, following LXX).

It is possible that the listed mountains represent ascending order (so Cook, p. 142). As in the case of the fictitious orchard (see commentary, 4:13) the symbolism is not literal – the named mountains indicate height and distance, but are somewhat separated from each other (see Murphy, p. 160). Lebanon is evidently the Lebanon range, Amana in the Anti-Lebanon, a rift separating the two. Senir and Hermon are in the south extremity of the Anti-Lebanon range.

4:9 "Sister-bride" – "Sister" was a term of romance in Egyptian and Mesopotamian literature (see Fox, p. 136). Falk, p. 122, feels that the inclusion of "sister" with "bride" clarifies that "bride," too, is a general romantic term here, not specifically referring to a wedding. "Sister" is not the only term spanning family and love relationships: *dod*, "lover" in the Song, indicates "uncle" elsewhere (e.g., Lev. 10:4).

* The transformation of the words from this verse in the following verses (with the exception of dens/wells) is noted by Fox, p. 135.

4:10 "Oil" – Oil was a preferred method of application of spices: "six months with oil of myrrh" (Esther 2:12).

4:11 "Your lips drip nectar" – The phrase, highly assonant, may have been a well-known description of sexual appeal. It is also used in Prov. 5:3.

"Honey and milk" – Some commentators connect this to the frequent descriptions of the land of Israel as a land flowing with milk and honey (Exod. 3:8, 17, etc.). The reversal of the terms, however, was probably done to avoid such an obvious application.

"Honey" – As a reference to speech, cf. Prov. 16:24: "Pleasant words are like a honeycomb, sweet to the palate and a cure for the body."

"Fragrance" – For pleasing fragrance of both the trees and the wine of Lebanon, cf. Hosea 14:7f. Both implications are found in the Song – wine (particularly 8:2) and trees (3:9).

4:12 "Cistern" – The term (*gal*) closely echoes "garden" (*gan*). (On the similarity of the *l* and *n* sounds in biblical Hebrew, see note, verse 7:1. That verse uses this similarity to create an echo.) The preference of the versions and some moderns for an emendation, repeating "garden," is unnecessary leveling. The root and parallel uses (Josh. 15:19, Judg. 1:15) indicate a water source, supported by an Ugaritic parallel (see Pope). The other uses indicate a desert location, and the applied adjectives "lower" and "upper" befit cisterns dug in the desert to catch the flow of flash floods through otherwise dry watercourses. Water being a precious commodity, the cisterns would be covered ("closed") by stone or other means to protect and to hide them.

4:14 For the import of spices as an adjunct to love-making, see Prov. 7:17.

Among the spices mentioned, imports include spikenard (from India), myrrh (S. Arabia), cinnamon (Far East), and perhaps others. Feliks, pp. 23–28, concludes that six of the nine spices were imported.

4:15 "Flowing" – The Hebrew may simply indicate a term for water (so Pope, and NJPS – "rill"). However, this term is clearly chosen for its root meaning, "flow," as a contrast to verse 12 and as a complement to her spices flowing in 4:16. The literal translation is therefore preferable.

4:16 This verse is followed by a chapter division, said division post-dating the writing of the Song by many centuries. Even though it seems to break the continuity of the text, it also reflects sensitivity, not unlike "blackouts" in some modern movies, since the act of sexual congress takes place between this and the next verse. The cantillation signs exhibit the same sensitivity, beginning chapter 5 with a prolonged emphasized sign (*zarka*), the only such use in Song, properly breaking the natural rhythm and continuity.

5:1 This verse has previously been interpreted as a celebration of sexual coition. "Thus the marriage has been consummated, and he calls upon his loving friends to eat and carouse in the wedding feast" (M.H. Segal, "The Song of Songs," *Vetus Testamentum* 12 [1962], p. 475). See also Landy, 1987, p. 316f. (See Overview, III H, on the structure of the Song.)

Leviticus Rabbah 9:6 (fifth century CE), homiletically reads 4:16 as the bride's invitation to the groom to the wedding canopy, and 5:1 as the groom's response.

Gerleman (Gerleman, Gillis, *Ruth Das Hohelied* [German], vol. 18 of *Biblischer Kommentar Altes*

Testament [Neukirschen-Vluyn: Neukirschener Verlag, 1965]) reads the last phrase of the verse as the poet's direct statement.

5:2 "Open" (as indicating his desire that she open herself to him) – Fox (p. 144) points out that the three uses of "open" in this section (here, 5, 6) avoid the use of the object "door."

5:4 "Stretched forth his hand" – *contra* Gordis et al. ("withdrew"). The context does allow for a motion toward, which is always the implication of the Hebrew *sh-l-ch*. For a parallel use of *shalach min*, cf. Ezek. 10:7.

5:6 "My soul went out" – as dying, Gen. 35:18, Ps. 146:4, as noted by Bloch.

5:10 "Ruddy" – as beautiful, see Lam. 4:7.

5:11 "Finest gold" – related to "fine gold " (*paz*, 5:15), the latter term here combined with another type of gold to indicate the superlative. However, these terms are not related by root to "gold" as it appears alone in the Song (1:11, 3:10, 5:14).

"Curls" – The translation, based on Mishnaic usage, is uncertain. Fox feels "curls" would be redundant, and suggests "fronds of a palm." Later rabbinic interpretation suggests "hill piled on hill." All translations are tentative, though the general sense of thick hair is accepted.

5:12 "By the full ponds" – an obscure phrase. The root indicates fullness. We follow several commentators (e.g., Gordis) in assuming the reference is to a pool or the like, translating "ponds" to avoid identification with other bodies of water, and maintaining the root "full" for reasons of cross-reference to other uses of that root.

5:13 "Bed" – There is no need to vocalize to the plural ("beds") (*contra* Murphy, who cites several translations and manuscripts), since the reference is to the scent, not the physical look of the cheeks.

"Towers" – There is no need to re-vocalize as a verb "that put forth" (aromatics) (*contra* Murphy and others, who base themselves on ancient versions), which would remove the implied connection to her body.

5:14 The description in this verse and the next lead many commentators to assume that there is an extended metaphor of a statue to which the lover is compared.

5:15 "Fine gold" – See note on "finest gold," 5:11.

6:4 "Awesome" – The term bothers many. ("Commentators have been sore abashed to explain the collation of beauty and terror" – Pope.) The term is used of fear of the enemy (Hab. 1:7) and is connected to war and theophany (Deut. 32:25, Gen. 15:12). Note, however, Isa. 33:18, where the root describes one's reaction to one's own city, where no element of terror would be involved.

"Visions" – The translation is chosen to reflect the other uses of the root.

6:5 "Overwhelm" – as Ibn Ezra, and several modern commentators.

6:7 "Smile" – see note, 4:3.

6:8 "Sixty...eighty" – The three-to-four relationship expresses a biblical "full" number (see Amos 1:3, 6, 9, 11, 13; Prov. 30:15, 18, 21, 24, 29; Job 5:19), here elevated by the multiple twenty. It is possible that that this multiple was used to achieve the number sixty, with the consequent implied comparison to the warriors.

6:9 "Pure" – the same term used in 6:10 (root *b-r-r*), though some commentators prefer the alternate meaning here, "chosen" (root *b-o-r*) (so Murphy, Gordis). The point, however, is not competition with other children, but that she is very special (a slightly different emphasis). This consideration, with the importance of relating this use to verse ten, makes the translation "pure" preferable, while the implication "chosen" remains an undertone.

"Acclaim...praise" – These same two verbs, in the mouths of others, are used to praise the "woman of valor" (Prov. 31:28). These are the only two verbs in the Song to use the conversive *vav* (a letter which changes the imperfect tense to a perfect), a form presumably outdated by the time the Song was written. This, plus the appearance of the phrase in Proverbs, may indicate that the phrase had earlier achieved independent epigrammatic status as praise, accounting for its later "archaic" use in the Song.

6:10   "Awesome" and "visions" – see notes, 6:4.

6:11   "Nut grove" – a *hapax legomenon* (the term appears only here in the Bible) of uncertain meaning. "Nut" is the most frequent translation (see Pope, pp. 574–579). Suggested implications range from sexual to sinister, and later homiletical literature uses varied attributes of the plant (form, shell, trunk shape, etc.) to derive implications ranging from regeneration to visibility. All remain matters of speculation.

6:12   All commentators struggle with this verse. ("The proper reading has never been successfully discovered" – Murphy; "I find it impossible to offer even a literal translation of this hopelessly garbled line" – Falk.) Underlying the present translation are the following understandings.

"Disoriented" – The phrase *lo yadati nafshi* indicates severe disorientation, as seen in the two other uses in the Bible, Job 9:21 and Prov. 19:2. Shalom Paul suggests a similar reading based on extra-biblical parallels (S.M. Paul, "An Unrecognized Medical Idiom in Canticles 6:12 and Job 9:21," *Biblica* 59 [1978], pp. 54–57).

"My soul" – *Nafshi* is to be read twice, a technique used elsewhere in the Bible (See commentaries 1:13, 14, 15; 5:1 for suggested similar double

readings in the Song.) Zakovitch also suggests the double reading.

"Mid" – *Sim*, "place," can be used without a preposition for the indirect object, as in Exod. 40:29 (*contra* Murphy).

"Chariots" – used as noble transport, not just for war; cf. Gen. 41:43.

"Nobility" – following Ginsburg's suggestion (see Pope, p. 589) that it is a construct form, approximately, "noble people."

Most vexing to commentators has been the challenge of making sense of the images. However, it is precisely the poet's intention to present an "out of focus" picture, a fantasy in previously unknown surroundings, a scene that will only be clarified several verses later (and then to the exclusion of many details). The confusion, then, is not a result of our inability to understand. Confusion is the message intended by the poet! The reader is meant to appreciate this confusion, not to remove it, and certainly not to emend it away.

7:1   "Encore" – As correctly noted by many commentators, *shuvi* does not mean "turn," but "return," or "again." This translation captures that meaning in the context of a performed dance.

"Shulammite" – Most commentators note the possible connection of the Shulammite, by root, to "Solomon," even if assuming an ultimate derivation from a place name (girl of "Shunem" or "Shulem"), from the name of a pagan god or from the root "perfection." Ibn Ezra saw the name as derived from Jerusalem. Note also – "This...epithet may have been chosen by the poet precisely for its echoes of *shalom* and *shelomoh* [Solomon]" (Bloch, p. 198). The poet's reliance on root repetition (see Overview, III E, "Guide

Words: Repetition as the Key to Meaning") confirms this association and relegates the origin of the term to secondary importance. For an overview of approaches, see Pope, pp. 596–600, Fox, pp. 156–8, Murphy p. 181. See our Overview, II B, on "Solomon (*Shlomo*) – The Antihero of the Song."

"Two Towns Twirl" – The translation attempts to mirror the repetitive nature of word use in this verse. The three key letters in "dance" (here translated "twirl") are *m-ch-l*, and the name "Two Towns" begins with the three letters *m-ch-n*. The two different letters – *l* and *n* – had similar "liquid" pronunciations in ancient Hebrew, as attested by a number of terms wherein the two are interchanged: note *lishkah/nishkah* (office, chamber), *nakat/lakat* (gather), *layl/lun* (spend night) *lachats/nachats* (urge) and *sansan/salsal* (palm frond). The reader in antiquity would have heard the echo. (Indeed, the poet puns on these two letters in 4:12, *gan* and *gal*.) Thus "Two Towns" echoes "twirl." The term "Two Towns" as a place name is based on similar modern uses (e.g., the "Five Towns" in suburban New York, the "Twin Cities" in Minnesota). For *machol* as a "whirl dance" see Mayer Gruber, *The Motherhood of God and Other Studies* (Atlanta: Scholars Press, 1992), p. 170f.

"In" – Many manuscripts and early translations read *bimcholat* for the Masoretic text's *kimcholat*, and that reading is accepted by many modern commentators. It is possible, though difficult, to interpret that even the received Masoretic text has temporal implication ("on the occasion of" – so Pope, p. 605). In either case, the translation remains the same, "in."

*The verse as a whole – Keel, p. 229, senses the sharp erotic tone as being bereft of love's emotion here: "The…words brutally reduce the woman to a mere sex object."

7:2 "Sandals" – Hakham points out that sandals were the privilege of the rich. The dancing girl here is identified with nobility.

7:3 "Navel" – as attested by biblical parallel usage. Some critics would read "vulva" based on an Arabic usage, but such is not attested in Hebrew. (Pope suggests that the description must move up the body, following the progression, and "belly" must therefore follow vulva. This ignores other description of terms at the same body level of the ones previously described, 4:2–3; 5:11.)

"Hedged with lilies" – We have no indication that a mound of wheat would be surrounded by plants of any sort, hence our assumption that the reference is to lilies on the body of the Shulammite. On flowered belts on figurines, see Pope, p. 622.

7:5 "Nose…tower of Lebanon" – as Goulder (*The Song of Fourteen Songs*), p. 56: "The ancients did not admire enormous noses any more than we do. The parallel is with the steep fallaway of (Anti-) Lebanon on the east side facing Damascus, not its height."

7:6 "Crimson Carmel" – As it happens, even the two English terms derive from the same root. Pope accepts the double implication of the single Hebrew term. There may be, in addition, a subtle reference to vineyard (*kerem*) of the same root (so Cook, p. 143).

7:7 "Love" – From the Vulgate on, some translations have preferred to see this as an address to the woman. An assumption of metonymy, the abstract for the concrete, is needed, but one finds no other such biblical use of "love." It is therefore most unlikely, if still possible. Hakham suggests

that both meanings (abstract, metonym) are implied. If so, the two meanings coalesce. Physical love is praised, but in his terms, this ecstasy resides in a special one person – his beloved.

7:9 "The palm" – The definite article requires a change of a vowel from the Masoretic text. It is reflected in the LXX and is preferred by most modern translations.

"Nose" – does not indicate an Egyptian nose kiss (*contra* Murphy). (Even in Egypt, mouth kissing was prevalent by the late second millennium BCE – Keel, p. 41.) Rather, the kiss in the Song is an intimate, exploring kiss, involving all parts of the mouth (see commentaries, 7:10, 5:16 and particularly the "Rereading" commentary, 4:3). In such a kiss, breathing will take place through the nose, as here reflected.

7:10 "As it should" – with a double entendre, "as strong wine" – see Gordis on this verse and on 1:4.

"Stirring" – as Gordis, Zakovitch.

7:11 "And I am the object" – literally, "And for me is his desire." The Hebrew places the object first for emphasis, and the slight revision in the translation was made to reflect this.

"His desire" – The balance to the "desire" in Genesis 3:16 has been recognized by several commentators, among them Zakovitch (p. 13), Bloch.

"The henna," alternatively, "in the villages" – Fox notes the double entendre.

7:14 "Loving plant" – The root is *dod*, "loving." The plant is commonly identified as the mandrake, associated with aphrodisiac-like powers in several cultures, an appropriate background reference to this verse and its only other biblical reference, Gen. 30:14–18.

8:1 * Other commentators have noted the summariz-

ing nature of chapter 8 – it is "a recapitulation of motifs" (Exum, p. 74).

8:2 "I would make you drink" – The sound play with "kiss" is also found in Gen. 29:10, 11.

"Juice" – The term is used as wine, Joel 1:5.

8:4 "Must" – We take the change from the previous *'im* to the negative *mah* as an indication of the greater strength of the negative. Pope (p. 661) calls it a "change from adjuration to prohibition."

8:5 "Beneath" – the earlier (erotic) references in the Song: 2:6, 4:11, 8:3.

"Became pregnant" – We use this term rather than "conceive" to differentiate from another root used in 3:4. The verb in this verse can apply to various stages, from conception to labor (see Ps. 7:15, Isa. 13:8). The former seems to be implied here.

For the lifestyle of hinds and gazelles for childbirth, see Feliks, pp. 13–18.

8:6 "Seal" – Zakovitch describes the seal as "a most personal item, a symbol of one's identity, from which one would not be separated." Hakham also emphasizes that the seal is forever next to one's person.

"Death" – Trible, p. 160, connects this to the creation account: "Death belonged to the creation of Eros" (Gen. 2:17), human disobedience bringing this disintegration of life. "In the closing moment of the Song of Songs, this tragedy is reversed." We feel that had this been the poet's intention, the terminology and other details would have adhered more closely to the language of Genesis.

"Jealousy" – Several commentators, uncomfortable with the idea, translate either "passion" (Gordis, Pope) or "ardor." However, "jealousy" is the proper translation (see Fox) and properly describes a concomitant of love (so Bloch).

"Furious flame" – literally "god-flame" which could indicate just a superlative with no reference to the Deity, as in parallel biblical structures. However, in two such cases there is an association with the Deity – in Jeremiah 2:31, the land of "deep gloom" is a hypothetical symbol applying to God, and in Ps. 118:5, God lifts the supplicant to the ultimate free expanse. In addition, some traditions here (and in Psalms) isolate the end syllable as a direct reference to God (though this too may just be a superlative – see Ps. 80:11). We feel that a secondary implication of "divine flame" is possible here.

8:7 "Multitudinous" – the same term *rabbim* as in *Bat Rabbim*, 7:5. For the waters as the primal force of chaos, cf. Herbert G. May, "Some Cosmic Connotations of *Mayim Rabbim*, Many Waters," in *Journal of Biblical Literature* 74 (1955, pp. 9–21) and comments in Murphy, p. 192.

8:8 On the responsibility of older brothers for their sisters in marriage, see Gen. 24:50, 55; Jud. 21:22.

For "speak for" as "speak against," see Num. 12:1, Ps. 50:20. For "speak for" as betrothal, see 1 Sam. 25:39.

For "do with" as acting to the detriment of, see Gen. 9:24, Exod. 18:8.

8:9 The varied interpretations of the two verses (8:8, 9) are discussed by commentators, each opting for one view or the other (e.g., Gordis sees the brothers opposing the girl, Pope sees them protecting her). The power of the verse, however, is in maintaining both levels of meaning simultaneously.

8:10 "Appeared in his eyes" – this phrase in Hebrew, *hayiti bi'enav ki...*, indicates a *lack* of correspondence to objective reality. ("Appeared" would have sufficed as a translation – the inclusion of "in his eyes" was to allow reference to other uses of "eyes" in the Song.) See Gen. 19:14, 29:20; Num. 13:33; 2 Sam. 4:10; Ezek. 21:28. This holds also in Gen. 27:12, when Jacob fears he will "appear" to deceive his father, for he must feel basically justified – either because his mother was the true culprit, or because he had "legitimately" purchased the blessing.

"Finding," possibly also "producing" – as Pope.

"Shalom" – Murphy is aware of the connection to Solomon and to the Shulammite, although he terms it only "probably" a deliberate play (p. 193).

8:11 "Had a vineyard" – the Hebrew *kerem hayah* (he had a vineyard), which begins this sentence, also begins two other biblical sections (1 Kings 21:1, Isa. 5:1). It was possibly a known opening line of stories or parables.

8:12 "Before me" – For *lifne* in this sense, see Gen. 34:10.

"Thousand" – Many commentators have noted the reference to Solomon's wives – among the most recent: Fox, Bloch and Zakovitch.

For the pairing of "thousand" and "ten thousand" in the Bible as the superlative amount – cf. 1 Sam. 18:7, Mic. 6:7 and Ps. 91:7.

* For another antiphrastic use, cf. Num. 14:44: Moses (*Moshe*) and the ark did not stir (*mashu*) from the camp. In somewhat similar fashion, Naomi (Ruth 1:20), whose name means "pleasantness" asks her friends not to use that name due to the bitterness she has experienced.

* Possible comparison to King David – Tournay (on chapter 8), whose approach to the Song is radically different than our own, notes the significant thirty-three appearances of *dod*. He also cites David's fame as a shepherd and king.

8:13 For other verses which similarly end in an incomplete manner, if for different reasons, see Ps. 27:13 (note NJPS) and Gen. 4:8a.

8:14 "Be swift" – The verb can indicate flight to or from (as Gordis, *contra* Fox, Bloch). Alternatively, if one accepts the limitation of the verb as "flight from," the implication remains "from amidst the fellows," and therefore, secondarily, "to" me (Fox, Zakovitch). In either case, it is the movement toward the lover that is of the essence.

The view that this verse is a quote said by the lover is found in Ibn Ezra, and in many modern commentators.

The insight that the close of the poem dismisses the very audience that was invited in at the beginning is as per Trible, p. 152.

Overview —
The Song of Songs:
A Woman in Love

We here review and annotate those assumptions and understandings which underlie this commentary and translation. We also provide a summary of selected aspects of the Song which require a more detailed articulation than that possible within the context of the commentary and the notes. Again, bibliographical references including only the author's names refer to works listed in the Selected Bibliography.

I. THE NATURE OF THE SONG

The Supreme Poem – this is the basic connotation of "Song of Songs." No idle boast, this. Few poems, indeed, have merited so much attention. In 1977, one commentary summarizing previous interpretations of this short book stretched over seven hundred tightly written pages – and since, much has been added! While we seek to add new insight, this work is but a small addition to centuries of enlightening interpretation.

A. A Unique Book

1. Parameters. The Song of Songs is a love poem, a part of the third section of the Hebrew Bible ("Writings," or "Hagiographa"). A relatively short work (eight chapters, one hundred and seventeen verses – though this is a later subdivision, not necessarily reflecting the author's intentions), it is the only biblical book devoted to human love. It therefore includes many unique words and phrases (proportionally more than any other biblical book), and

it departs from the Bible's usual reluctance to dwell on anatomical beauty.

2. Unity. Until recently, most modern approaches saw the Song as an anthology of short poems and fragments. That has changed. An increasing number of researchers appreciate the Song's unity. Years ago, H.H. Rowley already wrote, "I am not able to distribute the poem amongst several authors," citing others who agreed.[1] Since then, many have acknowledged the guiding hand of a single author. Some emphasize form or repeated patterns as a clear indication of unity,[2] while some cite repeated words, phrases, formulae, themes and/or motifs.[3] Other scholars also detect a "sense of the whole." As one writer put it, "Through the careful selection and structuring of images, metaphors and motifs, the author of the Song has created a unique expression on the

---

1. Rowley, p. 222.
2. Pope, pp. 44–54, summarizes these views, while not accepting them.
3. Murphy, pp. 67–91.

subject of love."[1] Others note a "loose narrative framework" and point to the consistency of character portrayal.[2] Many, then, see the Song as the unified work of a single author.

This commentary accepts and supplements those arguments. In particular, we demonstrate that the numerous repetitions perform definable functions. Furthermore, this unified reading leads to more than a "sense of the whole": it reveals the poet's commitments and a story behind the poetry. By relating each section of the poem to others, one gains deeper understanding of the text. In that sense, this commentary is itself an argument for unity.

The "anthologists" have cited two principle contentions: (1) supposed different dates of composition of subsections and (2) the different genres of literature. Concerning the former, below we note that the composition date is late, and befits a single author. Concerning the latter, one can easily accept the ability of a late and highly skilled poet to take advantage of varied forms and genres of writing. Even recent "anthologists" acknowledge that the text minimally reflects an active and skilled late editor, since the sections as they appear take account of one another.[3]

3. Beauty and Subtlety. Poetry speaks best for itself. No statement of the Song's beauty can have the effect of actual reading. However, some of the subtlety of the Song is not immediately apparent to the first-time reader. As another commentator noted: "All of Song of Songs is a consummate work of art, seen to be so in every sentence and word, in each literary allusion.... The understanding of this literary work demands many rereadings in depth.... The complexity of the creation as it stands does not allow for true comprehension on a first-hearing basis..."[4]

B. The Poem of a Woman in Love

Below[5] we note that the Song was written in the fourth or third century BCE. Its "attribution" to Solomon (tenth century BCE) does not indicate the authorship.

But if not Solomon, then who is the author? Ultimately, one must accept the familiar "anonymous" as our poet. However, we accept a relatively new proposal – that the author was

---

1. K. Gros Louis, *Literary Interpretation of Biblical Narrative,* II (New York: Abingdon Press, 1962), p. xx.
2. Particularly Fox, in a detailed explication, pp. 209–222.
3. Zakovitch, introduction, and particularly sections 16–27 therein.
4. Zakovitch, p. 23. Our translation.
5. This section, paragraph D, "Date of Composition," p. 149.

a woman, or minimally, a male seeking to capture the female voice. We have in the Song an articulation, rare (but not totally absent) in the Bible, of the words of a woman.

Among arguments made in support of this recent contention are the following:

1. The dominant voice is female. Nearly two-thirds of the verses are spoken by the woman, and even some of the male lover's words appear as quoted by her. Appropriately, her words open and close the Song.

2. She seems the more assertive of the two, initiating lovemaking (4:16, 7:14), boldly searching through the night streets (3:1–3, 5:6f.), successfully fending off the competition of the Girls of Jerusalem (2:7, 3:5, 8:4f.), etc.

3. The leading group of "others" is female (the "Girls of Jerusalem"), and the constant model is the mother, not the father. This is also reflected in the appearance of "mother's house" as a reference to the home (3:4, 8:2), as opposed to the frequent use of "father's house" elsewhere in the Bible.

4. Equality between the sexes is not only reflected, but also clearly emphasized. The point is made frontally in the statement "My lover is mine, and I am his" (2:16) and it is developed through the Song.[1] Nowhere else in the Bible is there such a clear emphasis.

5. Some of the metaphoric descriptions of the woman emphasize strength, even drawing on military references (e.g., towers).[2] This is not a unique biblical usage, but unusual nevertheless.

6. All of this is noted against the background of biblical literature, which is highly patriarchal and androcentric, most often concerned with women only in secondary and supportive roles. Again, the text is exceptional.[3]

None of these contentions prove that a woman wrote the poem. Either gender might adopt the positions noted, and great authors in all cultures often associate with and describe the positions and feeling of the other sex. The author, then, remains anonymous, but the enlightened positions are clear. Certainly there are adequate grounds for leaning

---

1. See commentary, 7:11, and below, "Love in the Song of Songs," II C-5, on "Mutuality," p. 156.
2. This is the principle point in Carol Meyers, "Gender Imagery in the Song of Songs," *Hebrew Annual Review* 10 (1986), pp. 209–223.
3. See Zakovitch, pp. 11–13.

toward the assumption that the author was a woman.[1]

In any case, the author wished to *present* the feminine voice. Inherently, this effort is fascinating and worthy of close attention. To the degree that the author succeeded, we here find a unique insight into antiquity. Today, as we search our imaginations for the unspoken reactions of women in so much of the Bible (How did Sarah react to Isaac's binding? What was Miriam's view of the exodus? How did women react to pagan child sacrifice? etc.), we can here discover the authentic voice of a woman.

C. An Overview of the History of Interpretation

1. Canonization. The final stage of the acceptance of the Song as part of Scripture is well documented. A late-first-century CE controversy on the subject is recorded, reflecting reservations, evidently, about either the Song's theme or its lack of explicit theological concern. Then, Rabbi Akiba's view carried the day. He declared: "Heaven forbid [that the Song not be included in canon]! No one can challenge the Song of Song's canonicity. No day is as great as the day it was given Israel. For all Scriptures are holy, but the Song of Songs is the Holy of Holies."[2]

In all probability, Rabbi Akiba had a symbolic approach in mind (briefly, that the Song is a symbolic tale of the love of God and the people Israel). However, there are indications of acceptance of the book well before Akiba's time,[3] and it is less clear that an allegoric approach was the original motivating factor. Some connect the acceptance to the poem's inherent appeal and worth[4] and some to the title's assumed attribution to Solomon. In his time, the position of Akiba, a leading rabbinic figure, gained general acceptance. The canonicity was not challenged again.

2. Allegory. Among both Jews and Christians, the dominant approach to the Song across two millennia has been allegorical, carrying the symbolic approach to its ultimate degree, assigning specific meaning to

---

1. For others so inclined, in varying degrees, note Bloch, p. 21; Schwartz, Leo W., "On Translating the 'Song of Songs,'" *Judaism* 13 (1964), p. 76. Also, note within Brenner: S.D. Goitein, "The Song of Songs, a Female Composition," pp. 58–66, as well as Brenner, Athalya, and Beekencamp, Jonneke and van Djik, Fokkelien, p. 28, 79 (two articles).

2. *Mishnah Yadayyim* III:5.
3. To be detailed below, section I E, "Canonization Reconsidered," p. 164.
4. "It entered the canon…because of its inevitable human appeal. Love is sacred even in passionate manifestations…" – M. Jastrow, as cited in Gordis, p. 43.

each of the Song's images. This mode of interpretation is indeed logical,[1] for the Bible does use the symbol of love and marriage as a metaphor for the relationship of God to His chosen people.[2] Furthermore, the Song is clearly committed to layered and multiple implications.

The range of allegorical understandings has been enormous, reflecting the lack of restraint inherent in the approach. The varied themes proposed include the history of God and the people Israel, the relationship of Jesus and the Church, a love affair between Solomon and "Wisdom," and the relationship of the soul to the Divine Word.[3] By way of illustration, we note three verses, with two allegorical interpretations each, one Jewish followed by one Christian:

1. "I am black, but beautiful" (1:5) — *black in my deeds, but beautiful through the deeds of my forebears* (Rashi); *black through sin, but beautiful through baptism* (Origen).
2. "A bag of myrrh is my lover to me, lying between my breasts" (1:13) — *God's Presence, above the ark, between the two cherubim* (Ibn Ezra); *Jesus between the two Testaments* (Cyril of Alexandria).
3. "I sought him, but found him not" (3:1) — *speaks of Israel in the desert* (Rashi); *speaks of the women seeking Jesus' body* (Cyril of Alexandria).

The allegorical approach has been largely abandoned in our time.[4] The Song itself bears no clear sign that it was written as an allegory, nor have scholars ever found anything resembling an agreed meaning. (We shall, in an excursus to this work, propose a new appreciation of the potential of using the Song as a symbol of divine love, though not an allegory. One can find in the Song words, phrases, situations, themes, etc., which can be applied beneficially to spiritual matters. That differs, however, from the claim that each term, person, etc., was created to stand for something other than itself, as allegory would hold.)

3. Drama. Already in antiquity many were sensitive to the dialogic character of the Song, but the view that this was a dramatic script gained popularity in the nineteenth century. Because the speakers change frequently, scholars began to see the Song as a script.

---

1. See Gerson D. Cohen.
2. See, e.g., Jer. 2:2, Hosea 2:21f.
3. For two successful and detailed surveys, see Rowley, pp. 198–212; Pope, pp. 93–132.
4. The closest recent commentary would be Tournay, who denies that his view of the book as longing for the Messiah is an allegory. Rather, he describes his approach as an enlarged double entendre.

Again, there has been no agreement concerning the story, speakers, number of characters, etc. Indeed, all interpretations depend on stage directions not provided, addition of a plot otherwise not detailed, and placement within the cultural milieu of Israel of a form otherwise not attested. The approach has been largely, if not totally,[1] abandoned. Some translations do identify the speakers of lines of the poem.[2]

4. Cult. This approach sees the Song as an evolution of pagan liturgy. Not surprisingly, there are texts within pagan literature (where gods mix, match and mate frequently) that shed light on the Song. However, the book as we have it is a secular love song, with no hint of ritual. Furthermore, as in the case of the drama approach, proponents of this theory have established no agreed meaning. At best, one might say that there is pagan background to some of the Song, a background now secularized, nationalized (the geography of the Song is all based in the land of Israel, not to mention the royal Israelite themes and setting) and camouflaged. Any stronger relationship involves assumptions so complex as to be unrealistic. What is left, then, is not a viable theory of origin, but a recollection of regional cultural milieu.

5. Poetry. We know that from ancient times there were those who saw the Song in the simplest of terms – as love poetry. Two rabbinic period texts already rail against those who sing the Song in bars, as secular ribald lyrics.[3] Even among ancient and medieval proponents of the allegory, there were those who split their commentaries into levels, including one relating to the text as a love poem between man and woman. The poetic appreciation of the Song, then, has a long history.

Since the late nineteenth century and until recently, literary poetic approaches have tended to see the Song as a collection, or anthology, of individual love songs, possibly reflected in the title, Song *of* Songs. We recall, however, the growing number of commentators acknowledging the Song's unity and their contentions.[4]

Some anthology proponents point to the large number of sharp changes in subject,

---

1. See Guilder. Also see Robert Graves, *The Song of Songs: Text and Commentary* (London: William Collins and Sons, 1973).
2. E.g., Gordis, Murphy, Fox.
3. *Tosefta Sanhedrin* 12:10 and Talmud *Sanhedrin* 101a. (The latter: "Our rabbis taught that one who makes a verse of the Song of Songs into a kind of ditty…brings evil to the world, and the Torah dons sackcloth, falls before the Holy One, Blessed be He, and says to Him: 'Master of the Universe, your children have made me into a harp for fools.'")
4. Above, A-2, p. 143.

but these "breaks" are only that: changes in focus. Some of them are so mild that there is no agreement among "anthologists" on the location or number of divisions. Some breaks are indeed clear, and are explained either by necessity (e.g., things get too intimate, as 2:7, 3:6, 5:1, 7:14) or another principle (e.g., the purposely staccato style of chapters 1 and 8).[1] In addition, many types of literature, from folk songs (in many cultures) to psalms, to narratives, exhibit similar breaks.[2]

Ultimately, anthology theory will rest on the failure to show a unity. Hopefully this commentary will strengthen the contention of a single author of a unified poem.

D. Date of Composition

There are two principle criteria for establishing the date of a text – historical references and language. However, early historical references can be dismissed as antiquating or classical allusions, and late language can be dismissed as a revision of an earlier text. Hence, much is left to the good sense of the inter-

preter. The Song has been dated practically everywhere across an eight-century span, from the tenth to the second century BCE. There is, however, a best approximation.

1. Historical References. The clearest historical reference is in the poem's title, seemingly attributing the book to Solomon (died c. 922 BCE). However, many do not attribute the title to the original text, and many who do see this either as a purposeful antiquation, a false attribution or a sentence indicating something other than authorship (see commentary). It is not clear that other citations of Solomon in the Song relate to him as a living or an historical figure. Still, there are some commentators who attribute the entire work to Solomon's period.

The text itself, however, belies that contention, for the other "clear" date in the text is the paired reference to Tirzah and Jerusalem (6:4), capitals of North and South Israel, respectively, only decades *after* Solomon's death. If both "Solomon" and these two cities are living realities in the text, perforce the Song is an anthology.

They were not necessarily living realities, however. This first pair of North-South capitals, even though Tirzah was capital only for one generation, can easily be seen as a frozen metaphor of beauty (as a modern might cite the "glory of [ancient] Athens" without

---

1. Note Cook, p. 132: "Nor do its [the Song's] breaks fragment it, since every break can be assigned to the clear changes of voice from the fourth verse on."
2. Note Zakovitch, p. 17, on Sumerian love songs: "… similar structural elements to the Song of Songs: surprising changes of speaker and locale, and insertion of a choir in the ongoing context…"

implying that it still exists), or a purposeful antiquation. Neither this reference to the two cities, nor those to Solomon, necessitates an early date of composition. In any case, the author does create a *pretension* of the time of the early monarchy, and the inclusion of such references would therefore be appropriate.

Other place names in the Song demonstrate a similar antiquating tendency. In terms of political control, the locations named were all under Israelite control only under Solomon and his father, David. Other emphases similarly fit that early period, such as the emphasis on spices (see 1 Kings 10:10f.) and cedars (1 Kings 10:27). In short, the poet times the poem in that golden age.

However, the poem never conceals its fictional character. The poet "constructs" an orchard of plants that grew in different countries.[1] The poet locates his lovers across the map, from Ein Gedi in the south to the mountains of Lebanon in the north. One need only understand that the poet is not reflecting contemporary reality, but creating a fiction, to realize that historical figures reflect the scene, not the date, of writing.

2. Language. The language of the Song is post-exilic, third or fourth century BCE. Included is at least one loan word from Persian ("orchard" in 4:13), and possibly a second ("litter" in 3:9) – an influence possible only from the late sixth century BCE (Cyrus' conquest). The Hebrew is laced with Aramaisms (Aramaic was the lingua franca of Israel from the fifth century BCE, though known and used in north Israel well before) and the Hebrew seems close to (postbiblical) Mishnaic Hebrew.[2]

Most telling is that our text cannot be a rewriting. The complex alliterations, puns, word plays, cross-references, etc., would require a rewriter of greater genius than an original poet. The commentary makes this obvious. The linguistic evidence, therefore, is decisive. Our text is post-exilic, fourth or third century BCE.

E. Literary Parallels

Various studies have found parallels to the Song in widely varied cultural milieus: ancient Indian (Sanskrit), Sumerian, Acadian, ancient Egyptian, ancient Greek and modern Arabic.[3] One could scarcely deny a priori the possibility of influence, and even if the connection is not derivative, similarities can

---

1. See below, II D-3, p. 163.

2. See summaries, Bloch, pp. 23–27 (though we tend to reject their sense of a Greek influence), Zakovitch, pp. 18–19, and especially Fox, pp. 187–190.
3. See for survey, Pope, pp. 54 –89, and, subsequently, Fox, passim.

be enlightening. However, in no case has dependency been demonstrated, and caution is therefore in order.

II. LOVE IN THE SONG OF SONGS

A. Is There a "Message"?

Dialogue is the chosen format of the Song, primarily that of the two lovers. Theoretically, the poet may have sought simply to reflect on these two, not to speak of love in general. The poem, however, has an encompassing tenor, and whether intentional or unplanned, an overview of love emerges. The poet's subject is reflected in the most repeated words: "love" (*ahavah*), "loving/lover" (*dodim* and *dod*, a more physical term) and "darling" (*ra'ayah*, with its near-partner, "shepherd," *ro'eh*).[1] Indeed, the concluding chapter includes a rapturous encomium of love. Throughout, the Song presents a positive model of love set against a negative one, as we detail below. The rejection of the latter goes beyond any one relationship.

Whether this poet's views reflected the mores of the society is a separate question, to which we shall return. (This being a feminine perspective, one could expect some difference from the male-dominated society.) In any case, the implications seem to stretch beyond the couple. Here we find an ideal of love.

B. Solomon (*Shlomo*) – The Antihero of the Song

The use of a guide word, a term which reveals the theme and message of a text through its uses in repetition, is an acknowledged literary technique of biblical texts. In fact, the poet of the Song raises this technique to new levels, as we shall detail.[2] Not surprisingly, the poet also reveals the main themes of the Song through repetition.

In describing the rejected view of love, the poet repeats a letter combination not technically a (three-letter) Hebrew "root," but rather a three-letter combination found in a number of longer terms. Repeatedly, the author uses the combination *sh-l-m*, as found in Solomon (*Shlomo*), Jerusalem (*Yerushalayim*), Shulammite (see 7:1)[3] and shalom (peace).[4]

---

1. See "On Translating and Interpreting the Song of Songs," below, section III E, p. 169.

2. See "On Translating and Interpreting the Song of Songs," below, section III E, p. 169.

3. The connection of the Shulammite to Solomon has long been noted. H.H. Rowley, seeing this as a feminine form of Solomon's name, cites already in 1939 another thirty-nine commentators who adopted that view ("The Meaning of the Shulamite" in *American Journal of Semitic Languages and Literature* 56, pp. 84–91).

4. Hebrew words have three-letter base roots. Properly speaking, *sh-l-m* is not the root of all these terms. Jerusalem is a pre-Israelite name, possibly

Overview – The Song of Songs: A Woman in Love · 151

Together, the terms appear eighteen times (an identical number to the uses [each] of both *'-h-v* ["love"], and *ro'eh-ra'ayah* [two nearly identical roots meaning "darling" and "pasture"]). Of these repetitions, "Solomon" and the "Girls of Jerusalem," terms connected to each other in 3:9f., are each repeated seven times (a particularly meaningful number[1]). Furthermore, a connection between Solomon and "shalom" is the best explanation of the difficult transition from 8:10 to 8:11.

To elucidate this use of *sh-l-m*, we turn first to the final chapter, in which the poet resolves the meaning of many terms. "Solomon had a vineyard in Ba'al Hamon.... My very own vineyard is before me," one of the lovers declares, "the thousand is yours, O Solomon (8:11–12)". This last mention of "Solomon" implies competition and rejection. The speaker prefers his/her vineyard to Solomon's, which brings in one thousand (pieces of silver). Many have noted the less-than-subtle reference here to Solomon's one thousand wives (seven hundred chief wives, three hundred concubines, 1 Kings 11:3). Indeed by chapter 8, "vineyard" represents the love relationship itself (see commentary). The poem, in short, seems to reject Solomon's multiplicity of relationships, preferring the one.[2]

This model of rejection also befits the "Girls of Jerusalem." These women hover in the background, occasionally as partners in dialogue with the woman, sometimes a standard of beauty, and often a potential bother. Three times the woman adjures them to nonintervention (2:7, 3:5, 8:4). They are to be kept at a distance. Even in seeking their help to find her lover, the woman hesitates, lest they become too involved. She emphasizes that he belongs exclusively to her (5:16, 6:3) and gives them "directions" to him which are meaningful to her in symbolic terms, but are useless in terms of really finding the lover. She even hints that she wants them not to find him.[3]

Who are these Girls of Jerusalem? Their history is reflected only in 3:10, which indicates

---

honoring a pagan god. Nor is there agreement on the origin of the name Solomon. In any case, the Bible elsewhere connects these terms: peace and Jerusalem, in Ps. 122:6; and an implied connection between Solomon and peace, 1 Chron. 22:9.

1. See Robert Gordis, "The Heptad as an Element of Biblical and Rabbinic Style," *Journal of Biblical Literature* 62 (1943), pp. 17–26. The only other seven-fold repetitions in the Song are of "mother," to which we shall refer below, and "my soul."

2. What Zakovitch, who sees the Song as an anthology, says of one poem (3:7–11) in fact holds for the entire work: "This song is nothing if not a mockery of this king [Solomon], and his love of wealth and women, a love which cannot lead to happiness" (p. 11).

3. See commentary, 5:8 and 6:1–3.

that Solomon's litter was "inlaid with love" by them. The words contain multiple levels of meaning, including the feelings of those doing the work ("lovingly wrought by…"), pictures of lovemaking engraved in the litter, and possibly acts of love performed therein. The Girls, then, seem to be "experts" in matters of love, even on a "mass" basis. Such an understanding befits the Girls' presumed expertise in beauty (1:5f.) and helps explain the woman's fear of having them too near her lover. These are city girls, girls of a thousand loves, women of the court, possibly the same "damsels" (6:8) grouped with the queens and concubines. Their efforts at intervention are constantly rejected. Verse 8:4 focuses on the contrast. The Girls are adjured for a final time not to intervene, while in the very next verse the woman exults that she has successfully done what she told them not to do – she has roused her lover.

The dance of the Shulammite (6:11–7:9) further elucidates the implication of *sh-l-m*. Many commentaries have mistakenly equated the Shulammite with the beloved. The poet makes no such contention, and in fact indicates the opposite. In a vision, while semi-conscious, the male lover sees a dancing woman, a twirling figure. The body description is the *reverse* of all previous ones: beginning from the feet up, the description begins by using totally new terms, departing from previous style. Even the locale is totally different – all takes place amid the chariots of the nobility (6:12).[1]

As the Shulammite dances, an onlooking crowd expresses its appreciation, its words eventually blending into those of the lover. Slowly, he begins to recall and use terms associated in the past with his beloved's body. Eventually, the identification with his beloved takes over, as all new terms are abandoned, and he finally recites a staccato list of descriptions used before. When he recalls her palate, symbol of the central kiss (see 1:2), she interrupts him with a cry of joy (7:11) as she realizes that her lover's desires are specifically directed at her.

The Shulammite, then, is his sexual fantasy. While he ultimately clarifies that his desires are directed toward his beloved, it would be inaccurate to identify the Shulammite with the beloved. The former was a tantalizing vision, a scantily clad woman dancing in a public display, divorced from intimacy. Certainly there is no better title for this vision than

---

1. Athalya Brenner, "Come Back, Come Back, the Shulammite (7:1–10)" in Brenner, pp. 234–257, shows sensitive awareness of these differences. Her conclusion that this is a parody, however, is based on misreading of key words, and is totally out of keeping with the poem.

Shulammite, girl of the root *sh-l-m*. Once again we have a potentially competitive model, one based heavily on raw sex appeal, and a model that is, in the final analysis, rejected.[1]

But is the model rejected? It is patently absurd to claim that the Song of Songs is either puritanical or prudish. Few works of literature have so successfully celebrated the rapture of physical love. Even the Shulammite is incorporated into the beloved!

Nevertheless, the world of *sh-l-m* is rejected in the Song of Songs. To understand the rejection, one must differentiate, as the Song does, between the type of relationship represented by *sh-l-m* on the one hand, and by the two lovers, on the other. The world of *sh-l-m* is a world of multiplicity of sexual relationships, of sex divorced from emotional love, devotion and/or commitment. It is a world of sex dances and a thousand "loves." The love ethos of the two lovers is other. They clearly prefer their own single relationship. *All multiple numbers*, from the doubling dance of the Shulammite to sixty to eighty to one thousand to ten thousand are rejected in the Song.[2] "One" is emphasized and praised.

The Song, then, while celebrating a sex-ual relationship, grants it *full* worth only in context, one we shall immediately detail, but one which clearly is exclusive: "My very own vineyard is before me. The thousand is yours, O Solomon."

Indeed, the previously cited allusion to Solomon's thousand wives in all probability inspired the poet in the choice of this symbol. There, in 1 Kings 11, it is stated that Solomon's wives led his heart astray (toward idolatry) *in Jerusalem*, and that Solomon's heart was not *"completely"* (*shalem* – fully devoted) with God. The author of Kings offers a daring pun – Solomon, *Shlomo*, in Jerusalem, *Yerushalayim*, was not *shalem*, not complete.[3] This is an example of antiphrasis, a rhetorical device using a word in a sense opposite to its proper meaning. The poet of Song of Songs adopted that pun as an underlying theme, constantly repeated throughout the Song.

Lest the internal repetition and the final rejection of Solomon not suffice to clarify matters for the reader, the poet took the precaution of articulating the guide word for all to see. This, the poet declared, is the Song of Songs *asher lishlomo*, concerning Solomon (1:1), or, if one would prefer, concerning the

---

1. The relationship to "shalom," 8:10, requires close analysis of Hebrew terms. The reader is referred to the commentary.
2. See 4:7, 5:10, 6:8f., 8:11f.

3. For a similar pun on Moses' name, see Num. 14:44.

world of *sh-l-m*.[1] The poet's message is that this world is *in*complete. At the end of the Song, that final rejection is followed only by the lovers' intention to be together in physical embrace.

We proceed, then, to the model of love and lovemaking the couple shares.

C. Love, Sex and the Single Maiden

1. Unmarried Lovers. We know little of the male lover. His beloved is clearly single and young, her physical maturity subject to differing evaluations (8:8–10). She is still under her brothers' protective care (8:8, 9; 1:6), as was the custom for single women,[2] and is closely attached to her mother's house (3:4, 8:2), another indication of her single status.[3] When they meet, they do so secretly, and they long for the day when this will change (8:1). Presumably, the lover is also single. While it is of historical interest to note the pious attempts of commentators across centuries to marry off the couple, one cannot accept their efforts as an accurate understanding of the text.

2. Sexual Relations. Explicit touching and hugging mark the Song, as there are many beautiful metaphoric descriptions of the body. The lovers long to lie with each other (1:13, 7:12), kisses dominating their dreams (1:2, 8:1). Is there more intimate contact?

Coition does occur within the Song of Songs, or, to be more precise, between the lines of the Song. (One need not search for it through allegoric interpretations of given lines, as some do, e.g., of 5:4 – "My lover stretched forth his hand through the hole."[4]) Even a superficial reading of the end of chapter 4 reveals that in verse 16 she agrees to (or initiates) sexual intercourse ("Let my lover come to his garden, let him eat its delectable fruits"), as has long been recognized. In the next verse, he celebrates after the fact ("I have come to my garden"). Similarly, at the end of chapter 7, having heard her lover identify his sexual fantasy[5] with her, she openly invites him: "Come my lover, let us go out to the field, let us lie (i.e., spend the night) among the henna.…There I will give you my loving" (7:12, 13). (*Dodim*, "loving," always bears physical implications.) Indeed, from its beginning the Song celebrates physical love – "Your loving is better than wine" (1:2). Toward the end,

---

1. Note: "The characteristic biblical strategy, clearest in the convention of the *leitworstil* [use of guide word], is to call explicit attention to the verbal repetition" (Alter [1981], p. 94).
2. Gen. 24:50, 55; Jud. 21:22.
3. Gen. 24:28, Ruth 1:8.

---

4. Pope, pp. 517–519.
5. As above, Overview, II B, on the Shulammite, p. 151.

the physical is celebrated explicitly: "How lovely you are, O love ecstatic" (7:7).

One should note, however, that the Song's language of love, erotic as the poem may be, is "never prurient or pornographic."[1] This is poetry of love, ever the more erotic for its resort to gentle symbols and metaphors. Lovemaking is described in circumlocution. It is seen from the perspective of the lovers, who bring to their lovemaking, in their heightened sensitivity, the flowing beauty of all that surrounds them.

Still, as clarified above, the Song rejects the love-sex model of "Solomon," a model which disconnects emotional and physical love, and which involves a multiplicity of relationships. The lovers of the Song have different values, as we continue to detail.

3. Love. The context of all that happens sexually between the couple is love. The terms "loving," "love" and various terms of endearment dominate. This is one of the bases of the rejection of the Solomonic model (above) — not only the multiplicity of the relationships and the lack of commitment, but also the lack of true emotion.

4. Exclusivity and Loyalty. Not only is the "thousand" of Solomon rejected (8:11–12) — so, too, is every plural number in the Song (apart from naturally doubled body parts). All such plural numbers are attributed to the others, the groups that observe the couple but are not part of their intimacy.[2] "One" is emphasized (6:8f.), once almost absurdly so — "You have stolen my heart with *one* of your eyes" (4:9). Accompanying that exclusivity is loyalty, as she declares on inviting him to lie with her again: "All delicacies, new — also old — my lover, I have kept for you" (7:14).

5. Mutuality. The clearest expression of the mutuality and equality of their love is through direct expression. "My lover is mine and I am his" (2:16), she declares, providing both sides of the equation. Lest one misunderstand, assuming sequential significance to the order of the two devotions, the verse is inverted when repeated: "I am my lover's and my lover is mine" (6:3). If that were not enough, the sentiment is restated a third time, with a remarkable change. After she realizes that he associates his sexual desires with her, she exults: "I am my lover's, and it is I whom he desires" (7:11 — literally, "and his desire is for me"). To understand that this is a restatement of the mutuality found in the two cited verses, we take note (as do several commentators) of another appearance of the term "desire" (one of two in the entire Bible). Eve, on receiving

---

1. The felicitous phrase of Murphy, p. 102.

2. See page 154, note 2.

her punishment for eating the forbidden fruit in Eden is told, "Your desire shall be for your husband, and he shall rule over you" (Gen. 2:16). The Song of Songs comes centuries after Genesis finally to correct its imbalance. Now *his* desire is also for *her!* This is, indeed, a perfect parallel and enlargement of the equality and mutuality articulated in the two previous statements of belonging.

This theme of mutuality is emphasized throughout the poem.[1] In the opening, she asks him to draw her after him, and in the end, she tells him to be swift in coming to her. The all-important kiss is mentioned explicitly twice – in 1:2 he gives the kiss, in 8:1, she gives it. She is a lily among brambles, he an apricot tree in the forest (2:2, 3). He is a cedar (masculine gender – 5:15), she a palm tree (feminine gender – 7:8, 9). She dreams of his bringing her to his chambers (1:4), and of herself bringing him to her mother's chambers (8:2). His fruit is sweet to her palate (2:3) and her palate is sweetness (5:16). She is more awesome than great sights ("things seen" – 6:4, 10); he is "seen" above ten thousand (5:10). He is to "circle" over the hills (2:17); she "circles"

_____

1. Note Phyllis Trible, *God and the Rhetoric of Sexuality* (Philadelphia: Fortress Press, 1978), p. 161: "There is no male dominance, no female subordination, and no stereotyping of either sex."

through the city (3:2). Myrrh flows from her fingers (5:5) and his lips (5:13).

Identical terms are applied to both – "indeed, you are beautiful" (1:15, 16), "your love is better than wine" (1:2, 4:10), "the fragrance of your oils" (1:3, 4:10). She is "totally" beautiful (4:7); he is "totally" a delight (5:16). Her lips "drip" honey (4:11), his "drip" myrrh (5:13). She wants to "hold" him (3:4), just as he wants to "hold" her (as the palm tree – 7:9). He calls her to "come" from Lebanon (4:8) and she calls him to "come" to his garden (4:16). She is "darling" (often) as is he (5:16). He "pastures" (often), as does she (1:8). "Doves" describes both their eyes (1:15, 5:1). Her mother is the one who "bore" her (6:9) as his "bore" him (8:5).

On occasion, so often do they dialogue and so close are their views, that the text is unclear as to which is speaking – perhaps indicating that both share identical sentiments (1:16; 4:15, 16a; 7:10c; 8:14).

From the earliest moment, with her call (1:4), "Draw me after you," it is delightfully unclear as to who leads whom.

All of these techniques, of course, are over and beyond shared values and commitments. One is hard put to imagine how the poet could have emphasized the mutuality more than s/he did.

6. *The Horizon of Marriage.* As noted, the

Song's lovers are not married. The poet, however, significantly includes marriage as hope on the horizon, as follows.

Marriage is the alternative to the shallow, external glory of Solomon. In 3:7–10 there are descriptions of Solomon's bed and litter, the former surrounded by an impressive army guard (sixty greatest warriors), the latter made of the world's best materials – gold, silver, royal purple yarn and cedar. Indeed, this litter is "inlaid with love" by the Girls of Jerusalem. All this is dismissed. The Girls of Zion are told what to note (3:11) – the crown his mother gave him on his *wedding* day. There lies true glory!

Marriage infiltrates the Song's terminology. In the central section (4:8–5:1), his love term for her is "sister-bride," a unique usage for love relationship, clearly drawn from weddings. In fact, three times she refers to him as "king" (1:4, 12; 7:6), also a term drawn from weddings, where grooms would be crowned (see commentary).

Further, the marriage dream is reflected in frequent references to "mother," one specifically related to Solomon's wedding (3:11). In fact, "mother" is used seven times in the Song, a particularly meaningful pattern,[1] and a distinction shared only with the central

terms "Solomon," "Girls of Jerusalem" and "my soul" (see commentary, 6:12). The motherhood concentration reflects the woman's dream of marriage.[2]

7. The Horizon of Childbearing. The emphasis on "mother," however, points to more than marriage. Using metaphor and word play, the poet hints that the dream centers on the role of childbearing. This emphasis is carried out first through a bold word play, which sets the framework for the repetitions of "mother" in the Song.

In 3:4, the woman expresses longing to bring her lover to her *mother's* house, the chamber "of *her who conceived me*" (*horati*, Hebrew root, *h-r-h*). This parallelism is not jarring, and is found elsewhere.[3] In 6:9, the poet repeats the parallel structure, with a different term: "the only one of *her mother*, the delight of *her who bore her.*" In 8:2, however, as she restates her desire to lead him to her mother's house, "mother" is set parallel to "she who taught me." This is an unusual Hebrew form, lead-

---

1. See page 152, note 1.

2. Edward F. Campbell, Jr., *Ruth* (Garden City: Doubleday, 1975), p. 64, suggests that the twice mentioned mother's house is specifically connected to marriage: "I propose that in some circle of custom…the 'mother's house' was the locus for matters pertinent to marriage, especially for discussion and planning for marriage."

3. "Their mother has played the harlot, she that conceived them has acted shamefully" (Hosea 2:7).

ing several ancient translations and modern commentators to emend and/or reread the text. Such suggestions miss the basic point. We have here an audacious word play. The Hebrew of 3:4 (*horati*, translated above "her who conceived me") is interpreted twice, once (6:9) from the root "conceive" (*h-r-h*) and once (8:2) from the root "teach" (*y-r-h*). Thus the term brilliantly plays back on itself. In her role as one who gives birth, the mother serves as instructor, as model for her daughter.

Two verses emphasize that "mother" recalls childbearing. Verse 6:9 states that the woman is "one [i.e., unique]...to her mother, pure to her who bore her." In 8:1 she longs for him to be like a brother, "suckling of my mother's breast." Both mentions of her mother specifically recall offspring.

Clearest, however, is the final use of "mother." The beloved delights, in 8:5, that she has succeeded in rousing him beneath the apricot tree: "there your mother became pregnant with you, there she became pregnant, she who bore you." The verse reaffirms that "mother" emphasizes childbearing. It also refers to the apricot tree, to which she had compared him (as an apricot tree among forest trees – 2:3). The greatest advantage of the apricot over forest trees, of course, is that the former bears fruit! This verse, 8:5, weaves images of intimacy, comparison and moth-

erhood all into a single context – childbearing. Just as she dreams of marriage, then, she also dreams of motherhood. Both are on her horizon.[1]

8. Love and Sex in the Song. The Song of Songs is a poem, not a diatribe, nor an argument, nor a prescription. One can describe the couple and their attitudes with some degree of certainty. There is less certainty as to what the poet would prescribe for others. Still, the lovers (and, through them, the poet) clearly celebrate their relationship. There seems to be an implied ideal.

We summarize, then, the view of the couple. They reject multiple loves and indiscriminate sex, the model associated with Solomon and the Girls of Jerusalem. Instead, their framework weaves loyalty and exclusivity, mutuality and equality. Within that, there is a sexual relationship, including coition. They are single young people, but dreams of marriage and childbearing are clearly on the horizon.

This is the view of a woman in love. How accurate this is to most women, or how different from most men, is a subject far beyond the scope of the present work.

---

1. See Segal 2000.

D. Articulating Love

To offer the Song of Songs' insights concerning love in prose summary is to debase it. The power of this poetry lies in its subtle inferences, in the truth revealed as images and words interact and clash, in its circling patterns and in its layered interior. Yet one is moved, not in place of the Song but in its honor, to recall a few of the themes the poet connects to this couple's love, while offering, evidently, an ideal model to the reader.

Any such list will be subjective and, perforce, selective. We choose to emphasize certain elements not frequently noted previously. What here follows is an addition to emphases detailed above (mutuality, loyalty, etc.). We also do not comment below on some of the most obvious messages, including that love is both spiritual and physical, that it is joy, that spring is the time of love, that love involves praise and admiration, and that poetry is, indeed, its language. We choose three additional descriptions.

1. The Motion of Love. The Song is dominated by motion of many kinds. These never impose themselves on the essence of love. There is no movement from loyalty to disloyalty, from optimism to pessimism, or from commitment to doubt. Yet, even if there is an "all-embracing mood...[of] joy...of a viva-cious affirmation,"[1] the poem often dwells on moments of separation (e.g., 1:7–8, 5:2). The poet would seem to indicate that while love is strong enough to conquer all, little is static, as follows.

Part of this motion is *physical*. The lovers constantly move across the landscape, and call on each other to be in motion – "Draw me after you, we shall run. The king has brought me" (1:3), the Song opens. Throughout, all is in motion: "Hark! The voice of my love! Behold – he comes, leaping across the mountains, skipping over the hills" (2:8). "Circle about my lover, make yourself like a gazelle" (2:17)." Who is this, ascending from the desert...?" (3:6). "O bride, come with me from Lebanon, trip down from atop Amana" (4:8). So the poem proceeds, to the very end: "Be swift, my lover...on mountains of spices" (8:14).

There are other motions. The strongest of them is a pulsating rhythm of *togetherness and separation*. The moments of union are fewer, but intimate – "his left hand underneath my head, and his right hand embracing me" (2:6), "let us go out to the field" (7:12). Separation is more common, either physical – "my dove, in the crannies of the rock, in the covert of

---

1. Cook, p. 132f.

the terrace, let me see your appearance, let me hear you voice" (2:14) – or temporal – "until the day breathes, circle about, my lover" (2:17). Even when there is contact, however, it is too often across some barrier – "there he stands behind our wall, gazing through the windows" (2:9), "my lover stretched forth his hand through the hole" (5:4).

Part of the motion is a *grand movement of change*, as former situations, previously used words and prior accounts continuously reveal themselves anew, with different implications. Terms continuously unfold, forcing reconsideration of their previous appearances. Apparent objective descriptions later gain symbolic complexity. Among terms developed in this manner are: wine, vineyard, lily, mother, garden, dove, shepherd and apricot. Even verbs, such as hold, see and bring, share this quality. In fact, the poet's basic technique is the use of such "guide words."[1] Concerning such words, Martin Buber commented, "the variation patterns interrelate to create a growing movement as it were. One viewing the text as a whole can sense waves moving to and fro between them"[2] The poet seems to suggest

that this constant re-revelation of the past is part and parcel of love.

Yet another motion is found in the dynamic between *dream and reality*. This is less a matter of sequence than of interaction. As a recalled circumstance flutters between fact and fantasy (e.g., their meeting at the wine house, 2:4–7, and her search through the city for him, 3:1–5), one senses not a frustration but a message; namely, that this confusion is inherent to the love relationship.

The general movement of the Song, of course, is *toward the future*. While the text pulsates with references to past, present and dreams, the concentration is on hope. This is love's province, and anticipation marks the Song not only as its dominant tone, but also in its structure. Three times the poet repeats a recollection while omitting a basic element. The reader is struck by the element's absence – the absence of finding him and bringing him to her mother's house in the search (5:5–7), and the absences of her breasts and of her lips in the praise of her body (6:4–7). That these are all resolved in later verses (7:4, 8, 10; 8:1, 2) is a reassurance, but also a reward for the

---

1. See below, "On Translating and Interpreting the Song of Songs," section III E, p. 169.
2. Buber, Martin, "The Use of the Guide Word in Biblical Stories" [Hebrew] reprinted in *Darkoh Shel*

Mikra' (Hebrew, "The Method of Bible") (Jerusalem: Bialik Institute, 1964), p. 284. For expanded quote, see below, "On Translating and Interpreting the Song of Songs," section E, p. 156.

positive act of anticipating. (Perhaps love has much to do with delayed fulfillment!)

This meta-message of love as motion is ultimately carried out by *the Song as a whole*, for the poem simply cannot be understood in a first consecutive reading. It is doubtful that the poet meant the title "Song of Songs" to be a hint that the text grows and changes with every reading, but we might adopt that understanding as a guide. (Indeed, we have added a chapter of reinterpretations inherent in a second reading for that very reason.) Each discovery grants new depth, even if the revelation is of more complexity and ambiguity.

Love, states the poet, as it creates and dominates reality, exhibits motion. These movements – between dreaming and consciousness, union and separation, present challenge and future hope – are of love's essence. Movement is love's field of play.

2. The Exclusivity of Love. True love, states the poet, is only between two. Exclusivity must apply. The poet emphasizes this contention in three ways.

The two lovers are set against all others in the Song, often through tension, even conflict. The Girls of Jerusalem are kept at a distance, adjured from interfering and misled when they ask to help find her lover. (See commentary, 6:1–3.) Her brothers are at odds with her – they set her to guard the vineyards,

something she does not usually do, and they have a markedly different conception of her and of her readiness for a relationship. (In fact, in 8:8–10, they offer to help her, while she hears a threat. The same words bear two totally different levels of meaning.) Another group, his "fellows," suggest that she stay with them (1:8) and are said to seek out her voice (8:13). True, occasionally these outsiders support them – in celebration of their love (5:1) or in praise of her (6:8), but they are always "others," outsiders.

The very form of the Song is unique – it is presented almost exclusively in dialogue.[1] All is a matter of exchange, and most often, between the two lovers. They speak to one another, listen, respond and are moved by each other's words. Sometimes they echo one another, often after a time.[2] Love is not an internal emotion of one person, but something that occurs between two.

In fact, the lovers share a special, symbolic language. When she "directs" the Girls of Jerusalem to her lover – "my lover had gone down to his garden, to the beds of spices, to pick lilies" (6:2) – they are really treated only to a

1. This paragraph is based on the groundbreaking observation of Fox, pp. 263–265 and 315–322, who notes that earlier Egyptian love poetry makes practically no use of dialogue.
2. As above, II C-5.

recollection of the couple's love: "his garden" is none other than the woman (5:1), "the beds of spice" none other than his description of her (4:13, 14), "pasturing among lilies" not a reference to shepherding sheep but to erotic contact (2:16, 4:5 — see commentaries). His imagery for her body is similarly unique, and when he has a sexual fantasy of a dancing (Shulammite) girl, it is his eventual use of those special terms that both wake him and inform her that she is the true object of his desire (7:1–9, see commentary). Even language, then, sets them apart.

3. The Scope of Love. Nothing shares the scope or power of love. The poet says this in many ways.

One is first struck by the imagery of nature, more specifically, its fragrance. It is reborn nature (the spring) that signals the time of love. "The fig tree puts forth its young fruit, and the vines, in blossom, give forth fragrance" (2:13). Pleasing odor is cited eight times, the final reference being to the loving plant, a reputed aphrodisiac (7:14). However, these nature references move far beyond fragrance. There are over thirty mentions of animals in the Song, and over seventy of plants and spices.

Furthermore, closer observation reveals a plethora of similes and metaphors, beyond animate nature. Images include precious metals (gold, silver), rare materials (ivory, marble, scarlet thread, purple yarn), expensive woods (cedar), jewels (lapis lazuli, beryl), cities and their parts (towers, pools, ramparts, Jerusalem), water sources (cistern, spring) and celestial bodies (sun, moon). To describe love, varied and multitudinous images must be used.

While Jerusalem (a principal guide word) dominates locales, the range is enormous. All places named were under Israelite control only once, the glorious expansion under Kings David and Solomon. The list includes such far-flung locations as Ein Gedi in the Judean desert, peaks in the Lebanon and Anti-Lebanon mountain ranges, Damascus in modern Syria, Heshbon in Trans-Jordan, Kedar in the Arabian desert, the Carmel range near the Mediterranean Sea, etc. Again, love seeks to encompass all.

Even the fragrances point in the same direction. She is described as an orchard (4:13f.), but a fictional one, for the plants therein grew in the widest possible array of places. Spikenard was imported from India, myrrh from south Arabia and cinnamon from the Far East. As one scholar summarized, here were gathered "the most expensive and fragrant spices and incense of the ancient world, plants whose origin was Africa, Arabia, Nepal, India and China, with only three growing in Israel."[1]

---

1. See notes on 4:14.

Fragrance, one of the Song's leading metaphors of love, is also all-encompassing.

Indeed, the poet says so directly: "For love is as mighty as death, jealousy as relentless as the grave" (8:6). In surrounding societies, death was a god-like power. For mortals, it is the unvanquished victor — but love, declares the poet, is stronger. Love's "darts are fire darts, a furious flame — multitudinous waters cannot quench love, nor can rivers sweep it away" (8:6f.). Those waters, in ancient myth, were the primal force that the gods overcame to create the universe. The poet makes use of the most powerful imagery available to state that love is greater than all.

E. Canonization, Reconsidered – The Song Vs. the Biblical Ethos

While the process of canonization, acceptance of books into the Bible, is unclear, we do know of the final debate on the Song of Songs.[1] We recalled Rabbi Akiba's (first–second century) strong defense of the Song's status, probably on the basis of a symbolic interpretation. We also noted that some credit canonization to the attribution of the Song to Solomon.

There are various indications that the Song of Songs was popularly canonized prior to Akiba's time. Josephus (*Against Apion* 1:8), writing c. 100, makes reference to four books of the Bible with "hymns to God and precepts" which phrase seems to include the Song of Songs. The Ezra Apocalypse, written mid-first century, seems to know of twenty-four books of the Hebrew Bible,[2] the current full number. In Christian tradition, the book is listed as canonical in a source near the end of the first century.[3] Much earlier, parts of the Song are found among the Dead Sea Scrolls.

Indeed, this scattered testimony to the early acceptance of the Song might indicate that official sanction postdated general popularity. While a symbolic reading may be part of the background of the official sanction, the underlying popularity, reflecting the appreciation given the book by the masses, may have been just as important.

Popular acceptance may reflect even more, for the Song presents a love-and-sex

---

1. As above, Overview, I C-1 "The Nature of the Song," p. 146.

2. Edgar J. Goodspeed, Edgar J, *The Apocrypha: An American Translation* (New York: Vintage, 1959), p. 97, verse 14:46.
3. Murphy, p. 7, referring to Jean Paul Audet, "A Hebrew-Aramaic List of Books of the Old Testament in Greek Transcription," *Journal of Theological Studies*, n.s., 1 (1950), p. 149.

ethic authentically Israelite. Like other biblical sections, which rework other cultures' texts into authentically Israelite molds (creation, flood story, psalms of praise, law codes, etc.), the Song of Songs would represent the Israelite sexual ethos. (One can so argue without claiming that this was the *poet's* intention. The Song bears no polemical tone. It may reflect a sexual ethos, without arguing for it.)

The Bible sees heterosexual sex as a positive side of life. While certain relations are strictly banned (adultery, incest, rape, etc.), others are prescribed: sexual relations, for example, are a wife's right (Exod. 21:10). The first humans were to "be fertile and multiply" (Gen. 1:28). Proverbs highly recommends marital sex: "Find joy in the wife of your youth – a loving hind, a graceful mountain goat. Let her breasts satisfy you at all times; be infatuated with love of her always" (5:18f.). These emphases befit the biblical inclusion of the Song.

Further, the consistent condemnation of adultery in the Bible blends well with the Song's emphasis on loyalty. The Bible's earliest reflection on marriage – "hence a man leaves his father and mother and clings to his wife, so that they become one flesh" (Gen. 2:24) – mirrors the Song's emphasis on exclusivity and its dreams of marriage. (While polygamy is permitted by biblical law, there is a monogamous emphasis, with all leading models, with the marked exception of ancient ancestors and kings, intending originally to marry only one woman.)

This biblical ethic of love-and-sex certainly differs from the general cultural milieu of the time. In pagan literature, indiscriminate sex is a part of the gods' lives, and it is graphically portrayed. For surrounding pagan cultures, sex was often a part of the holy ritual of rebirth and the land's fertility. (In fact, it might be suggested that the absence of "God" in the Song partially reflects radical opposition to this pagan ethos.)

On the other extreme, perhaps in reaction to that pagan world, celibacy was offered as an ideal, as Paul held: "To the unmarried and the widows I say that it is well for them to remain single as I do. But if they cannot exercise self-control, they should marry. For it is better to marry than to be aflame with passion" (1 Cor. 10:8f.).

The Hebrew Bible (as well reflected in the Song) celebrates sex, within a context of love, exclusivity and mutuality.

One cannot ignore, however, two apparent conflicts with biblical norms: the acceptance of unmarried sexual relations in the Song, and the nonsexist nature of those relationships. These would seem to be not only a radical break with the surrounding cultures, but with the Bible as well.

In the Song, the lovers are unmarried. Surely chastity is the biblical norm! That is certainly so, but two observations are in order. First, the actual moments of union in the Song occur, as stated above, *between* the lines. They are never fully articulated.[1] This perhaps allowed early religionists to turn a blind eye, even to the obvious.

Second, the Bible, when it wants to ban a sexual activity, does so in the clearest of terms, as we see with adultery, incest, bestiality, and so on. Premarital, loving sexual relations merit a different treatment. They are nowhere explicitly banned. Virginity seems prized, but the only instance of severe punishment connected to the subject is within a context that also involves deception and financial loss (Deut. 22:13–21), not the lack of virginity alone.[2] An

earlier text treats deflowering as an economic crime.[3]

Silence, of course, does not indicate approval, and later Jewish tradition did prohibit premarital sex, but given other clearly disapproved acts, one can minimally state that the Bible does not see such relations as an "abomination," on the level of other misdeeds. If adultery was a felony, unchastity was a misdemeanor.

A second apparent area of conflict is the egalitarian approach of the Song to sexual relationships. The Song departs from the Bible's androcentric view of love relationships, as emphasized in recent feminist and other writings,[4] and the Song is certainly revolutionary in that regard.[5] However, there may be biblical parallels to this approach. Some feel that the Song's egalitarianism reflects the original harmony of another story – the Garden

---

1. Magnificently summarized by Trible, p. 144: "It speaks from lover to lover with whispers of intimacy, shouts of ecstasy, and silences of consummation."

2. Deut. 22:21 is an extremely difficult verse. It calls for a death penalty for fornication without witnesses, a break with consistent biblical norms, and sharply contradicts other biblical law (where the death penalty is specifically for adultery). It also provides the reader with an easily fabricated way out. It would seem either to be limited to circumstances not articulated (e.g., engagement) or not

intended to be an applied law. See Jeffrey H. Tigay, *The JPS Torah Commentary: Deuteronomy* (Philadelphia: Jewish Publication Society, 1996), "Accusations of Premarital Unchastity," p. 476f.

3. Exodus 22:15f.

4. Trible, passim; Pardes, p. 118f.; Fokkelien van Dijk-Hemmes, "The Imagination of Power and the Power of Imagination," in Brenner, pp. 156–170; and others. Note Landy, 1987, p. 317: "The dominance and initiative of the Beloved are the poem's most astonishing characteristic."

5. Falk, p. 86: "[the Song] offers a thoroughly non-sexist view of heterosexual love."

of Eden.[1] Indeed, there are sufficient models of female assertion and centrality in the Bible to allow for canonization of the Song.[2]

In short, both the sexual and gender ethics are "at home" in biblical tradition, even as they remain exceptional and radical expressions in these matters.

Further, even if one were to conclude the opposite, that in both instances the Song markedly contrasts other parts of the Bible, it still should be noted that canonization does not seem to demand a narrow field of agreement.[3] A variety of approaches, even basic disagreements, exist among biblical texts. Job's challenges exist beside the calm assurance of Psalm 23. Jeremiah blames the people for the destruction of the Temple while the author of Lamentations cannot understand why the disaster came upon them. There is a broad range of acceptable views in the Bible. Given this range of opinions, the Song, which does match many of the biblical emphases in love relationships, can be seen as fitting well in the biblical landscape.

There is, in the final analysis, no certain reconstruction of the process that led to the Song's popularity and ultimate canonization. We should not minimize the appropriateness of the love metaphor for the relationship between God and humans. Still, the poem's model of human love would have to have been sufficiently acceptable to be used as a metaphor for the divine, and therefore it would have to be within the range of the society's values.

The canon, then, has preserved for posterity not only a poem of beauty and subtlety, but also an admirable ethic of love and sex, which fits well with what we know of biblical culture. It is presented as the view of a woman. Whether it remains an advanced ethic for today is a question the reader is encouraged to engage.

III. ON TRANSLATING AND INTERPRETING THE SONG OF SONGS

A. The Literal Bias

Translation technique is commonly divided as either "literal" or "idiomatic."[4] Because we are convinced that the Song proceeds primarily

---

1. This is the central thesis of Trible.
2. *Contra* Brenner, Introduction, who suggests that the equality of the Song was a major stumbling block in the process of canonization.
3. Pardes, p. 121: "The canon-makers gave expression… to voices which negated the uniformity of religious practice."

---

4. Edward Greenstein, "Theories of Modern Bible Translation," in *Prooftexts* 3:1 (January 1983), p. 10.

on the basis of root repetition,[1] we have translated accordingly (literally), seeking (to a maximal extent) to use the same term in English for parallel root uses in Hebrew, and different English terms for each Hebrew root. Thus, the reader, with effort,[2] is able to hear the echoes that dominate the Song, and to constantly re-read early verses in light of later ones.

We clarify by example. Three roots indicate sight in the Song. We have translated *d-g-l* variously as "viewed" (2:6), "visible" (5:10) and "visions" (6:4, 10); *r-'-h* with various forms of "see" and "sight;" and *ch-z-h* as "observe" (7:1). The separate translations reflect our tendency *not* to connect parallel meanings – only parallel root uses. Thus we treat the three terms for sight as unrelated.[3]

---

1. See below, section E, p. 169.
2. "The literal translation resembles the voice of the author, but muffled. The author's sense may be difficult to discern, but the reader who wishes to hear it will make the requisite efforts" (Edward Greenstein, "Theories of Modern Bible Translation," in *Prooftexts* 3:1 [January 1983], p. 20).
3. The differentiated translations still allow the reader, of course, to explore relationships through meaning as well as root. In one case only, verses are related by meaning, not root – the parts of the mouth – on which we comment below. To illustrate our approach to root usage, we note that Pardes, p. 138, does relate the woman to the "watchmen" (3:3) because she too "guards" (1:6), while we do not connect the uses, because the verses use two different Hebrew roots.

Echoes are sometimes represented by near translations. Thus "atop" Amana and "top" spices reflect a single Hebrew word (*rosh* – 4:8, 14). ("Top spices" might have been better translated "choice" or "finest spices," were one not reflecting the echo.) Similarly, "gone away" and "come away" (2:10f.) reflect an echoing use of a single emphatic adverbial form.

Not always was it possible to use identical English terms. By way of example, the oft repeated "darling" echoes the similar "shepherd," but this is left unreflected in translation. In such instances, we cite the Hebrew echoes in the commentary or notes.

In rare instances, we detected no meaning to a repetition. Nevertheless, we maintained the echo in translation, hoping other readers may find such implications. By way of example we note "multitudinous" (7:6, 8:6), and "chariot/chariotry" (1:9, 6:12).

B. Double Entendres

Double entendres are among the poet's favorite techniques. Where possible, we included both levels of meaning in the translation itself. By way of example "crimson Carmel" (7:6) represents two translations of a single Hebrew term. More often, the alternate or complementary reading was indicated in the commentary. In such cases we were guided by what we felt would be the instinctive first understanding as the translation, with the second level clarified in the commentary. In the cases of "Janus" parallelism, wherein the double entendre involves one meaning of a term with what comes before the word and another with what comes after, if we cannot translate both, we translated the former and noted the latter in the commentary.

C. "Love" and "Loving"

In using the translation, the reader is reminded that "love" and "loving" represent two different Hebrew roots in the Song. "Love" is used in our translation for *'-h-v*, a general term, one less often associated in Hebrew with physical lovemaking and/or coition (though it can be). "Loving" is the translation of *dodim*, a term which always has physical overtones in the Hebrew. The word "lover," *dod*, is related to "loving," not "love."

D. "Lover" and "Beloved"

The woman is the more active and assertive member of the couple. Nevertheless, for reasons noted in the introduction, we felt compelled to readopt the more usual usage: "lover" for male, "beloved" for female.[1]

E. Guide Words: Repetition as the Key to Meaning

The discovery of meaning through repetition is one of the oldest techniques of biblical interpretation, a prominent method in the Jewish homiletic and heuristic literature known as Midrash. (E.g., Jacob is "deceived" when Laban gives him Leah instead of Rachel in marriage [Genesis 29:25] – justly, it is said, because Jacob "deceived" [same Hebrew root – *r-m-h*] his father when he took Esau's blessing [Genesis 27:35].)[2] There are numerous examples. The lack of application of this approach to the Song of Songs across the ages can partially be attributed to the early and nearly universal acceptance of the allegorical understanding.

Modern biblical commentaries are also aware of possible implications of a repeated word or phrase. We deal here, however, not with a single repetition, but with repetitions as a pattern. In that regard, we note in particular the sensitivity shown by Martin Buber. In an essay on biblical narrative, Buber articulated his approach to a repeated word or root. "By 'guide word' we mean a word or a root which is repeated within a text (or consecutive texts, or a series of texts) in a meaningful

---

1. As Landy (1987) p. 306.

2. *Midrash Tanhuma, Vayyeitsei,* 11 (Vilna: ed. Buber), p. 152.

pattern; one who carefully traces these repetitions will find one level of meaning of the text deciphered, clarified or at least more fully revealed.... The variations of the (stem) word often intensify the dynamic effect of the repetition. I say 'dynamic' because the variation patterns interrelate to create a growing movement as it were. One viewing the text as a whole can sense waves moving to and fro between them...."[1]

The Song of Songs uses patterns of repetition as its basic literary technique. (Note that Buber and others studied this technique primarily in *narrative*, while the Song is *poetry*.)[2]

Many have seen the large number of repetitions as a prime indication of the poem's unity.[3] A few interpreted some repetitions, but did not go beyond that. One researcher wrote, "It almost looks as if somebody would have sprinkled repetitions throughout the Song in a planned way."[4] Indeed, somebody did – the poet!

We have, above, noted the poet's use of the root *sh-l-m* in indicating the Song's theme, the repetitions of *'em*, "mother," and the repeated use of *ahavah*, "love." We have also noted the use of identical terms to indicate mutuality, and the echo of the similar words "beloved" *ra'ayah* and "shepherd" (or "pasture"), *ro'eh*.

While we shall here illustrate with three other repetitions, these are examples only. In fact, *every* repetition in the Song can be seen as meaningful and we have, in our com-

1. Martin Buber, "The Use of the Guide Word..." p. 284 – translated here from the Hebrew. Cf. the comments of Weiss, Meir, *The Bible and Modern Literary Theory* [Hebrew] (Jerusalem: Bialik Institute, 1967), pp. 24–26. Cf. also the extensive treatment of this technique in Alter (1981) pp. 92–97, who noted also that the technique has been applied well beyond Bible. He cites Bruce F. Kawin, *Telling It Again and Again: Repetition in Literature and Film* (Ithaca: Cornell U.P., 1972), "[the words carry] the meanings they have acquired in earlier contexts with them into their present and future contexts, immensely complicating and interrelating the concerns and actions of the play."

2. Indeed, the Song exhibits at least three elements which Alter (1981) identifies as elements of biblical prose – the repetitions, the preference for dialogue (note his chapter, "Between Narrative and Dialogue," pp. 63–86) and the use of one typical prose formula: "The formula of rising up and

going off to a different place...is one of the prevalent biblical conventions for marking the end of a narrative segment" (p. 65). This deserves further consideration, particularly in light of the conclusion in Alter (1985) that the Song is "untypical of biblical verse" (p. 185).

3. See above, Overview, I A-2 (Unity), "The Nature of the Song," p. 143.

4. R. Kessler, "Some Poetical and Structural Features of the Song of Songs," *Leeds University Oriental Society Monograph Series VIII* (1957), p. 49.

mentary, explored possible connections in each instance. It is moot to argue whether the poet intended them all, or whether some were subconscious even to him or her. The poet's unqualified reliance on repetition in many cases leaves all such repetitions as potentially meaningful. Each instance must be judged on its own merit.

The term lily, *shoshanah*, appears eight times. As so often, the first use seems natural, with no hint of future importance. She calls herself a simple lily, and he responds that she is a lily among brambles, emphasizing her singularity (2:1, 2). However, in the next reference, he is already termed the one who pastures among the lilies, imagery drawing him (his mouth?) to her person. This process accelerates. In 4:5 her breasts are termed "harts pasturing among the lilies," and in 5:13 his lips are equated with lilies. The symbol joins their bodies in intimate embrace. Subsequently, this intimacy is used to fool the Girls of Jerusalem, who are told that this man is "the one who pastures among the lilies" which they understand as location, while she is only recalling their contact (6:2, 3)! Finally, in the Shulammite fantasy, it is appropriately this intimate symbol that first reminds him that his physical desire is specifically for her (7:4). "Lily" is never fully understood without reference to all previous uses; later references shed retrospective light (and shadow!) on the preceding.

Sometimes term repetition is used to indicate comparison. In one concentrated section, Solomon's "sixty" "warriors" are "held fast" to their swords, are in fear "at night," and are "taught" (trained for) war (3:7, 8). In comparison, *she* is praised by "sixty" queens (6:8f.), "holds" her lover (3:4), circles fearlessly through the city "at night" (3:1, 2) and is "taught" love by her mother (8:2). Appropriately, the "warriors'" shields end up as decorations in *her* necklace (4:4).

The terms for "mouth" present a particularly complex repetition pattern. They are surrounded by the only two mentions of "kiss" (1:2, 8:1). A central part of the mouth, the palate, is mentioned three times. In the "innocent" first use, the apricot tree (a metaphor for the lover) has fruit that is sweet to her palate (2:3). "His palate is sweetness" (5:16) already hints that the lovers engage in an intimate kiss, and that the earlier use was more meaningful than it first seemed. The third use seals the image: "your palate, like the best wine" (7:10), for wine is clearly connected to kisses ("let him kiss me with the kisses of his mouth, for your loving is better than wine" – 1:2).

Indeed, only in the case of the mouth is so wide a variety of terms used (mouth, lips, palate, tongue, teeth, cheeks, smile and organ of speech [4:3][1]). This exception to the rule (of repetition by root only) may well prove the rule. This very variety emphasizes and isolates the mouth, perhaps reflecting the poet's intention to involve all aspects of the mouth in the intimate contact, the erotic kiss. So central is the image, in fact, that "palate" will be used as a parallel, in 5:6, to "his entirety."

Throughout the Song, term after term gains depth and complexity in repetition. It is through the guide words and less complex repetitions that the reader must seek the meaning of the Song. We have concentrated on these repetitions in the commentary.

F. Reading and Rereading the Song, and This Commentary

All great literature bears rereading. In the case of the Song, the consistent use of guide words and repetition is sufficient reason to argue that the Song can *only* be understood on rereading, and that, several times over. Only then will the reader begin to appreciate the interaction of terms, phrases, situations, etc. In fact the interweaving of meanings may be so complex as to deny any sense of total completion.[2]

The poet evidently wished to reveal these layers of meanings gradually. In translating and commenting, we have tried to walk the thin line between revealing too little and too much. In order to appreciate future readings, however, we added the final chapter, "On Rereading the Song of Songs." There we have reviewed many verses that change significantly on a second reading. For readers who will return to the original commentary at a later date, we indicated each verse that is reviewed in the chapter "Rereading" by a double asterisk in parentheses after the first commentary.

G. Against Reductionism

How much ink has been spilled on arguing which of two meanings was a poet's intention, and how poorly thought out that very inquiry is! Were the poets less aware of the range of meanings than we? Is a poem similar to a do-it-yourself guide, to be judged first and foremost by single meaning and lack of

---

1. See commentary, 4:3.

2. "Its dynamic forward movement that always turns back on itself becomes timeless." (Francis Landy, *Paradoxes of Paradise: Identity and Difference in the Song of Songs* [Sheffield: The Almond Press, 1983], p. 141)

ambiguity? Is a poem successful if it can be retold in simple prose?

There are two possible initial assumptions when encountering a range of meanings in a sentence: that the poet intended only one, or that the poet was aware of the range itself. We may never reconstruct original intentions, but of those two assumptions, it is almost always better to choose the latter. Hence this commentary has included, at times, alternative or "complementary" understandings, second and third levels of interpretations which are carried by the text along with the first.

We also have preferred open translations. By way of example, in 1:11 the lover proposes making an item of jewelry, the root implying "turn" or "circle." It is variously translated "wreaths," "pendants," "earrings" and "bangles." We chose to translate "circlets," which, while less clear and definite, allows for the various interpretations.

Consistent with the above, we were willing to accept an uncertain range of possibilities. On several occasions the reader has found unanswered questions – these are not rhetorical, but open considerations. Similarly, in several places the reader has found the term "perhaps." This is not an attempt to insert a less well-founded interpretation, but a worthwhile conjecture, which remains precisely that.

H. In Appreciation of Previous Commentaries – A Note on Notes

Our purpose is not to survey prior works, but to suggest new insight. A commentary must walk the thin line between providing the reader with a comprehensible complete overview, on one hand, and avoiding unnecessary repetition of previous scholarship and overabundance of detail on the other. Given the large number of commentaries now available, and their wonderful contributions, we have felt free to refer readers frequently to earlier commentaries for details that might not be of immediate interest to all.

Because accessibility is an issue for those interested in pursuing the more academic background, we have referred to more recent and comprehensive studies rather than to the earlier works where ideas might first have been mentioned. We have emphasized currently available commentaries, most in English, with some reference to unique Hebrew commentaries. (Medieval Hebrew commentators are readily available in assorted compendia.) We do wish to note particularly the significant contribution of Marvin H. Pope, whose 1977 commentary was truly comprehensive. It is highly unlikely that any future researcher will be able to do without it.

We also chose not to repeat arguments

for what have become well-accepted interpretations. In 7:6, by way of example, it is agreed that *dalat roshech* means "the hair of your head," "the locks" or the like, based on a parallel usage in Isaiah. This interpretation is already found in a biblical dictionary in 1907, and yet the derivation is still detailed in many commentaries.[1] In such cases, we make no comment at all.

Where a significant degree of controversy exists, we have cited either the reasons for our interpretation or a scholar or scholars who have detailed the same. We also make an effort to credit others whose original recent contributions are reflected here.

I. Structure

1. Elements of Structure. Structure is often related to meaning, in the Bible and in other literature. The Song seems to defy all efforts to identify structure. The amount of work necessary even to approximate a structure is itself evidence of the relative absence thereof.[2] The poet's heavy reliance on repetition, ironically, serves to mask any intended structure based on words or phrases.

That said, there are indications of one basic structure, as follows. The reverse movement of the beginning and end has been noted – in the beginning, he brings her to his chamber; in the end, he is to be swift in moving toward her. Indeed, the use of Solomon in the title and near the end (8:12) has a similar enclosing effect.

This feeling of enclosing is echoed by the style of the opening and closing sections of the Song. Chapters 1 and 2, on one hand, and chapter 8 on the other, share a similar style of rapid movement from one subject to another, what one might call a "staccato" effect. (Testimony to this style is the division into subunits by modern proponents of the anthology theory. They find in these three chapters more poems than in the other five combined.[3]) The opening two chapters evidently establish the themes of the Song. Chapter 8 is, in the words of one scholar, "a recapitulation of motifs."[4] (The commentary

---

1. See Pope, Murphy, Zakovitch, Bloch, Hakham, Fox, and others.
2. The reader is referred to the most successful such effort – that of Exum, pp. 47–79. She finds a very complex structure, elements of which we accept below. As a whole, however, her analysis is so dependent on form that it creates sections that do not exhibit continuity or logical sequence. See

the reservations of Murphy, p. 62f. and Fox, pp. 207–209.
3. Gordis finds sixteen units in the three chapters, thirteen in the other five; Zakovitch seventeen and twelve; Falk eighteen and thirteen; and NJPS, which divides the Song into sections, has twenty-three in the three chapters, seventeen in the other five.
4. Exum, p. 42.

has shown that it is more than that. It is the resolution of the word development of many of the Song's guide words – Solomon, vineyard, rouse, kiss, wine, etc. – and it is there, most appropriately, that we find the poet's encomium of love, and the beloved's final call to her lover to join her.)

All of the above points indirectly to the middle of the poem, and in fact the first and clearest moment of sexual coition occurs in the middle of the book, between chapters 4 and 5.[1] It has been noted that "the major incision exists behind verse 5:1"[2] and one recent structural study finds that the themes and phrases of the first half of the book are echoed in the second half.[3] A number of the surviving medieval manuscripts of the Song have only one break – after 5:1![4] This is clearly appropriate. As per one commentator: here is "the entrance of the Lover into the garden of love which is the Beloved in 5:1; his possession and enjoyment of its fruits constitute the one act of consummation in the poem, and hence its emotional center."[5]

The import of the center is reflected in its being a dividing line. Any repeated scenes occur in the two different halves, and the phenomenon of "delayed fulfillment,"[6] wherein a missing central term is omitted in a repetition but inserted later, occurs only in the second half of the poem. Other changes also take place. The flight enjoined by the woman in 2:17 changes from a flight across cleft mountains (indicating separation) to being swift across mountains of spices, symbolizing closeness to her body (8:12). One might beneficially compare other partially parallel uses of phrases, which have different contexts and associations: "I am lovesick" (2:5, 5:8); "his left hand under[neath] my head" (2:6, 8:3), the ascent from the desert (3:6, 8:5), "bring you to my mother's house" (3:4, 8:2) and the adjuration to the Girls of Jerusalem (2:7 and 3:5; with 8:4). In general, in the second half of the poem there are more sweeping statements (e.g., 8:6–7) and the woman is more

---

1. See above, Overview, "Love, Sex and the Single Maiden," II c-2, p. 155.
2. R. Kessler, "Some Poetical and Structural Features of the Song of Songs," *Leeds University Oriental Society Monograph Series VIII* (1957), p. 42.
3. Exum. Similarly, the more complicated attempt by William Shea ("The Chiastic Structure of the Song of Songs," *Zeitschrift fur die Alttestamentliche Wissenschaft* 92 (1980), pp. 378–396, divides the poem at this point. Note Landy (1987) p. 315: "There is a certain circularity in the Song; the second half reflects the first."
4. Noted by Cohen, p. 33.

5. Landy, 1987, p. 316f.
6. See above, Overview, II d-1, "Love in the Song of Songs," p. 160, on the emphasis of the future.

assertive (e.g., 7:12, 8:10). We have commented on changes in the commentary.

All this points to the one clear structural implication of the Song: after 5:1, nothing can be quite the same.[1]

2. The Subdivisions. We wish to repeat a caution from the introduction. In this commentary, we have divided the Song into smaller units. These units should not be understood as separate poems. In no case did we intend so to imply. Rather, we sought to accommodate the need to read longer works in smaller sections. In order to emphasize that these are not self-contained poems, we have labeled each only with a short quote from the text itself, numbering each as a consecutive chapter, as of one book.

J. In Conclusion

We conclude with a restatement of one of the medieval texts we cited at the end of the brief introduction. Ibn Ezra (eleventh century) begins his commentary:

"This is a noble book, entirely a delight, and none of Solomon's one thousand and five songs can match it, for which reason it begins, 'The song of songs of Solomon...'"

---

1. J. Carlebach, *Das Hohelied, ubertragen und gedeutet* [German] (Frankfurt am Main, 1931) labels the two sections as "engagement" and "marriage." See Cohen, p. 10. We detect no marriage, but appreciate the awareness of the strong sense of change.

Excursus:
Love Human,
Love Divine

*F*or two thousand years, most Jewish and Christian traditions understood the Song of Songs to be an allegory, the human love story really implying a love relationship on the human-divine level. Often, terms were interpreted as symbols of historical acts and personalities; sometimes, of philosophic principles. While the Song was certainly not originally written as an allegory,[1] the basic insight was healthy – for the metaphor of love is apt for spiritual relationships.

One is moved to consider, then, whether an attempt to apply the love story of the Song as presently understood to the human-divine level might prove enlightening. Whether a modern reader be committed believer or devoted atheist, the possibilities inherent in application of this human love model to matters beyond opens avenues of contemplation worthy of attention.

A. Might Human Love Clarify Matters Divine?

The metaphor of "love" is rooted in tradition.
The first uses of the metaphor of shared love to symbolize the relationship of God and the People Israel occur in the Torah (Pentateuch), the first five books of the Bible. Israel must love God (Deut. 6:5, 11:13, etc.); God loves Israel (Deut. 23:6, as in Isa. 43:4 and elsewhere). This metaphor was expanded by the prophets, and marriage became the *leitmotif* of the relationship, adultery or infidelity the symbol of leaving God. Even in reassuring Israel, the second Isaiah, speaking during the exile, used this imagery: "'Can one cast off the wife of his youth?' said your God. 'For a little while I forsook you, but with vast love I will bring you back…. With kindness everlasting I will take you back in love.'" (Isa. 54:6f.)

The prophet Hosea beautifully expressed a knowledge gained through love. Looking forward to a theoretical "remarriage" of God and Israel, he wrote (in light of the practice of sanctifying marriage by gifts given from groom to bride), quoting God speaking to Israel: "I will betroth you to Me forever; I will betroth you to Me with [gifts of] righteousness and justice, with goodness and mercy; and I will betroth you to Me with faithfulness – and you shall know the Lord" (Hosea 2:21f.). Knowledge comes second, gained through the experience of the gifts of love.

So, too, the devotion inherent in the human-divine combination is well expressed through metaphors of love and marriage. Biblically, devotees of God are termed lovers (Exod. 20:6, Ps. 97:10, etc.); God is said to love Israel, both in the past (Mal. 1:2) and

---

1. See Overview, I C-2, p. 146.

in the future (Deut. 7:13). The total infatuation of first love, of early marriage, provides a particularly powerful image by which the Bible recalls the desert period, as the Jews left Egypt: "Thus said the Lord: 'I remember the devotion of your youth, your love as a bride — how you followed Me in the wilderness, in a land not sown'" (Jer. 2:2). The application is mutual, as the same prophet speaks of God's feeling at that time: "I loved you with an everlasting love; therefore I continue My grace to you. I will build you firmly again" (Jer. 31:3). Human experience provides the necessary and comprehensible metaphor for expressing connection to the divine.

The metaphor of "love" is helpful.

It is therefore natural that the inheritors of the biblical culture would adopt the greatest of human love poems, the Song of Songs, as a symbol for the divine love relationship. Celebrating and elucidating that adoption, Gerson Cohen wrote:

> One metaphor that cannot be found in the literature of any ancient religion outside of Israel is the description of the god as lover or husband of his *people*.... Absolute fidelity on the part of Israel to one God, come what may, is the sum and substance of the message of the Bible.

Now in the life of the ancient Israelite there was only one situation reflecting that kind of absolute relationship, and that was the vow of fidelity of a woman to her husband.... No other ancient people entertained such notions or metaphors of its gods, for no ancient people conceived of itself as having the same intense, personal, and exclusive relationship with its god that Israel did.[1]

Indeed, human language must make use of metaphor to describe ultimate religious concerns. Any purported comprehension of the divine (or articulation thereof) is human, and therefore limited. Just as the comprehension is not restricted to knowledge gained through reason, so too the articulation is not restricted to theology. Both are facilitated by the concept "love."

The metaphor of "love" requires clarification.

But if the acceptance of the love in the Song of Songs as a metaphor for the relationship of the people and God was culturally natural and theological useful, it was also necessary. For if "love" can enlighten, it can also confuse. Few terms, today as in antiquity, suffer

---

1. Cohen, Gerson D., pp. 6–7.

more overuse[1] and diminution of effect in the hands of the masses. In this light, the Song of Songs as symbol for divine-human love could serve to define and limit. The Song is a specific situation and model, a rejection of other approaches, and it therefore can serve to clarify what is meant by an ideal love.

(We mention that the divine-human love with which we deal here was not conceived, in the Bible or in Jewish sources beyond, as in any way contradictory to law. The opposite was the case. In the classic expression of Jewish prayer, said daily, "You have loved Your people Israel with eternal love; Torah and commandments, laws and statutes have You commanded us." While this insight goes beyond the scope of this chapter, we include it lest readers assume otherwise.)

B. Love Human, Love Divine – Initial Inquiries

Below we explore possible lines of thought derived from considering matters divine in light of the love depicted in the Song. The first two considerations reflect matters covered at some depth in the "Overview." Thereafter, we include a number of lines of inquiry that might be pursued, to indicate the potential available. Detailed discussion would be well beyond the scope of this commentary.

Movement is love's field of play.[2]

We do not remain stationary. The Song pictures lovers who are constantly in motion, and in doing so, foreshadows love relationships in general. Motion is so constant that love is defined as a category within its bounds. The "other" cannot be appreciated only within a given environment or context — that, essentially, would not be love.

How challenging such a view is, not only to our human relationships, but particularly to divine. To understand that both partners are in motion is to know that every new connection is in a context unlike yesterday's, and that even the same words must be reapplied and re-understood. That holds both for humans considering God (e.g., prayer) and for humans as object of God's concern and devotion (e.g., as they seek to rediscover through reading holy texts). They can learn to appreciate that what is new to them is not necessarily detachment from previous love, but part and parcel of a process that only exists in motion.

Part of the change emphasized in the

---

1. It is of some fascination that there are more references to love than any other term in the index of the Oxford Dictionary of Quotations (London: Oxford University Press, 2nd ed., 1955).

2. See Overview, II D-1, "The Motion of Love," p. 160.

Song is the pulsating rhythm of presence and absence. This is far beyond the aphorism that "absence makes the heart grow fonder," which would imply that true love is within "presence." Here love transcends distance, even as its physical restraints are sorely felt. This is not obvious – in fact, it runs counter to intuition and experience. The Song would seem to imply that it is essential. Can one achieve such a love?

The absence of the Deity is certainly felt too often. As in the Song, people seek, and find Him not. Perhaps one must search this human description of love for clues. What elements allow for love while apart in the human condition, and how might they be applied to the world of the spiritual?

The Song also conveys, through its form, that change applies to prior events, as the past (terms, experiences, memories, etc.) is altered through reexamination, new happenings and developed depth. Within love, the Song's form would seem to imply, present and past are constantly in dialogue, changing one another. Forms remain as content evolves. How often have we proved reluctant to changing yesterday's understanding, to allow for, and to delight in, new vistas!

So it might be even with love divine. Whether the past be national-and-ancient (e.g., the giving of the Torah on Mount Sinai),

or a recent personal life cycle moment, one should be open to re-viewing it, for that this is the essence of the relationship.

Mutuality – My lover is mine, and I am his.[1]

In multiple ways, the Song describes a love that is mutual and equal. Happily, such a picture is easily comprehended, even if not easily accomplished, in our time. Across the centuries this was not so, even on the level of understanding. We now accept this mutuality and equality as goal.

These principles are harder to understand – even shocking – if applied to categories of relations between the human and the divine. Surely there can be no equality or mutuality here! Yet we find, even in ancient sources, surprising contentions of this type. By way of example, from Talmudic times, Jews already understood that every day one was to don phylacteries – leather boxes with text inside, with straps attached, near one's head and arm, as an act of devotion. The text inside reads, in part, "Hear O Israel the Lord our God the Lord is One [unique]" (Deut. 6:4). How striking, then, that a Talmudic era rabbi would state[2] that God donned phylacteries every morning. "What is the text inside?" he

---

1. See Overview, II C-5 (Mutuality), p. 156.
2. *Talmud Berakhot* 6a, citing 1 Chron. 17:31.

asked, replying, "Who is like Your people Israel, a unique nation on this earth?" (II Sam. 7:23). Even earlier, the Bible equated the loves through identical terminology: "You have *affirmed* this day that the Lord is your God... and the Lord has *affirmed* that you are His treasured people" (Deut. 26:17f.). Centuries later, a liturgical poem recited at the New Year used that image, along with terminology from the Song: "We are Your darlings, You are our lover [terms from the Song]...We are Your affirmation; You are our affirmation."

The application of mutuality and equality to love human-divine, then, is not without precedent, at least as metaphor. What might it mean? Even if texts describe God at times anthropomorphically, with body (the hand of God) or emotion (even anger), no one would seek to equate God and humanity. Yet in the love metaphor, the devotion is precisely that. This would imply a mindset for humans not only as recipients of love, but as actors in a love relationship. Receipt implies obligation on both parties. Devotion is not only an expression of acknowledgment of a gift, but part of a living, two-way exchange.

Other lines of inquiry — Examples.
Human-divine communication is often articulated, from the human side, as prayer, from the divine, through ancient text. Several aspects of the Song can enlighten that process. First, the mass of repetitions in the Song imply that reiteration may be of love's essence. One can perhaps gain sympathy through the love metaphor for prayer and holy texts, which by nature are repeated. Second, if the Song's emphasis on dialogue and exchange is applied also to love divine, prayer and holy texts must constantly take on new content as part of ongoing dialogue. Finally, if the Song implies that the poetry of love is layered, in its communication and in its essence, could not one argue that if the divine human relationship is love, the communication should seek complexity, not simple clarity?

In the Song, love leads to praise, which seems less a requirement than part of love's essence. Whether the praise is true or not, each partner is raised to new levels by the admiration of the other. The Song is a wonderful challenge to our praise of the divine, for most often we conceive of that in royal terms — the vassal praising the king. But if this praise derives from love, it should be neither doxology nor flattery, less "holy" and more intimate.

"Until it so desires" — has love its own pace? The Song seems to imply that love grows and has its own calendar and season. Are we willing to grant a divine love that seems so absolute and complete the same assumption of growth and temporary partiality? There would seem to be an implied danger in closing too soon.

The Song magnificently combines an appreciation of the wonder of today with an expectation and anticipation of an even better future. The potential application to divine love is powerful. As ideal as achieved love might be, there seems to be completion only beyond today. A view of love with God, as being "on the way," engaged, totally committed yet looking forward to a better tomorrow, is a soberly rapturous understanding of the present.

The story behind the poetry of the Song did not proceed smoothly. Could one also say that human-divine love inevitably suffers such lapses, such missed opportunities, such miscommunication, such pain? Is there enough strength in recalled union to allow one to bear renewed absence?

Even when the lovers meet and achieve their fondest desires, the poem proceeds to further separation. Perhaps in this section we find the epitome of applicability of the human to the divine – following fulfillment, there is only partiality. Yesterday's perfection allows one to live through the next day's shortcomings, in hope.

In the Song, the woman shares part of her story with others, but keeps other aspects to herself. Part of love is its personal history, a secret language, hidden memories, etc. Could the same be true of divine love? Is there, in the final analysis, a very personal relationship that cannot or should not fully be shared with others?

In the Song, all plural numbers are negative, only "one" is positive. This is not just a description, but a goal, and a difficult one. Anthropologists constantly speak of the unnaturalness of human monogamy. We are surrounded by choice and competition.

Neither is monotheism a natural or easy achievement. The worldview of paganism is not silly – despite prophetic mockery, there is much in life experience to argue for a world of competing ultimate powers. Single loyalty is an accomplishment, constantly played out against competing attractions. The central statement of Jewish worship, for example – "Hear O Israel, the Lord our God, the Lord is One" – is not simple piety, but a grand goal.

Clearly the woman in the Song is not married. This ideal love exists before the wedding ceremony, certainly no surprise in modernity, when love is most often considered a desired prerequisite of marriage, not its result. This is extremely enlightening and challenging as a metaphor of divine love. This perfect relationship exists, to a degree, as the stage of "not quite," before the pinnacle of the bond.

There are plans to be made. The relationship does not exist at a stage of full completion — and perhaps in this case of human-divine love, it never can be. Perhaps to view the love of God and humanity as frozen at a wonderful, but incomplete, stage, can lead to the patience, understanding and forgiveness necessary to the relationship.

It is astounding that this, the greatest of love poems, ends not in a typical "happy ending," the couple walking off into the sunset, but in a final dialogue, a call to action, a vision of the future. Love most complete still exists in a finite world with all its limitations; hence, love forever looks forward to a future ideal. As divine love, then, the Song seems available for religious stances that are not static, but dynamic, which see progress in the future, which see an ideal well beyond present limitations — a future commonly thought of as messianic. Even in moments of fulfillment, when perfection of the relationship seems almost palpable, one senses that the moment is only a "taste of the world-to-come." True love is ever retranslated to challenge and opportunity, achievement to hope. One feels achievement not on reaching a plateau, but only if one is climbing.

Appendix:
The Style of the Poet

We here offer a literary profile of our author. In doing so, we do not suggest that all of the techniques employed are unique — indeed they are not, with some exceptions. Rather, they place the author within the biblical literary landscape. By noting the repeated use of specific techniques, however, we do add yet another argument to bolster the claim of a single author.

The outstanding literary technique of the author, of course, is the use of repetitions of roots, words and phrases to carry the themes and meaning of the Song. For further comment on this technique, see the Overview, section III E on "Guide Words" and numerous references throughout the commentary.

Because this use of repetitions is reflected in well over half the verses in Song, it is particularly difficult to identify more specific patterns based on repetition. By way of example, "inclusio" indicates the opening and closing of a section with the same term, but because of the plethora of repetitions, it is difficult to identify that usage with certainty. Similarly, other commentators have noted chiastic structures (a-b-b-a), some of them quite complex, in the Song, again based on repetition. We note neither inclusio nor chiasm below, in light of the general use of repetition. Where repetitions serve a specific purpose that we feel is of note, we do record that usage.

In each case we shall describe the technique,

and then in the subsequent paragraph, make brief reference to terms, phrases or verses that illustrate the technique. In each case, the reader interested in detail should refer to the commentary and to the chapter "Rereading the Song of Songs."

1. The poet will use a word or term that can be understood in at least two different ways.

Illustrative verses: 1:1 (Song of Songs — multiple meanings); 1:2 (of wine/than wine — so also 4:10); 1:4 (rightly/good wine; inhale/recall; "you" as masculine or feminine); 1:7 (where/how; pasture/feed); 1:8 (by/above; pasture/feed — and so throughout the poem); 1:13, 14 (is my lover to me/my lover is mine); 1:14 (from/in); 2:3 (his/its shadow); 2:7 (whole verse — non intervention or patience); 2:8 (hark/voice — so also 5:2); 2:12 (singing/pruning); 2:14 (address to dove/address to woman); 2:17 (reference to morning/evening); 3:4 (conceive/instruct — see commentary and Overview, IIc-6, 7); 3:6 (perfumed/clouded); 3:10 (inlaid with pictures of love/acts of love/lovingly wrought by); 4:2 (befitting/twinning); 4:12 (direct address/statement to self); 4:13 (limbs of plant/of body); 5:1 (loving/lovers; also, dual direction of the address); 5:8 (if/that you not); 5:15 (choice/young man); 7:2 (steps/feet); 7:6 (crimson/Carmel); 7:7 (love/metonymy for lover); 7:10 (rightly/good

wine – as 1:4); 7:12 (henna/villages); 8:1 (fraternal brother/lover); 8:2 (she/you [instruct me]); 8:8 (do for/do against; marriage/speak against); 8:9 (fashion/besiege); 8:10 (then/therefore; find/produce).

2. A particularly complex application of these double meanings occurs when a set of such double meanings results in parallel, different understandings of a verse or verses.

Illustrative verses: 1:8 (statement of the lover or statement of the shepherds); 6:1–3 (her recollection of him in poetic terms/girls hear directions of where to find him); 8:8–10 (brothers and she hear two different messages, same words).

3. Terms are read twice, once with what comes before and once either independently or with what follows.

Illustrative verses: 1:4 (after you); 1:13, 14 (is my beloved to me); 1:15 (my darling you are); 5:1 (lovers, with loving); 5:2 (my beloved); 6:12 (my soul, disoriented); 8:13 (for your voice).

4. The poet purposely blurs the identity of speakers, sometimes having one person's statement blend into the statement of another (in the cases of overlap, indicating that the two parties agree).

Illustrative verses: 1:4 (see commentary); 2:15 (the two lovers); 3:7–10 (unclear transition,

him to her – see "Rereading the Song of Songs," end of commentary, 3:9–10); 4:15, 16a (the two lovers); 6:10 (she and the Girls of Jerusalem); 7:2–7 (noble observers blend into the lover – see commentary, 7:7); 7:10 ("stirring the lips of the sleepers" – the two lovers); 8:14 (the two lovers).

5. The author subtly attributes all plural numbers to outsiders, not the two lovers.

The multiple numbers occur in 3:7; 4:5, 9; 5:10; 6:8f. 8:11f. Also note the use of doubling in the Shulammite dance, 7:1, and the association of masses with the Shulammite and Solomon, 7:5 and 8:11.

6. The poet tends to end a list with an all-embracing term or number.

Illustrative verses: 4:7 (totally); 4:14 (all top spices); 5:16 (totally); 6:10 (visions).

7. Repetitions are often used to compare the lovers to others.

Illustrative verses: 3:9f. to 5:14–16 (four different terms – lover to Solomon); 3:2 to 3:7 (circling – beloved to the warriors); 3:1–4 to 3:8 (holding and "at night" – lover to the warriors); 3:8 to 8:2 (teach – beloved to the warriors); 3:9 to 4:8, 5:15 and 7:5 (Lebanon – Solomon to the lovers); 1:11 to 3:12 (silver and gold – Solomon to the lovers); 3:10 to 7:6

(purple – Solomon to the beloved); 8:2 to 8:7 (house – beloved to anonymous other); 8:7 (give, in contrast to all previous uses – see commentary there).

8. The poet indicates mutuality by using the same phrase or term for both lovers.

Illustrative verses: 1:2, 3 and 4:10 (your loving better than wine); 1:14 and 7:9 (cluster); 4:13 and 8:2 (pomegranate); 4:7 and 5:16 (all); 5:10 and 6:4, 10 (view); 2:14 and 5:15 (the sight of); 1:16 and 7:7 (lovely); 3:4 and 7:9 (hold); 2:10, 13 and 7:12 (come).

9. The poet makes slight changes to indicate significant development or difference.

Illustrative verses: 2:17, 4:6, 8:14 (cleft mountains/mountain of myrrh, hill of frankincense/mountains of spices); 2:16, 6:3, 7:11 ("my beloved is mine," with its inversions); 3:11 (Girls of Zion for Girls of Jerusalem); 3:4, 6:9, 8:2 (the development of "she who conceived me" – see Overview, II C-7, "The Horizon of Childbearing"); 5:7 (the "watchmen of the ramparts" for watchmen).

10. A unique structure is the threefold repetition of a structure in which the poet asks "who is this" without providing a direct answer – 3:6, 6:10, 8:5.

11. On three occasions, the poet breaks away from a description which has become too intimate by turning to an outside party, followed immediately by a radical change of subject – 2:7, 3:5, 5:1.

12. Like many biblical poets, the author enjoys occasionally playing on the sound of the words.

Illustrative verses (partial): *shir hashirim asher lishlomo* (1:1); *shemecha* and *shemanecha* (1:3); *tson* and *tse'i* (1:8); *hevi'ani* and *ahavah* (2:4); occasional alliteration (e.g., 1:6: *she'ani sh'chachoret sheshizafatni hashamesh*); *tsiyon* and *tse'enah* (3:11); *shekulam* and *shakulah* (4:2); *libavtini* and *Levanon* (4:8f.); *eshakcha* and *ashkicha* (8:1f.); *ta'iru* and *te'oreru* (2:7 and elsewhere.). See "Rereading the Song of Songs" on 4:8 for a series of five such plays on words.

The Song of Songs:
Selected Bibliography

The following bibliography is not comprehensive. Rather, it combines recommended reading with volumes cited frequently in the introduction and in the notes. A complete bibliography is found in Pope. For subsequent publications, see Bloch.

Alter, Robert. *The Art of Biblical Narrative.* New York: Basic Books, 1981.

————. *The Art of Biblical Poetry.* New York: Basic Books, 1985. See esp. "The Garden of Metaphor," 185–203.

Bloch, Ariel and Chana. *The Song of Songs, A New Translation.* Berkeley: University of California Press, 1995.

Brenner, Athalya, ed. *A Feminist Companion to the Song of Songs.* Sheffield: Sheffield Academic Press, 1993.

Cohen, Gabriel. *Studies in the Five Scrolls: The Song of Songs* [Hebrew]. Jerusalem: Ministry of Education and Culture, 1984.

Cohen, Gerson D. "The Song of Songs and the Jewish Religious Mentality," in *Studies in the Variety of Rabbinic Cultures,* 3–17. Philadelphia: Jewish Publication Society, 1991.

Cook, Albert. *The Root of the Thing: A Study of Job and the Song of Songs.* Bloomington: Indiana University Press, 1968.

Exum, J. Cheryl. "A Literary and Structural Analysis of the Song of Songs." *Zeitschrift fur die alttestamentlichte Wissenschaft* 85 (1973): 47–79.

Falk, Marcia. *Love Lyrics from the Bible: A Translation and Literary Study of the Song of Songs.* Sheffield: The Almond Press, 1982.

Feliks, Yehuda. *Song of Songs: Nature, Epic and Allegory* [Hebrew]. Jerusalem: Israel Society for Biblical Research, 1983.

Fox, Michael v. *The Song of Songs and the Ancient Egyptian Love Songs.* Madison: University of Wisconsin Press, 1985.

Ginsburg, H.L. "The Song of Songs," in *The Five Megilloth and Jonah: A New Translation,* 1–2. Philadelphia: Jewish Publication Society, 1969. Also incorporated in subsequent Bible translation volumes.

Gordis, Robert. *The Song of Songs: A Study, Modern Translation and Commentary.* New York: Jewish Theological Seminary of America, 1954.

Guilder, Michael. *The Song of Fourteen Songs.* Sheffield: JSOT press, 1986.

Hakham, Amos. "Commentary on the Song of Songs" [Hebrew]. In *Hamesh Megillot*

[The Five Scrolls], edited by Aharon Mirsky, Feivel Meltzer and Judah Kiel, 1–76. Jerusalem: Mosad Harav Kook, 1990.

Ibn Ezra — commentary of Abraham Ibn Ezra, d. 1167.

Keel, Othmar. *The Song of Songs: A Continental Commentary* Minneapolis: Fortress Press, 1994. Originally published as *Das Hoheleid* (Zurich: Theologischer Verlag, 1986).

Landy, Francis. "The Song of Songs." In *The Literary Guide to the Bible*, ed. Robert Alter and Frank Kermode, 305–320. Cambridge: Harvard University Press, 1987.

LXX — The Septuagint, oldest Greek translation of the Bible, third to first century BCE.

Murphy, Roland E. *The Song of Songs*. Minneapolis: Fortress Press, 1990.

Pardes, Ilana. *Countertraditions in the Bible: A Feminist Approach*. Cambridge: Harvard University Press, 1992. See esp. chap. 7, "'I Am a Wall, and My Breasts like Towers,' The Song of Songs and the Question of Canonization."

Pope, Marvin H. *Song of Songs: A New Translation with Introduction and Commentary*. Garden City, NY: Doubleday, 1977.

Rashi — commentary of R. Solomon ben Isaac, d. 1105.

Rowley, H.H. "The Interpretation of the Song of Songs." Chap. 6 in *The Servant of the Lord*. Oxford: Basil Blackwell and Mott, 1965. First published 1952 by Lutterworth Press.

Segal, Benjamin. "The Theme of Song of Songs," "Repetition in the Song of Songs," "Double Meanings in the Song of Songs" and "Literary Patterns in the Song of Songs." *Dor le Dor* (Journal of the World Jewish Bible Center) 1986–88 (four articles).

———. "To Bear, To Teach: Motherhood in the Song of Songs." *Nashim: The Journal of Jewish Women's and Gender Studies* 3 (Winter 2000): 43–55.

Tournay, Raymond Jacques. *Word of God, Song of Love: A Commentary on the Song of Songs*. New York: Paulist Press, 1988. Originally published as *Quand Dieu parle aux hommes le langue de l'amour* (Paris: J. Gabalda, 1982).

Trible, Phyllis. "Love's Lyrics Redeemed," in *God and the Rhetoric of Sexuality*, 144–165. Philadelphia: Fortress Press, 1978.

Zakovitch, Yair. *The Song of Songs: Introduction and Commentary* [Hebrew]. Tel Aviv: Am Oved Publishers, and Jerusalem: The Magnes Press, 1992.

"How beautiful you are,
How lovely you are,
O love ecstatic."
–Song of Songs 7:7